W9-DCL-696

CARMELITE MONASTERY
LIBRARY
SARANAC LAKE, N.Y.

MONASTIC RENEWAL

MONASTIC RENEWAL

Columba Cary-Elwes, O.S.B.

Monk of Ampleforth

CARMELITE MONASTERY
LIBRARY
SARANAC LAKE, N Y

HERDER AND HERDER

1967
HERDER AND HERDER NEW YORK
232 Madison Avenue, New York 10016

Nihil obstat: Aelred Graham, O.S.B.
Imprimatur: Joseph Cardinal Ritter, Archbishop of St. Louis
December 9, 1966

The Scripture quotations are in the translation of Monsignor
Ronald A. Knox, copyright 1944, 1948, and 1950 by
Sheed and Ward, Inc., New York. With the kind permission
of His Eminence the Cardinal Archbishop of Westminster.

Library of Congress Catalog Card Number: 67–17621
© 1967 by Herder and Herder, Inc.
Manufactured in the United States of America

DEDICATION

To all those Benedictines
old and young
who have helped the writer
in his search
for the authentic Benedictine spirit
this book is gratefully
dedicated,
but especially to those
of St. Louis Priory.

CONTENTS

ACKNOWLEDGEMENTS

It was in the summer of 1966 at St. John's Archabbey, Collegeville, that the thoughts contained in this book began to take final shape, and I am most grateful to all the monks and sisters there at the time who assisted me in facing the problems. Then I wish to thank most particularly the team of young monks of St. Louis Priory, resident there or at Ampleforth, England, who helped me prepare the manuscript for printing, not only by typing much of it and clarifying its style, but also by giving straight and constructive criticism. I thank, too, Sister Mary Agnes, of the Visitation Academy in St. Louis, who took over much of the burden of typing the final version; also Dom Alberic Stacpoole of Ampleforth; he in the midst of his own intensive studies gave me of his time at Oxford and led me to All Souls where together with Dr. Southern we grappled with the question of the history of Benedictine schools. It is customary, and in this case most just, to say at this point that all the errors of fact and failures of insight are my own.

C. C-E.

PREFACE

THE WHOLE PEOPLE of God has been encouraged to question their ways of life: the bishops, the priests, the laity, and also the religious. Monks and nuns too, and all those who follow the way of the vows, are questioning their way of life. This is right. The Church, at the Second Vatican Council, encouraged them to do so.

All were instructed to search the Scriptures and their own traditions in order to find the authentic spirit of the Gospel and that of their particular Order. They were also encouraged to see their own spirit in the light of the modern situation, to abandon what was no more than a passing fashion and to relate their lives to the Church of today.

This book is a contribution to the Benedictine *aggiornamento*, written in a discursive way, in a form much like a travel log of someone going back over his tracks in a great journey. So we start with the present, as the point of arrival. Then we go back to the beginning and retrace our steps, attempting to recognize those elements in the journey which contributed most to our way of life.

Thus, in the historical sections, the reader must not expect to find a compendium of monastic history. The attempt there has been, rather, to note and comment on significant events, personages, and new elements along the way that have influenced the monastic tradition.

As we proceed, it becomes evident that certain subjects need special treatment in themselves as significant elements of traditional monastic life, and this they receive in the second part of the book: obedience, poverty, prayer.

The aim has not been to provide all the answers. These have to be discovered for each individual by himself, and for each community by itself. Rather, the author has described the situation and presented its themes as he sees them, with some pointers, some judgments—but not so many that the readers themselves are frustrated in making up their own minds.

The only thesis of the book is that the Benedictine way of life, as it has been known and developed for centuries, is a true monastic tradition. There is no claim whatever that it is the only one. Many others abound, particularly the splendid Cistercian tradition, from which the Benedictines have always much to learn. There is room for all of us in the many mansions of the Church, as I hope can be seen from the pages of this book.

MONASTIC RENEWAL

CHAPTER ONE

MONASTIC AGGIORNAMENTO

THE WHOLE CHURCH is astir, from a great wind blowing, which is filling the sails and carrying her along. We are now, as it were, out on the high seas, and the new land-fall is not yet in sight. Every member of the Church, no matter what his position, is alive to the fact that, since the Pentecostal experience of the Second Vatican Council, things cannot be the same. This is as true for religious as it is for laity and priests and bishops.

A number of words to describe this awakening are in common currency: *aggiornamento*—the favorite of Pope John; *adaptation*—a key word in the Council; *renewal* and *reform*—words favored by the theologians. The first two have an immediate connection with our world as it is today; the second two are primarily a description of an inward change. The last in particular is one most easily misunderstood. There are reforms and reforms. It does not follow that, because the Reformation led reform in one direction, there should be no reform again. On the contrary, the Church has now appropriated the idea of reform as a permanent policy, recognizing in it a theological principle—*Ecclesia semper reformanda*—which owes much to the experience of the Reformation four hundred years ago. The Catholic Counter-Reformation was, of course, a real renewal, but the Church shied away from a

15

number of reforms proposed then, since they seemed dangerous.

The words *renewal* and *reform* might be used interchangeably, but this is not, on the whole, the use of the conciliar documents. In these documents, they usually have distinct meanings and represent quite distinct attitudes to the Church's approach to change. We will attempt to give them here their precise sense. But often they are used interchangeably.

Reform means restoring a form that has been de-formed— in other words, a return to the original form. This idea makes us look back to our origins, to the rock from which we were hewn (Is. 51, 1), to the holy Gospel of Jesus Christ, to the revealed word of God, and also the holy rule of the founder of the Order. That any reform can justifiably occur implies that deformation in the Church should not surprise us, whether in the life of the Church as a whole or in a particular Order—seeing that the Church is made up of sinners, be they popes, bishops, priests, religious, laity. All are sinners and are in continual need of reformation in their lives. They are reformed through the restoring sacraments of confession and the holy Eucharist, through new responses to the word of God in whatever form it may assume.

The difficulty is not really to admit the fact in theory or in principle or as a possibility of failing to live up to the demands of Christ. But it is difficult to recognize those areas in our own lives, individually and corporately, where this is true, and sometimes quite difficult to put the reform into effect. History proves that each generation glosses over its own abuses.

Renewal, on the other hand, instead of looking back to the past, looks to the present and the future. Renewal means making something new, up-dating, the taking up of new attitudes in liturgy and education and pastoral work, because the old ones, no matter how good they were for past cases, have become less able to help the faithful of the present. Both in matters of technique and in spiritual outlook, renewal and revision are a rule of life, provided they are genuine developments.

Aggiornamento is a similar word, popularized by Pope John's use of it, so that it is a memento of his spirit and ideas. It means up-dating and making relevant for *today,* and we may see in it a spiritual reference to that Today which is always God's gift, the time to choose and answer, lest our hearts be hardened (Heb. 3, 13).

The word *adaptation,* of all this group of words, is the one that probably appeals most to the young; it has an existential tang. The situation and values associated with it are these: here we have two entities, the Benedictine or religious life on the one hand and the world and Church on the other. These are to be taken as they are, as facts of experience. Religious should face these other realities, and should with complete objectivity grasp what is relevant to their life both in the way of the world and in the way of the Church. We do not live in a vacuum but in a particular historical situation with all its complexity, but also with all its opportunities.

The aim should not be simply to conform to the world or to be absorbed in all the active life of the Church, but to have that supreme prudence of choosing what is relevant to us according to God's will.

This approach may sound narrow or selfish. In a sense it is, but not viciously. There is the vice of selfishness, and there is the Christian virtue of self-love. We have to love others as we love ourselves: no love of self, no love of others. It is by all having a true reverence for their vocation that we will all truly serve the world and the Church. Consequently, the first objective in the life of any man or any institution is to know itself, to love itself sufficiently to coordinate itself rationally and then it can go out to help others. Else it would be like blind leading blind. Adaptation must flow from our own vision of the light of Christ, in response to our own particular vocation from him.

This attitude, then, takes it as axiomatic that the world has something to give religious. It takes for granted that Benedictines are totally separated neither from the Church nor from the world. It takes as basic that it is a distinct and particular kind of life in the Church.

17

Monastic Reform and Renewal

Several times in the *Decree on the Appropriate Renewal of the Religious Life* the Fathers of the Council stress the idea of a return to the principles of the founder of the institution, a return to the source, to that initial insight which set the Order off on its way through time. The ultimate source of all reform for religious Orders is the Gospel, then their rule and the spirit of their founder, and then a careful examination of the sound tradition of the Order. This backward look for the Benedictines will require several chapters.

It is not the aim of the Church to reduce all Orders and religious institutions to a common way of life. It is one of the glories of the Church's life that she allows the Holy Spirit to work in her, generation by generation, in ever new ways to fit new circumstances.

Religious Orders therefore should return to their origins and all the insight that that charismatic time had for the institution. The founder was being guided in a special way by the Spirit; this inner light was codified and sealed by the approval of the Church. We must not aim at standardization but at that splendid variety which proves the Church's vitality. St. Vincent de Paul would not allow a priest from another Order than his own give his own Order a retreat because, he maintained, no other than members of his own institution could truly understand the spirit of his Order.

To look back is not enough; we have to look both ways. We have also to be aware of what is coming upon us today and tomorrow, and this is where the tensions begin to arise. Tension is not a sign of infirmity but of life, for it is with the powers of life that an organism faces problems and responds to challenges. The aim of the Church in the world is to witness to Christ. If she remains totally separate from the world, hidden from it, this witness would be impossible. To cut herself off absolutely would be to fail in her mission.

Monasticism, in this regard, is in a peculiar and delicate position, since it is always an association of persons more or

18

less cut off from the world. Yet it would be false to maintain that monks and nuns have no relationship with the world and with the Church. A wrong answer here could drag the monk or sister from their cell, or at the other extreme could concentrate them too much upon their own personal salvation. A balance has to be sought for those whose vocation is neither just active nor just comtemplative. No one would deny that the primary aim of the Benedictine is the seeking of God, nor that this very act lived out through a whole lifetime is a sign to the world of faith in God. Nor would one deny that by self-sacrifice and by prayer and penance the monk and nun, especially the contemplatives, help to draw down graces upon the Church and the world. What we are here asking is this: In the world of the twentieth century should monks and sisters do more?

It was Pope John's deep conviction that the Church was not keeping pace with the times, even though he did not quite know how to bring it up to date. This was an immense task. The Council Fathers agreed that monks and nuns also needed updating. Naturally, it is within their own competence to examine their lives. But getting up to date means change. No Order, even the oldest, can avoid that disturbing business of change. Institutions are made of people; and the former too have to change. Few institutions can be less inclined to change, even in the smallest thing, than monasteries and convents. How should one set about it? There are two considerations.

1. Before change, one wants to be very sure what elements in the present time have true relevance to the monastic life, including elements of Church life and of secular life. This is the broad subject of the present state of affairs: things as they are in monasteries, in the world, in the life of the Church. To give briefly an example: In Church life, the new spirit of the liturgy could make an enormous difference to the way a particular religious group lived. Or again, from the side of the world, new reflections on the human person and all his freedoms create a new situation in monasteries and convents.

2. Before change, one also has to be quite sure of what is

essential to the spirit of the Order and what is not. For this we have to examine the sources, as was said above—not simply to discover what was done and was thought in fact, as a historical inquiry, but (and this is far more difficult) to examine which parts could be scrapped as merely part of a historical situation and which parts are truly evangelical insights and therefore precious and to be preserved.

The first consideration, that of the present situation, is the subject of the present and the following chapters. The second topic, the spirit of the Order, will be dealt with at length in the third chapter. Then various incidental topics of great importance in themselves will be treated individually in later chapters.

One of the areas of *aggiornamento* which especially affects Benedictines is that of the liturgy. It would be rare to find a house which was not attempting to implement the *Constitution on the Sacred Liturgy*. But there are problems.

It is still possible to confuse liturgy with ritualism. We could still imagine that the more liturgy we had and the more ornate it was the more liturgical we were. This is an error, or at least an exaggeration, from which we are not all free. Today we recognize that the liturgy has an inward life and various outward forms. It is the inward life that should occupy our attention, and the outward expressions can be left much freer than we used to think. The fact is that the whole Western Church had become far too interested in outer forms, and far too little concerned with the inward meaning. It follows that we should re-examine the meaning of liturgy in the light of the Council's Constitution, and come to an awareness that it means a communal prayer to the Father by his Church with Christ, centered on the memorial of the Last Supper. What will count will be the extent of the participation, the making real of the sign, the simplicity—one might say the humility—of the approach.

One thing associated with this problem is the accumulation

in most monasteries and convents of pious practices, which now clutter up the schedule. They were good in their day, since they provided precisely that communal, simple approach to the Father which the liturgy should have been giving—but had ceased to do, either because it was no longer meaningful or because the Divine Office had been abandoned and even the conventual Mass. Now, all that should be re-thought. Is there any need today for repeated Benedictions? Devotion to the Blessed Sacrament is good, but perhaps it was an over-emphasis (necessary in its day) upon one aspect of the Eucharist, and that not the most important, namely, the fact that Christ is really present. Then there are all the novenas and litanies whose use multiplied in the nineteenth century—they should be quietly pruned. This will be painful to some members of the community, and it is difficult to see how the change can be made without some distress. Perhaps the devotion could be made optional; but the difficulty with doing that is that the scrupulous inevitably think that it is more perfect to go than not to go. In fact, the opposite is the case: it is better to pray well and briefly, than to multiply prayers and be weary.

Is there anything sacrosanct in having seven distinct periods of Divine Office a day and one at night? It is true that the "seven" derives from a biblical quotation mentioned several times in the Rule: that we should pray seven times a day. The Benedictine way of life in the twentieth century, which admits of a considerable amount of work for the community, does not readily fit into a seven-times-a-day division of the Divine Office. The result is that Matins and Lauds are crowded together, Prime and Terce, Sext, None, and Vespers possibly, and then Compline by itself at the end. Combined with these in the public timetable will be a community Mass and perhaps also a half hour's meditation. This is spiritual indigestion, a cluttering up of prayer, which becomes a burden and not a refreshment to the soul.

What is to be done? The first thing to decide, and this has

been mentioned by Fr. Wilfrid Tunink in his excellent book *Vision of Peace*,[1] is the number of psalms we should be reciting a week. For, whereas St. Benedict said the 150 psalms would be sufficient for his kind of non-giant monk, the Benedictine breviary provides about 240. There is movement afoot, in fact several movements, for reorganizing the psalter so that we do only recite 150. There is also a scheme that Prime should be eliminated, since its proximity to Lauds makes it superfluous. Others would have only one little hour, which would come at the time when the community have a break in the middle of the day. Some feel that Vespers and Compline, for semi-active Benedictines, are a duplication of evening prayer. But there should usually be good room for both—Vespers before supper and Compline before bed. It would be possible either to make Compline a private devotion or, less good, to place it very soon after supper, in order that the evening may be unbroken for those who need it to study or work or even just to get to bed early. The revision of the lessons (including the "brief" ones) of Matins is of great importance. In this particularly, there could well be freedom for individual communities to have their own readings, chosen by qualified members: so much variety and range is possible that it would be a missed opportunity if all Benedictine communities were restricted to one set of readings.

All these possibilities are matters that should be thrashed out in a friendly way among the community members with the pros and cons openly expressed. This would be true dialogue and a good entry into this important part of the new spirit in religious and monastic life, where the monks and sisters are more and more considered adult enough to take part in the process of deciding community policy. The decision is actually taken by the superior, but his brethren should actively co-operate in providing him with a sound factual and human basis for reaching a decision.

The factors which contribute to the decision in this case include the relative importance of the Divine Office and the

1. New York and London, 1963.

work that the community has undertaken for the Church in the neighborhood. We are not concerned here with exceptional circumstances, in which monks or sisters are outside their monastic framework, but of work undertaken within that framework. It would seem reasonable that the Office should be given a central position because it is the most important public work of the community. Nothing should shake this pattern, and normally no member of the community should consider himself exempt from it. If he does, then the timetable may be adjusted or the work should be decreased or "monasticized," that is, brought into the ordinary compass of the community life. Thus, for example, if a religious has an apostolic work which takes him or her out late at night so that it is impossible to be present at the morning Office regularly, this would be an unsuitable work for that religious in ordinary circumstances.

But it would not be unreasonable to shift the times of the Office away from the traditional times, at least to a certain extent, because of the work undertaken. There is nothing absolutely right about Matins at 2 A.M. any more than at 3 or 6 A.M., nor about Vespers at 4, 5, or 6 P.M. What would be unfortunate is this: that all the Divine Office be piled up in the early morning or late evening. Work and prayer should be integrated in each person's life, and in the corporate life of the community by a reasonable timetable which allows each its natural scope.

When one is away from the Office for a legitimate reason is it necessary for one to make up Office? According to the traditional interpretation of St. Benedict's mind, he meant the monks away from choir to stop whatever they were doing and to recite there in the fields or on the road the hour which was then being recited in choir. They could do so because they needed no books: their first business as young boys and novices had been to learn the psalter by heart. Today it is even easier, with breviaries available. But one sees the picture of a busy monk who has missed much Office, at the end of the day, worn out, who then has to get through Matins to Compline. This ceases to be meaningful. Would it not be wise to say that he would not have to make all this up, granted that he could not have said the Office earlier? Making up Office can be a good sign of union with the prayer of the community; but the goal of praising the Lord in union with one's brothers should not be sacrificed to blank and hurried recitation of a scheduled group of psalms. It is a question of cases, really, and each monk should act in all responsibility when faced with such a decision. When the question is one of prayer versus recitation to the letter, no rule can be laid down for the right decision, since both claims have their own authority: the Spirit bids us pray, the Rule says recite. In fact, all recitation and all prayer are a human compromise between formal and informal elements; like a conversation with another man, one's conversation with God is somewhat conventional and somewhat spontaneous. Would it not be more Christian, and more humane, to leave the exact manner of saying office outside choir up to the individual? Of course, an answer is to abolish the rule of making up Office.

There is one area of conventual life where liturgy and spirituality are crossed in an artificial way—that is, in the practice of confession. The sacrament of penance serves for two purposes: authoritative forgiveness of sins, and (incidentally) spiritual direction. For people in the world, these two activities may be well combined. But the life of a community contains a large amount of daily and indirect spiritual direction through the mere fact of sharing the same values and reacting in similar ways to common experiences, through observation and conversation, through imitation and encouragement. A monk living in community does not need the *same* regular stimulus to self-examination that, say, a secular priest does; the atmosphere of a monastery or convent is not necessarily holier than that of a presbytery, but there is definitely a difference in the companionship of like minds pursuing prayer and a common work together. Since the need for spiritual direction is more diffuse in monasteries than in the world, the regulation of weekly confession, if *for this purpose,* could be reconsidered.

Confession as a sacrament for the forgiveness of sins (which is its real meaning) also needs to be discussed frankly. Convents experience this problem with particular acuteness: confession has become a wearying routine—there is such a large number of nuns with little or nothing to confess, and doing so every week. There is little evidence in the conduct of this round that a sinner is encountering the grace and forgiveness of Jesus Christ through the merciful attention of his Church. This wonderful sacrament would shine with a more radiant light if the absolution and penance were given publicly to the community after those who had gone privately. There seems little need to go privately every week, but all should be free to do so. Each house could organize its practice of spiritual direction and sacramental confession so as to avoid both regimentation and laxity. The requirement to go to confession can, like an exam at the end of a semester's work in school, force one to organize one's knowledge and reach a definite plateau where perspectives may be gained both backward and forward. But the requirement to do so once a week may be too much for many religious. The sort of failings that arise in community life are usually ones for which private prayer of contrition and the ensuing effort to rectify the fault and above all the common Eucharist are very effective. Most monks are aware of some call of Christ—some person, some task, some situation—which they habitually fail to answer; their prayer of contrition is a confession of weakness and reliance on the power of God, and the "penance" which one humbly accepts is to face that same call again with greater trust in God.

What is essential in the Rule and what accidental, what belongs to monks of all times and what to the sixth century? It is not easy to distinguish in the original concept or insight of the Benedictine life what is permanent and what ephemeral. Thus the period of history during which the Rule was written cannot help but have exerted a profound impression upon its spirituality. It is easy to point to other examples in history of the same thing: Orders steeped in Jansenist or anti-Jansenist thought, medieval clergy influenced by monasticism, and modern monks influenced by Jesuits or other Orders.

Let us take the timetable as an example of a physical detail in the Rule. In the summer the monks rose at 2 and retired to bed at 9, five hours sleep, plus a two-hour siesta between 12 and 2 o'clock. In winter, the monastic night sleep might be from 5 P.M. to 2 A.M., nine hours sleep in all. These variations depended, of course, on the early or later rising of the sun and the length of the days and nights. St. Benedict, as elsewhere, makes the comment that if the abbot thinks differently about the arrangements for sleep let him decide as he thinks fit. Fourteen hundred years later should we hesitate to take him at his word? The answer depends on what principles are to be discerned in the original timetable: are they accidental or still meaningful? The wisdom which is manifested in many small regulations of physical details of monastic life in the Benedictine Rule is to be seen here too. St. Benedict did not want his monks to be sluggards; he arranged the timetable to provide ample and natural space for prayer, work, and *lectio divina,* with meals and rests as circumstances allowed. What would he have done if there had been electricity in his mountain monastery? To rise at 2 A.M. would be today a difficult practice, even if we went to bed at 5 P.M. Is there any reason to choose this asceticism over others in order to be Benedictine? There is something appropriate in the general practice of early rising to pray, but the exact hour is not important. The monastic life is an ascetic life, and it is a great principle of asceticism that the outward forms should not be hard and fast, but the motive constant and enduring.

The same sort of considerations apply to the asceticism of food and drink, which are a fairly superficial element of the monk's religious life. Long ago monasteries modified the drink regulations of the Rule. Wine was easy to come by at Monte Cassino, not so easy in Minnesota or Tokyo or Mexico. For wine, then, read beer or rice wine or lemonade. The Rule is meant to have that flexibility to circumstances. On food, St. Benedict followed the traditional Church fasts and added some of his own. Here again he was flexible. If there was a lot of work, let the monks have more food and at easier hours. Food is to be cooked, various, frugal, vegetarian, and substantial once a day. With the possible exception of frugality, these are accidental provisions.

Meat has been a subject of contention in monastic history. In the sixth century, meat was a luxury; it remained so until the nineteenth century when some Staffordshire and Yorkshire farmers discovered the mangel-wurzel and winter feeding. The flocks no longer had to be slaughtered because of lack of food. Meat has become increasingly cheap and plentiful. Chicken was once a luxury but has now become a common staple. At Monte Cassino the hot climate made meat less needed to provide stamina against cold weather, but in cold climates it is important for well-being. Finally, in ancient and medieval times meat was supposed by most spiritual directors to build up concupiscence. Simple errors certainly do not belong to the essence of the Benedictine spirit. Still, one must admit that meatless meals are a traditional sign of an ascetic spirit; such a diet is less interesting and less sustaining, and so would provide a regular occasion for asceticism. The decision is the abbot's and community's and depends, as in most cases, on the responsible judgment of its usefulness in a particular situation.

St. Benedict was legislating and directing the lives not of ascetical athletes but of average men. He was more interested in obedience and in the spirit of generous service than in outward forms. He many times encourages the abbot to use his judgment and provides a model for responsible judgment when he considers cases where a custom is affected by climate or heavy work or just human nature. To keep to the letter of the Benedictine Rule now is to create a very ascetical life for modern men, one of extreme rigor, whereas St. Benedict was for moderation and prudence. The pace of life today is accelerated far beyond the slow-moving tempo of sixth-century Italy. In fact then, and rightly so, most monasteries see to their own ascetic practices, following the same spirit of frugality and simplicity which belongs to the Benedictine tradition.

Another case where the question of conformity to the times arises is the matter of dress. Here indeed we can say, *"De vestibus non est disputandum"*: there are many opinions on this touchy question. Clothes do not make a man, any more

27

than manners, but like manners they come very close. So it is right that there be discussion of the subject.

Most religious Orders have inherited a dress from the past. The older the Order the more antiquated and quaint the dress, until you reach Roman times and an archaic simplicity, which too is very unlike modern dress. Is this choice of peculiarity in monastic dress purely an accident of history, or is there a principle or perhaps a practical reason behind it? We know that communities taken as a whole are much more conservative than their individual members. It is when the community acts as a corporate body that it is most conscious of its origins and purposes, and so it is then, that it is most natural in its traditional habit: that is, at prayer together, at meetings and discussions, at meals. When an individual is acting as an individual then there is much less point to the habit; sometimes an individual is acting as a representative to the public of the whole community, and then the habit is fitting. The community consciousness of itself and its origins produces a strong tendency not to change. The original habit comes to be a symbol of the first vocation of the Order into the life of the Church, and such holy memories are treasured by the conservative sense of the past. But this is an inadequate reason for keeping it if it has become quite anachronistic and cumbersome. Such habits should be changed, even if their use is limited (as it rightly may be) to community activities.

A curious thing about the dress of religious is that in the course of time, inadvertently, the original design can have been changed, little by little, until it really is no longer the way the dress started off. The Sisters of Charity's "wings" are an example: they had become stylized and starched. But the Sisters of Charity have now in their wisdom abandoned them as useless and awkward.

In what ways is the Benedictine habit anachronistic? The scapular, which was originally an apron, has become like a sacred vestment: it is distinctive, it is simple, and it serves no useful purpose. True, it is a historical relic and is common to most old religious Orders. It could be scrapped. What of the hood or the coif? In ancient times monastic churches were very drafty; it was useful to put up the hood and keep the gales of January off one's neck. Monasteries with drafty churches could still keep their hoods; in warm climates (where they cannot be used at all) they serve no useful purpose. Nuns will probably want some kind of cap or veil, both to keep them from thinking of their hair and as a symbol of modesty.

Monks do not require quite the same kind of theological training that is needed by secular priests; nor nuns the same as monks. The only people who can really know what is needed are those who are engaged in the particular community's work. Most monasteries need less training in moral cases, social justice, and marriage law than do secular priests. They could instead study more Scripture, patristics, Church history, liturgy, and the theology of prayer. Here too it is important that the community enter into dialogue on the areas of study which would be most usefully and fruitfully enlarged. Only in this way, when each community takes such initiative, will the information and enlightenment be found to improve the monastery's training program.

A sensitive area in most communities is that of the art displayed, particularly religious art. This display is an index to the spiritual understanding of the brothers in the house. Or rather their acceptance is such an index; the works themselves represent the spiritual outlook of those who bequeathed what is on the walls and in the niches of monasteries or convents. A certain amount of ruthlessness is required, but also some tact, because it may emerge that the statue that has just been eliminated was the gift of the family of a sister, for whom that destruction is a great sadness. But all poor lithographs and soft Christs should go.

Now let us pass from the elements of monastic life today to the effect on monasteries of the world today. One of the outstanding characteristics of the modern age is its sophistication, its scientific knowledge, its broad and general education. People know much more now as a rule than any previous age—in terms of acquaintance certainly, if not of wisdom. The contrast with the age of St. Benedict is extreme, and with him personally even more so. We must not exaggerate his renunciation of learning, but neither should we ignore it. We accept the account of St. Gregory that he left Rome in the middle of his schooling to pursue a monastic life. Even when it was very civilized, the culture of ancient Rome was not Christian and had little to commend itself to Christian souls.

The evidence of the Rule, formed and guided by the spirit of St. Benedict, leads one to suspect that he was well read. It contains quotations from numerous Fathers of the Church and also from classical sources. Yet learning as such seems to have held in his eyes a low place, and the original Benedictine monastic regime was not studious, was perhaps quite unlearned. *Lectio divina* was not plain study. I am not at this point advocating the devotion of monks to study, but merely pointing out that the atmosphere of those days in monasteries was in no way intellectual to the degree that modern monasteries are. This is particularly true of America. Most monasteries will not take postulants who have not completed college, let alone high school. St. Benedict himself would not have qualified. The same is true for sisters: they either have done college courses or, immediately after their first monastic training, go to college to work for their degree. Certainly, all have received good high school educations. Among young and old, superiors and subjects, there is no fear of learning; the only fear is that a person is not sufficiently educated. Compared to the time of St. Benedict it would seem almost an idolatry of learning.

What difference does this fact of the modern world make for monasteries? The first difference is that manual labor has given place, in large part, to intellectual labor. This does not mean that manual labor is irrelevant to monks, but that it need not be done in the fields. Not all the benefits of using a spade can be gained from using a typewriter; and it is true that physical labor is a great relief to the concentration of prayer.

A second difference is that *lectio divina* has become much more intellectual than pious. This is all to the good, provided that it does not cease to be prayerful. *Lectio divina* is more a *way of reading* than a class of books; if one were to find that one could read intellectual books only in an intellectual way, then one's *lectio divina* should be pious books. But I believe that most monks and sisters can find food for prayer in many kinds of books. This subject will be treated in more detail later.

Another characteristic of the modern age is that people have a real sense of independence. This is developed by the executive experience which many young religious already have had before they entered the convent or monastery. Young people have often taught or held a responsible position in the business world, which gives them a kind of maturity. These considerations should make us wary of presenting humility, obedience, and authority in quite the same manner as we used to do.

Self-development, self-expression, achievement, creativity are all a prominent part of modern man's mental furniture. A spirit of authoritarianism or paternalism, which presents humility as a childish blind submission, is not likely to be approved, and is in fact a wrong spirit for modern men.

But the quarrel is not between the ancient spirituality as it is found in the Rule, and the modern mentality; rather it is between a recent and shallow spirituality, and the modern mind. The modern mind is, in these matters and others, realistic, honest, anti-humbug. The ancient spirituality has similar characteristics. It was simple, straightforward, realistic. Thus the teaching on, for instance, humility as stated by St. Benedict and the explanation of humility given by modern psychologists are very similar. Humility is not shown by being the most successful in going through a door last; nor is it evident in a person who refuses to admit the great gifts God has given him; nor in one who imagines great sins which were in fact peccadilloes. No, humility is a recognition that we are immediately subject

31

to the almighty power of God, and little in his hands, and this naturally expresses itself in our physical bearing.

Obedience we will deal with elsewhere. Closely connected with this issue is that of the sense of responsibility. The area of consultation between the superior and the community must be widened. This would not lead to a spirit of insubordination; quite the contrary. It is lack of contact which leads to criticism and murmuring. If the community is consulted, then it has less to be critical about and no excuses for any private nursing of regrets. St. Benedict put this idea very early in his Rule when speaking of bringing the community to council. He wants not only the elderly but also the young, and even defends free speech for the young because, as he says, God can choose to speak through them, and often does. But he warns the young not to hold obstinately to their views. Nor does he offer the anxious superior a sop by suggesting that he should satisfy their eagerness to cooperate by presenting to them matters for discussion of relatively slight significance. The contrary is true. The community should discuss the major issues, and lesser matters are to be left to the smaller advisory body, the council.

We have something to learn from modern psychiatry in the matter of maturity. One of the disturbing phenomena of the last decade in monastic life has been the greater instability of young religious. They come into the novititate, they take their vows, and, surprisingly, in a year or two or even earlier, they present themselves to the superior and say that it was all a mistake, they no longer have any inclination to be religious at all. They have no compunction about breaking their vows, which apparently have no deep significance for them. This is almost incomprehensible to the older religious, brought up in a different atmosphere.

The question is one of maturity. It is patent that these young religious, when they took their vows, really lacked maturity. How is that? They could have been twenty to twenty-five years old at the time.

Psychiatrists will tell us that the modern youth have been brought up in a very curious way, without the restrictions their fathers and mothers had when they were young. The later twentieth century has been fooled by those who have preached the gospel of complete freedom for the young: that we must not inhibit them. It is now clear that what the teenagers really need is—something to struggle against, and a challenge to respond to. Only in this way will he and she find themselves. All this we hear about loss of identity is important; it is not, however, losing but never acquiring an identity which is the problem. An identity can only be found by being forced back on one's own resources, by asserting one's personal conviction of real values against some restriction or other. The revolt of the young is an age-old phenomenon. It has become fantastically exaggerated today in its outward manifestations because no one objects to their "revolts." Really these extremes of the young are a cry for someone to resist, so that they can have something to fight for.

Consequently, these same young people enter monasteries and convents, grown up physically but still adolescent in spirit. The first time they really acquire identity is when they come up against the Rule. This they have to revolt against, this they feel they must reject. It is their first opportunity to assert their personality.

Here is an area of information that should make us pause to think not only about accepting the immature but also about our attitude to the rules we impose or do not impose in our schools and colleges. We have many things to learn from psychiatry.

Attitudes towards superiors do not spring only from conscious motives and convictions. Superiors can be the object of extreme animosity not necessarily from conscious disobedience on the part of the religious but from some early and ingrained parental relation. Unnatural cruelty or severity, an unhappy home life, can beget a deep spirit of resentment which can be transferred to a new authority. We must recognize the importance of the huge new documentation on the subconscious.

33

In view of modern psychological knowledge, the motives of postulants for entrance need more searching scrutiny: is it the desire to escape from home, or from life; is it the desire which a parent has imposed on the son or daughter to fulfill the parents' religious instincts to dedicate their child to God and not to another human being? The behavior of young religious in their early years in the monastery could display to an alert observer symptoms of on-coming mental malady. Excessive pressure on certain types could lead to a breakdown; some religious need and should have mental therapy.

Modern knowledge of the psyche may help to test other religious phenomena, including visions and pseudo-mysticism. Here is a story which reads like an extract from a psychiatrist's notebook:

In a certain convent there lived a nun, said to have been once possessed by a devil, and now making herself an object of contempt to the whole community. The other sisters took her at her word and treated her to blows continually, and would not permit her to eat with them. This sister was content to serve them their food. As a mark of her wretchedness she used to wear not the usual well-fitting veil as the others did but an old piece of rough cloth. She wore this while serving the other sisters, and ate as her private meal the crumbs and husks of bread left over and the water the community washed their hands in. She was, in effect, the community broom.

A monk, who perhaps thought himself more humble than his fellows, was inspired to go visit this convent where he heard there was one more humble than himself. He obtained permission to visit the sisters, but the one he was seeking was not present. "Is there no other," he asked; "the one I came to seek is not here." They said there was only one other sister, but she was of no account. He said, "Let me see her." They brought her in much against her will, wearing her ridiculous headgear. Straightway he recognized her as the sister he had traveled to see. He bowed down before her, much to the amazement and confusion of the assembled sisters. He said, "I entreat God to give me a share of this nun's holiness with her on the day of judgment." Then he left, and the community now began to venerate the sister whom they had previously condemned. But she, poor thing, not being able to accept this change, one day vanished from the convent and was never heard of again, nor is it known where she was buried.[1]

Were her actions religious or neurotic? Was she just odd or holy or both?

Finally, among the elements of the life of the modern world which might have a relevance to the Benedictine *aggiorna-mento,* we will mention what appears to be a trivial problem, but which exemplifies much of what has been said in this chapter about spiritual principles: that is, the television. The basic attitudes are well established: some say that a television should not be available to monks and nuns, because it is a waste of time, a wasteland of unimportant and unmonastic programs. Others would say that if they are going to deal with people in the world, they should know what they think, and the only way really available to monks and sisters is the medium of television. This is what the millions watch and it molds their opinions. In addition, the argument continues, the quickest way of knowing what is going on in the world is to watch a half-hour news program.

Most superiors would comment that the television has divided the community into those who watch and those who don't, and into those who want this program and those who want that. Experience invariably indicates that some spend too much time watching television which they might profitably use in other ways.

The problem is not merely a superficial one, but a concrete summary of community life in the modern world in the affluent countries. How is it to be solved? The answer to some of the remarks referred to above is that those who watch television too much would not be doing anything useful if they did not

1. *The Paradise or Garden of the Fathers. A Compilation,* Edited by Wallis Budge, vol. 1, London, 1907, pp. 147–148; from the *Rule of Pachomius,* by Palladius. The text has been somewhat shortened by the present writer.

35

watch; it is simply for them a relaxation of tensions and for that reason very useful. It would not be necessary to give complete freedom for viewing. Certain times could be specified, a certain number of hours per week set as a limit. But the cry might then be raised that monks and nuns ought to be mature people and it is a sign of immaturing either in the superior or in the community that such a limit is deemed necessary. Of course, there is something in this outlook, but then we have to recognize that even grown people are tempted to laziness, to pleasure loving, and that some pattern is a good thing. It is not necessary for this pattern to be rigid. The principle perhaps should be that the pattern provides the norm, what the superior considers reasonable in normal circumstances, and this is set in consultation with the community. On the other hand, individuals who find this ruling restrictive for some reason or another, for instance their driving need for relaxation, could be given reasonable permission to watch more. It would be a sad day for a monastery when the rules or the standard were set by those who were in fact the exception, and in every department: food, sleep, relaxation, clothing, going out, and so forth. In short, the discussion and solution for each monastery of this and many other contemporary questions is governed by the precepts of humanity and maturity, of prudent judgment and responsible cooperation. These are not inventions or discoveries of the twentieth century; their absence may even be a special mark of our own time. Such a judgment in either direction is beyond us. But that they exist as the norms for a sound religious and spiritual life is true at all times and is the heritage of the Benedictine tradition.

We have discussed, as preliminaries to change, the relevance of certain elements of modern monastic life and of the world itself. There are currents in the life of the Church as a whole which have a bearing on the Benedictine *aggiornamento*. The most prominent among these as themes which receive special attention today are the biblical basis for dogmatic theology, the morality of the Gospel and the prominence of love as its basic principle, the secondary status of ritual and law, the need for and the glory of God's grace, the goodness of the world and openness to it, the community—whether religious or parish or other, the liturgy and its special place in Christian life. The Second Vatican Council has consolidated these gains. Benedictines could reasonably rejoice because many of these aspects of Catholicism as it is preached today are part of the original Benedictine monasticism. Spirituality was then, and still should be in a monastery, liturgical and biblical in a special way. Benedictine life is basically communal, for it is by obedience to the brethren that we will go to God. This last point needs expanding; the others are treated elsewhere in this book.

Community life cannot be taken for granted like, say, the bark growing on a tree trunk. It has to be nurtured and this is particularly true in our time. Young religious will not accept a cold, forbidding indifference to their existence on the part of the older members of the community. The modern religious expect acceptance and respect, they expect love. And they are right. A convent or monastic community is supposed to have the basic element of family life, which is a very close and deep love, a mutual appreciation and consideration which takes the other members as one's very own brothers. Family love is not the love of friendship; it is a natural link, a bond of unity, which one can fail to respect, but which one cannot ignore. Family love is the love that can be taken for granted, though it should never be taken for granted.

If the young do not find this, they think—and rightly—that they are being starved of one of the ingredients of their spiritual food for which they came to live in community. The group is meant to be a mutual help, a living relation on which one can always rely.

An older spirituality (the attempt to date such things is very difficult and not very fruitful) might say, "But you have given up human love for divine love; this is the sacrifice expected of you." The young reply, "We have offered God our married love

37

for this other way of Love, we have not abandoned human love itself. To love one's brothers—that is, all men—is the heart of the Gospel, and if we do not find it in the monastery or convent we have been cheated. These people are not Christians, they are dried-up moralists and legalists, pharisees and worse, not true followers of Christ, which is all we have come here to try to become."

Is it true that the young do not find love in their communities? Yes, sometimes it is. Some of the old, in the first place, have less sympathy for them than they used to have. They consider their ideas revolutionary, absurd, disturbing, and even heretical. They refuse to budge when anyone suggests adaptation or up-dating. A marked instance is failure to cooperate in the liturgical changes. One can understand their mind, but it is not loving. A little interest expressed, a little warmth and humanity, a little encouragement and congratulation for the successes and interests of the young would make a world of difference, because these signs would show that the community does care. This is not an attitude to be encouraged only among the older members; indifference can possess the young as well as the old. All have to be on perpetual guard against such sins of omission. The sort of occasion where such a breach of community life can occur is, to take an example, the return of a young religious to his community after a few years of study away. He is full of various ideas, some good, some not really new, some perhaps even misguided, but all likely at variance with established custom. Perhaps in some matter he will obtain the approval of authority, but the "old guard" do not like change and so set up a delaying tactic, fail to offer any encouragement, complain to the superior, murmur among themselves, and show disapproval by word and by facial expressions. When this is once begun it is difficult to stop, and it is a serious breach of community life, for out of pride or insecurity a matter of ritual has been given a higher value than the respect and open response and even the allowance that is due to a brother. The conservative say that to change is not their mood and that the young should have more human respect for their situation; but the young are just as fully persons, and their mood also deserves respect. In this cooperation, this communion of different spirits, the older monks may think they possess the spirit of monasticism as a sort of right, for nothing replaces experience; but the young have as their prerogative the spirit of the times—the modern world and the contemporary mind of the Church—and the community as a whole must learn to listen to both of these spirits. Both deserve great respect, for in their different ways they are the voice of God. One thing is certain: modern religious houses will not survive in an ice-cold, inhuman, un-Christian atmosphere. The spirits of old and new must seize the essentials, and one of these is love of one another. Monastic *aggiornamento* is perhaps different from others in being the growth of a stable and permanent community, with each monastery setting its own house in order. Therefore, it is important above all that we possess a true spirit of community life and brotherly love, and that this spirit find expression in all our actions and gestures.

Some of the many subjects treated in this chapter may appear relatively trivial. This is in some cases true: dress, liturgical practice, timetables, and diets are not the subjects that really concerned Pope John when he moved towards a renewal in the Church. For him the change was deeper. His aim was to make the Church so Christ-like in all its members that those outside the Church would recognize Christ in their encounter with it, would love him there and want to link their lives with the Church. Consequently, for Pope John and for the Fathers of the Council he convened, the dominant aim was to renew the holiness of the Church. And the *aggiornamento,* the renewal and reform of the religious Orders are all aimed at making them more Christ-like.

The deeper *aggiornamento* will be a deepening of the spiritual life of monk and nun. Far more important, therefore, than the length of the skirt or the kind of hymn will be the realization of the true meaning of charity, obedience and love, of poverty, of prayer and humility and of all those parts of the Christian life that draw the soul into true union with the Saviour.

Once that has been achieved or partially achieved, then there will surely follow the desire of each Order, each diocese, each Christian to take their due part in the life of the Church and of the world around, according to the spirit of the dedicated life each has been called to. But the Church cannot go out to the world until it has first become fully conscious of its own nature. This applies to the Church as a whole, but also to organizations within it, and to each individual soul. Therefore, we shall next make a brief survey of the Benedictine Order over the world in all its variety. Then we will examine at length the real meaning and spirit of Benedictine monasticism, all in an effort of self-understanding to prepare ourselves for our present course of renewal and *aggiornamento*.

CHAPTER TWO

BENEDICTINES TODAY

1. The Facts

AT THE PRESENT TIME, mid-twentieth century, there are Benedictine monasteries spread through most of the world, from
Tokyo in Japan to Toumliline in Africa, to Woodside in California. There are monasteries of many races, but more inter-
estingly of an almost endless variety of work within the
framework of the Rule.

As Benedictines are in the process of reassessing their life,
particularly—but not only—with respect to outward activity,
it is valuable to have some idea of what those activities are.

In the United States and in Canada almost every known
variety may be found. The most common and the most popu-
lous are the monasteries and convents founded in the nineteenth century from Germany and Switzerland with the specific
purpose at the time of coming to the spiritual aid of the immigrants, chiefly German, then pouring into the Middle West.
So we find the great abbeys of St. Vincent's, St. Meinrad's, St.
John's, and St. Benedict's, the great convents of St. Benedict's
and St. Scholastica's, all dedicated to founding missions,
schools, hospitals, colleges, seminaries, and the like. These
monasteries still have these works and they flourish, particu-
ularly the colleges and the missions, and for the sisters the
schools and hospitals too. These are not the only ones through-

41

out the United States. The pattern is much the same, from St. Leo's, Florida, which has parishes, school, and college, to Westminster in British Columbia which has a small seminary. The emphasis is always on education and in helping the secular clergy.

Now in the second stage of their growth, they have themselves gone into the foreign mission field—St. Benedict's, Atcheson, in Brazil, St. John's in the Bahamas, Mexico, and Japan, others in Peru and Africa.

Nothing is so astonishing in the world of religious in the twentieth century as the success of the American Benedictine sisters. The American sisterhoods generally are the most remarkable side of American Catholicism. But of them all perhaps the Benedictines are outstanding. Almost without exception, where the monks have gone and settled, there the sisters are too, where the monks founded seminaries and schools and colleges, there the sisters did likewise—except for the seminaries; and as the monks spread into the neighboring countryside or neighboring towns to found missions or parishes, there too we find established small clusters of sisters, five, ten, twenty, three hundred, setting up parochial grade schools, high schools, and also hospitals. In other cases they have ventured out on their own, as in Bismarck where they have a hospital and school, or St. Paul's. There are plenty of others. They too are making foundations in South America, Central America, and Japan. A peculiarity of the Benedictine sisters in the United States is the unwieldy size of their communities; 300 is small, 1000 is large.

Recently, a different style of Benedictine monastery has emerged in the United States, in conscious reaction to the active houses; they are small but fervent: Mount Saviour in New York State, Pevely in Missouri, and a third in Arizona, and several others. The emphasis in these is the primacy of the contemplative life with external works kept to a minimum.

Among the Benedictine sisters the same reaction is taking place, particularly in Clyde (Missouri) and another house in the East, Regina Laudis and the daughter houses.

There is also a sprinkling of monasteries throughout the United States from other traditions, particularly the Anglo-American Houses: St. Anselm's Abbey in Washington, D.C., St. Gregory's Priory at Portsmouth,[1] and St. Louis Priory, Missouri. All three are small and holding a balance between great activity and purely contemplative living. Then also there is a Belgian House, refugee from China and now at Valyermo in California; a Hungarian house, Woodside, refugee from Hungary. These are still finding their feet, but are all genuine and often ancient expressions of the Benedictine ideals.

In Europe the pattern is not quite the same, but there too we find considerable variety.

To take England first, which people still tend to think of as a very Protestant country, there are 9–10 houses of the old English Benedictine Congregation which survived through the Reformation. Ampleforth has a monastic family of 160–170 monks; Downside, Douai, Buckfast all over 60; Fort Augustus, Worth, Belmont, and Ealing have under 50. All except Buckfast have thriving schools, all of them are boarding schools except Ealing. None of them runs a seminary, but many are engaged in parochial work away from the monastery, a legacy from recusant times that some abbots are loath to abandon. Up to the present none of these has missions in the real sense. But they all have a strong liturgical life—of fairly recent date—and at Downside a fine tradition of scholarship. These monasteries are examples of the mixed life.

Associated with them are a number of not so active nor so flourishing convents, also survivors from far-off recusant times. Not all thrive; Stanbrook does with a purely contemplative life and a strong liturgical and scholarly tradition. Talacre is the same, and its origins are Anglican. So there is the interesting contrast of flourishing men's abbeys living a fairly—sometimes very—active life under the Rule, and on the other side a handful of convents leading a strict contemplative life, but not flourishing as they should be. The picture for convents is much the same in continental Europe as in England. Though

1. These have all-American communities.

43

the monasteries may thrive, the convents are not flourishing, for lack perhaps of distinctive character and work. This is not true of those which teach—though up to recently the strictness of enclosure has hampered even this activity—nor of those assisting in the active work of the missions, for example the convent associated with St. André.

Besides all these monasteries and convents in England belonging to the English Benedictine Congregation, there are others, that sought shelter from persecution of one sort or another in their own country, in their "new island home." A good example of these is Quarr Abbey in the Isle of Wight, an offshoot of Solesmes in France, very liturgically oriented and with no external works, and in fact entirely English now and flourishing.

France, whose tradition includes Cluny, Corbie, and Clairvaux, to say nothing of the Maurists, has since mid-nineteenth century been the scene of a notable Benedictine revival similar to the German one of Beuron. Like most revivals of the nineteenth century it has an archeological character and antiquarian flavor; the leader was Abbot Guéranger of Solesmes, a nineteenth-century liturgist. The Congrégation de France has about twenty houses, the chief of which is Solesmes, whose great aim has been the revival of the liturgy and especially the Gregorian chant. Their life is strictly contemplative with very little exterior work, except scholarship and liturgical propaganda.

There are other houses in France of a different congregation, of which Encalcat is a good example. It has a small school for boys but it is primarily contemplative. However, it has recently launched out into missionary endeavor in Africa, a work demanding much energy and activity, much on the lines of a Boniface or an Ansgar. Already Encalcat has three foundations in Morocco and Central West Africa.

Belgium's monasticism is an interesting example of variation. There are two large monasteries, the abbey of Abbot Columba Marmion at Maredsous and another, St. André, outside Bruges. The former is much according to type: a large community with a flourishing boarding school, a good liturgical tradition, and strict monastic discipline.

St. André's is more diversified. It has a school like Maredsous, but it has a lively apostolate of the popular liturgy with its missals, and its weekly and monthly journals, but above all it supports a great missionary enterprise in the Congo.

A monastery of considerable interest is Mont César near Louvain; it was founded as a scholars' monastery, ideally suited for this, of course, near the great Catholic University. It has had considerable influence. But vocations have been very slow in coming. One wonders whether that is the way to do it. A monastery full of scholars is not sufficiently diversified. In the case of St. Anselm's Abbey, Washington, D.C., the purely scholarly activity has been mixed with running a day school. After all, not all aspirants to scholarship make the grade, not all are temperamentally suited, not all who enter are scholars. A third solution is that of St. Bernard's Priory, Madrid, Spain, which has remained and will probably always remain dependent on Sto. Domingo de Silos. Monks who wish to study, do research, or teach at the university can be sent there, but not necessarily for a life sentence. In England the great universities of Oxford and Cambridge have Benedictine houses of study for Ampleforth and Downside. These in time might become, like St. Bernard's, houses that monks from all over the world who wish to study may use as a common house of studies.

Chevetogne, founded by the wish of Pope Pius XI, in an early effort to get in touch with the vast flow of Orthodox pouring into the West in the wake of the Bolshevik Revolution in Russia in 1917, is *sui generis,* but all the more interesting and important for that very fact. Its whole work is ecumenical.

Germany is as diversified as America. There are great monasteries with schools or associated with universities; it has monasteries for seminarians' training, missionary congregations like the St. Otillien. But it also has the shrine monastery, or place-of-pilgrimage monasteries like Beuron or Maria Laach, just as

Switzerland has Einsiedeln, or like Monte Cassino and Subiaco in Italy. These places, which have become "national monuments," lose something of their monastic separateness. The great German monasteries, however, like the French and Belgian and St. John's in Collegeville, have been in the forefront of the liturgical movement and of the ecumenical movement, an apostolate for which monasteries in more recent times would seem ideally suited. The convents on the whole are more dated than the monasteries.

In Spain there are two major abbeys and several smaller ones, and two congregations. The most famous abbey, Montserrat of the Subiaco congregation, overlooking Barcelona in Catalonia, is a pilgrimage monastery. Thousands visit it every year. In order to accommodate pilgrims and retreatants, it has built an enormous hostelry. Montserrat is also a great liturgical center, a center for scholars and not unexpectedly a center of Catalan patriotism.

The monastery of Samos in Galicia (originally founded in the seventh century by St. Fortunatus of Braga), now of the Subiaco congregation, has made a foundation in Puerto Rico, not to have a school for the well-to-do, but for the poorest of the poor. This foundation hopes to become indigenous in time, unlike the old South American foundations which remained proudly Spanish.

Sto. Domingo de Silos, built originally in the tenth-eleventh century, and whose two-storey early medieval cloister still stands, was refounded from Solesmes in the late nineteenth century and still belongs to that Congregation. It has many of the characteristics of the nineteenth century revival—a contemplative atmosphere, a liturgical apostolate, and scholars at work.

In Madrid there is a dependent priory of Silos, whose life too is contemplative with an obvious apostolate of spiritual guidance, retreats, liturgical renewal in the capital, and scholarly work. This is St. Bernard's referred to above.

India has at least two monasteries founded by Benedictines

and on the Holy Rule. The most flourishing in Kerala, of which Fr. Bede Griffiths is a member, calls itself Cistercian. It has grappled with the problem of a different culture by a very flexible attitude to the details and spirit of the Rule, trying to bear witness in an Indian way—that is, one grasped by Hindus —to the perfect life of Christ, especially by particular practices of poverty and prayer. They are in the slow process of rediscovering the monastic tradition of the Syriac Church from which the Southern Indian Christian Church derived its faith and practice. Of all monastic experiments at the present time, this is the most original and radical and probably the most important. There is always a danger of binding oneself in a period of experimentation to the legal framework of a monasticism of a different culture and a different period of history. We need the spirit, but we need to clothe it in the manners of our time.

How is it that Benedictines present such a confusing array of "works"? Most Orders are founded for a particular work: Dominicans for preaching, Passionists for "missions," medical missionaries for what their name indicates, and so on. But Benedictines were not founded for any particular "work" or indeed for "work" at all. In a sense it can be said that it was the embryonic order of the Western Church, founded for no one work and so for all works. There is however a caution. Monks were cut off from the world and did not go back into the world except under dire necessity and usually at the command of the bishop or of the pope himself; so any work undertaken—except in the above circumstances—was undertaken within the monastery area itself. As the world became more socially and economically complex, so too did the variety or scope of monastic works increase and not necessarily to the benefit of the monastic spirit. The survey we have made so far provides us with a set of facts on which we shall make some comments. Here in summary is a list of the type of work monasteries and convents often undertake:

(1) Education: high school, colleges, seminaries.

47

(2) Liturgical apostolate: scholarship, the publishing of books, periodicals, and missals; conferences, retreats, the full liturgical life in the monastery.

(3) Parish work: monks living in twos and threes in parishes round the monastery or away from the monastery. Monks going out to parishes at the weekend; monks helping the secular clergy.

(4) Mission work: seminaries, schools, colleges, hospitals, centers in the missions where medical, agricultural, and other help is available, running parishes from a monastic center.

(5) Pilgrimage center: with retreats, conferences, sermons, confessions, ceremonies.

(6) Scholarship: theological, historical, liturgical; publishing, printing.

(7) Ecumenical work: writing, meetings.

(8) Agriculture.

(9) Family counselling.

(10) The town monastery: confessions, sermons, counselling, ecumenism, scholarship, retreats, conferences, etc.

(11) Hospitals.

2. Comments

In the life of the Church today there are a bewildering number of activities, of apostolates; there are endless ways in which the Christian can take Christ to his neighbor, as many almost as there are neighbors. Some of these apostolates are on our doorstep, some are far away in the missionary field. Some are intellectual, some economic, some social, others purely evangelical in the sense of preaching the word. But all of them have to be done, from priest's housekeeper to college president, to apostolate in the wilds of Africa or Asia. We cannot all do all, but each has to choose and fit into the general pattern, recognizing that God is all in all. He is the workman and we are his instruments.

Never before except in the sixteenth century and in the very early Church has the consciousness of the missionary impetus been so great. Yet in spite of this insight the number of missionaries is minimal. The areas are vast and include not only the pagan countries, African and Asian, but also the once Catholic countries like South America, all of these needing hundreds and thousands of priests and sisters in order to provide for the harvesting. That is the greatest need in the Church today. On the other hand, some countries of the old Western culture have tens of thousands of priests, monks, and sisters ministering to a small proportion of the Christians in the world. Repeatedly the popes of recent times have urged religious orders to send out missionaries into the mission countries.

It would be quite in keeping with the tradition of the Order to do so. Therefore, we should examine this new situation, see how Benedictines can best help on the missions—by establishing the monastic life? by schools? by hospitals? by being catechists? Should Benedictines abandon the work or at least some of it which they are now doing in the home land? It could be argued that only by abandoning some of it will the laity be forced to undertake certain works that they are perfectly capable of doing. The most obvious is that of education. The time has come to recognize that the Catholic laity, pouring through our universities and colleges, acquiring M.A.s and Ph.D.s, are ready and eager to take this responsibility.

The second great area of need is in the world of the underprivileged. In American cities and countryside there are vast numbers of Negroes and others who have none of the advantages that the affluent society could have brought them. Here is a work which a religious Order could well undertake in a specific place. Are monks and nuns particularly suited to this work? This again is a matter for examination and dialogue, in fact of experimentation.

But we should not forget one point in all this. The young are spurred on by such undertakings as missions and programs for the underprivileged. These seem to them the only work worth-while. This is a real error. Everyone has a soul to save and needs help, even the rich. Besides, the apostolate of the mind—education—is also one of the key works of today. The battlefield of the world is the mind, Pope Pius XI once said.

The mixed life as led by a great many Benedictine monasteries and convents must be carefully distinguished from the active life. The former is essentially and primarily a contemplative life in which outside activities have been accepted for the good of the Church but which are not such as to destroy the contemplative character of the institution. There is even room here for a further distinction between the Orders such as that of Preachers whose purpose is preaching and yet who remain contemplative in spirit, and the Benedictine Order not founded for any specific work except prayer and penance in a stable life, opening itself as it were to the possibilities of activity within the framework of its life. Then there is the so-called active life, which is primarily the active apostolate with the framework of regular prayer and the vows of poverty, chastity, and obedience. The last are "body and soul" part of the missionary active apostolate of the Church under the general direction of the pope and college of bishops and in detail under the ordinary of the diocese. Both the last case and the Dominican are fairly clear in this matter of relationship between prayer and work. The Benedictine case is difficult. In the various conciliar documents the description of religious is in terms of black or white; either a religious is in an active order and then must take in hand what the bishops decide, or he is entirely contemplative with no apostolic activity and he is praised and left to his own devices. This mixed life is not mentioned except once, though then with much emphasis.

In the *Decree on the Appropriate Renewal of the Religious Life,* the Council Fathers of the Second Vatican Council, after speaking of the purely contemplative "Members of those communities which are totally dedicated to contemplation [who] give themselves to God alone in solitude and silence and through constant prayer and ready penance" (Article 7), go on to say:

In the East and in the West, the venerable institution of monastic life should be faithfully preserved, and should grow ever-increasingly radiant with its own authentic spirit. Through the long course of centuries, this institution has proved its merits splendidly to the Church and to human society. The main task of monks is to render to the Divine Majesty a service at once simple and noble, within the monastic confines. This they do either by devoting themselves entirely to divine worship in a life that is hidden, or by lawfully taking up some apostolate or works of Christian charity. While safeguarding the proper identity of each institute, let monasteries be renewed in their ancient and beneficial traditions, and so adapt them to the modern needs of souls that monasteries will be seed beds of growth for the Christian people.[1]

Over and over again, from the time of St. Gregory the Great to this present century, Benedictine houses have answered the call of the hierarchy, come out of their monasteries for a time in order to undertake some real need of the church: the evangelizing of the Anglo-Saxons, the assistance to the nineteenth-century immigrants to the United States. But then the emergency has receded and the monks have remained in what were once merely temporary outposts.

In a Carthusian monastery there are no works other than leading the monastic life, so the Carthusians do not have the problem of integrating two distinct things. The Cistercian "works" are kept, normally, very subordinate; they are mostly agricultural and the heavy work is done by the lay brothers. In a Benedictine monastery the "works" are usually done by the priest-monks, and consequently, as with the Cistercian brothers, there is a conflict with their specific monastic choir obligations. But in the case of Cistercian lay brothers the choir obligation does not exist. They are excused from the Divine Office, and to the early Cistercians that practice did not seem to be a slackening of ideals. It is true that the lay brothers perhaps could not read and knew no Latin and so Matins would have been a poor form of prayer for them. Thus their labors

---

1. *The Documents of Vatican II*, General Editor, Walter M. Abbott, S.J., New York and London, 1966, pp. 472–473.

were taken to be the equivalent of prayer. Not so the Benedictine priest or sister. They are expected to do both. Indeed, most of them would consider not saying the Divine Office an impoverishment of their spiritual life, particularly if this gap in it lasted any considerable time.

We are therefore faced with a large and widespread problem for Benedictines who have accepted some fairly active form of work, whether it be school, seminary, college, hospital, or mission; and it has to be faced. One solution would be to eliminate these works. That solution is simple, possible, but unrealistic. The Benedictine vocation is generally to a mixed life, and the art of the abbot, his council, and on very crucial occasions the whole community, will be to relate meaningfully the monastic side and the active side with prudence. What are to be the principles upon which he should do this?

Perhaps the overriding principle is that no work should be undertaken or extended which would result in the vast majority of the monks not being able to live the full life. Obviously, we are here not thinking of crisis-action, such as the period of immigration into the United States or the times of persecution in England; even that should always be considered temporary. It is true that the community as a whole fulfills the choir obligation, but that is far too legalistic an attitude. Monks do not take on the choir as an obligation but as an act of worship, and that being so, every monk should normally be able to attend choir.

The problem could be short-circuited by (1) reducing the amount of choir praying, and (2) reducing the number of times that monks went to choir. (1), to the present writer, would appear to be an impoverishment of the specifically monastic side of the life at the expense of the outside work. The argument for (2) might continue: the modern world is so different from that of St. Benedict, or from that of any of the ancient monastic founders, that we have to make allowances; to hold out for anything else would be mere archaism. (We have spoken elsewhere about modifications in the Divine Office.)

In active monasteries a number of monks are excused presence in choir for one reason or another: the procurator, the president of the college, the headmaster and a number of his assistants. It is maintained that the community as such fulfills the obligation. That is true, but what is the effect on the individual monk? These same monks are likely to omit their *lectio divina* with the result of impoverishing their spiritual lives. These cases and the others which come to mind make one hesitate to approve of the huge monastic enterprises which have grown up in this century. The overriding principle which should govern these problems is this: for Benedictines prayer, prayer in common, the atmosphere of prayer is first. Of course, there are unexpected circumstances, but they should remain exceptional.

Now let us consider each of these different activities in turn, reviewing them as suitable to the monastic ideal, to the present needs of the Church, and of the world.

Scholarship. This work is eminently suited to the life of the monastery. It has a long tradition going back well beyond the Maurists, who were, of course, the greatest monastic scholars. Scholarship now needs even less mobility than it did in past ages. Mabillon did not refuse to carry out a number of literary journeys, visiting all the major centers where manuscripts could be found, particularly the monasteries of Germany and Italy and France herself. Today that is scarcely necessary. Given an efficient postal system, the liberal use of foundation money, and apparatus for microfilming and viewing manuscripts, a monk could be set up for life studying all the documents on his particular recondite subject without ever leaving the monastery, becoming another Venerable Bede who would not leave Wearmouth even at the command of the pope.

We said above that the likelihood of a whole monastery of monks being scholars was very remote and this is true. But in each monastery sooner or later one or two men will emerge with that exceptional combination of qualities that makes the real scholar. Too often these qualities are swallowed up in the activities of teaching. Many are capable of being teachers, but the real scholar like Mabillon, Henri Leclercq, or Cuthbert Butler is rare indeed. It should be on the conscience of the superiors to use these men for the good of the Church in an area where the supply is so short but the need is so great. It is one of the glories of the Jesuits that they have set aside such men to engage in basic study in those areas which are specially important in contemporary thought: Scripture, sociology, theology, psychology, archeology, and so on. Can it be that the Benedictines, who in so many ways are ideally suited to undertake these works, have failed to sacrifice men for this study? Benedictines have the advantage that men living permanently in the same house together could work as a team.

As nearly all Benedictine houses are nineteenth-century foundations or refoundations, most of the works that monks and sisters are presently engaged in were begun in that same century, so that they are not specifically twentieth-century works. It should be our concern to judge whether there is a work ideally suited to our monastic spirit but not yet undertaken by us, either at all or only a very little, a work which would also benefit greatly the Church or the world around us.

Undoubtedly, the most typical demand of today by the Church is *missionary work*. Some convents and monasteries are moving cautiously in that direction; one or two have been doing so for half a century. But considering the great number of convents and monasteries throughout the world and their large communities, it might seem that the effort has been half-hearted. Is there any reason for this?

The most obvious reason, and the one always given, is that previous commitments are already so considerable that to undertake another would overburden the community. This is almost always true. Should, however, the commitments now engrossing the communities be continued? This is particularly relevant in the domain of parishes and parish schools. The former are the business of the secular priests, the second might well be that of the lay people. Too much energy may well be

being exerted in schools on the home front, a too great concentration of dedicated personnel in one part of the Church
when the rest is being starved even of the very essentials. It
might prove part of the *aggiornamento* for the Benedictines
and other religious Orders to hand over their parishes to the
bishop, and the schools also. So long as the religious do the
work of the seculars, so long will young men, really meant for
the parochial clergy, become religious.

This is the age of the missions and it would surely prove
true that if the Benedictines had faith and undertook really to
go out into foreign lands, vocations would flow in. Nor should
we envisage in this missionary endeavors simply a repetition
of the school pattern in the home country. It should be true
missionary work, assuming the work of the mission apostolate
but with a Benedictine spirit and pattern. In this work the
Belgians and especially the French of Encalcat have led the
way. But let us beware of the mistakes of past missionaries,
not accepting native members into the community. A mission,
like education, is established so that in time it can become
superfluous.

Are *schools* really ideal from a monastic point of view?
Here the monk is not compelled to leave his present location
in order to exercise his apostolate. The boys or girls come to
the monastery. But it would be unrealistic to deny that together with the boy and the girl a great deal more comes into
the monastery. This is the most active time of life—innocent
activity, it is true, in the main—but what with games, the var-
sity teams, the dances, the social engagements necessary to
keep in touch with the parents, the normal extracurricular
activities: theatre, music, art, and all the others, the religious
will find themselves caught up at times in a fair amount of
activity. Besides this, to run a school efficiently, the teachers,
the religious, must attend the universities in order to study
secular subjects: science, mathematics, Latin, French, Russian,
and this for four years and even longer. Besides being a con-

siderable expense for the community, it means that many of its members are away for years.

If this is true for houses engaged in high-school work, how much more true is it of houses engaged at the college level? Here the intrusion of the world is likely to be even more intense and continuous. Such an establishment has to be very large or else it will not be financially or intellectually viable. Once one reaches this mammoth size, then the pressure on the individual religious becomes in some cases unbearable and the *quies* of the ancient monastic tradition is impossible.

We really must examine whether this multiplication of small colleges is wise. It is surely good to have some Catholic colleges of higher learning. John Tracy Ellis years ago suggested that they should become the joint concern of a number of religious Orders, rather than the private preserve of this or that Order. Perhaps we have reached the period of ecumenism even within the Church when the idea could be at least tried. But for Benedictines this might not be a solution, as they would tend to be cut off in a contemplative enclave. The administration of the establishments is something quite beyond the obligations that the ordinary monk or sister should be expected to undertake. Here surely is an impasse that is not easy to resolve. It may take several decades before the real answer is forthcoming.

The advantage of a school over a college is that it can remain comparatively small; it can occupy the energies of the majority of a community; its organization is not complex and is therefore financially easier to manage. On the other hand, the college seems more real. The college students are grown up whereas the school students are immature; for some this makes the latter seem a "Mickey Mouse" operation and not fulfilling their apostolic spirit. In fact, it is more likely that one can profoundly influence a youngster of fifteen through eighteen than one can the college student who is reaching out to complete independence. The question, however, is debatable.

In general, monastic schools are for the well to do. This has been a tradition going right back to when only the well to do had education anyway. Today, in an age very conscious of the underprivileged, it would certainly seem opportune to examine whether it might not be the time to launch out into work for these same underprivileged—the Negroes and the very poor. Such work would be in complete accord with the character of the young religious, who would like nothing more than engagement in the saving of the secular city. We must not go along with the fallacy that only the poor need saving nor maintain that only the rich can be saved. It would be advisable to have both works, perhaps summer schools for the underprivileged. This is an area where experience would tell us a lot.

A Benedictine community of its very nature is not large and so the type of education most suited to it is not mass education but an education of high standards for a comparatively small group. This type of school appeals to some and not to others. But it has its part to play, and no one should be excluded from receiving this education merely from a lack of means. That is the ideal towards which all institutions of higher education should strive.

Ecumenism, as noted above, has become the full-time work of one monastery—Chevetogne. This is an apostolate particularly suited to the Benedictine ethos. Their motto is "Peace." Besides, Benedictines have a traditional spirituality which is the nearest thing to the Orthodox, since Benedictine formation antedates the break between the East and the West. The whole atmosphere of a monastery is one of peace and recollection. Prayer is the chief agent of reunion and prayer is the center of a monastery. Not every monastery could make a major contribution to world ecumenism, but most could take a significant part in the local activity towards restoring unity. This could be done by individual contacts, by weekends of joint meetings with Orthodox or Protestants; by writing, by conscious prayer and penance.

Hospital work would appear to be eminently suited to a monastic community. It possesses a venerable tradition going back to St. Basil the Great in the fifth century. Here is a clear work of mercy; it can be done near the monastery or convent; it contains within itself the asceticism, the charity, the patience, the self-dedication which we associate with the life of holiness.

Once again we come up against the administration obligations which can be very heavy. This surely could be handed over to secular personnel. But there is another element which does not occur in any other work as far as one knows. This element is the relationship with the doctors. They naturally want the best nurse in charge of this ward or that floor. The reverend mother has to consider that aspect—it is important; but she also has to consider the spiritual dimension, the good of the sisters, the good of the life of the whole community. Not infrequently, the doctors find that their best nurse has been sent off to become novice mistress, or simply has not been found suitable as the head of the department from the monastic point of view. This leads to much acrimony, and is probably the chief problem in hospital work.

Nevertheless, hospital work is suitable for Benedictines. The social life associated with schools and colleges is not present; for one thing, the sick cannot take much part in such activities. These have almost as much *stabilitas loci* as the sisters. The variety of work in a hospital must be considered, allowing of many types of sister to find useful and fulfilling occupation.

We have been through a number of the works undertaken by Benedictines—all with their particular advantages and disadvantages. Still we can judge the whole matter from a different angle.

1. In St. Benedict's time the world was very slow moving; it was predominantly agricultural; St. Benedict himself was not interested in intellectual works. These we could assume reasonably enough as the chief characteristics of his time and his personality which are peculiar to them and need not be followed to the letter.

2. It follows that the very large areas of occupation, not

specifically prayer—even, we might venture to suggest, part of *lectio divina*—could be reapportioned, to pursuits more in accord with our time and not his. In his day there were four hours of *lectio divina* which included study even then—and about the same amount of manual labor. Today much of this time, say six hours, could be taken up with studies and works for God.

These works could include any of the above works of Benedictines today. The only caution one should make is this that the work should not be allowed to swallow up all the time and it should not take the sisters or monks very frequently away from the monastery where they have *quies* and opportunity for the other elements of their life: prayer in common, solitude, community life, etc.

3. We must either stop talking about the contemplative life, or always remind ourselves of what we mean by it.[1] Contemplative life cannot mean a life where the Benedictine monk or sister has contemplative prayer. That could occur, but it is a gift of God; it could be expected, but it is not an inevitable result of living in a so called contemplative community. St. Teresa when speaking about one of her communities remarked that not a single one of the sisters there experienced contemplative prayer; and she did not say this in any condemnatory sense. So, all we can mean by the contemplative life, or contemplative community, is that these are conducive to contemplation.

4. We have now to admit that contemplative prayer can be found in any walk of life; that it is a gift of God and will be given—perhaps in new forms—to any who really *give* themselves to God asking for union with him.

5. Since there is no guarantee that a sister will be a contemplative, she *has* to have activity, work to do, for her own good. A Benedictine pattern is established to provide a setting in which many different types of monks or sisters can live together happily serving God, some more, some less intimately

1. St. Benedict never used the term at all. The contemplative life is one orientated entirely or mainly to union with God in prayer.

aware of God. The important thing is that it be possible for those called to a more contemplative way to be able to practice it.

It will not always be possible for the superior to arrange it, and then surely God will not let the soul suffer, if for the common good he has to go on working more than he would like. Obedience in this is certainly grace-giving.

Having surveyed the manifold works of Benedictines in our time and before comparing all this with the past history of the Order, one final consideration should be borne in mind. Benedictines are not committed by their Rule to any one of these works. From this it follows that as the history of the Church unfolds, the Benedictines undoubtedly as occasion arises will undertake new and important works in harmony with their way of life. But, just as one cannot make a great ocean liner suddenly change course, right about, neither can the Order nor an individual house precipitously change its allotted work.

CHAPTER THREE

BACK TO THE SOURCES

1. The Scriptural Basis for the Monastic Life

(I)

WE IN OUR generation are not the first to undertake an inquiry into the scriptural bases for the monastic life. The Fathers of the Councils have told us to do it; but it has already been done by St. Basil in the fourth century.[1] He was dissatisfied with the way monastic life was going, unsure of the grounds of it, so he painstakingly undertook a private research in the Bible and this he published. By and large it is a *vade mecum* for the good Christian and at first reading has no particular relevance to the monk. But this is precisely the burden of St. Basil's message. All Christians should strive after the perfect life. He would not separate the Christian from the monk. Nor did he make that separation in real life. The Scripture passages he picks out in his *Moralia* begin with those on the attitude of penitence, much as the Gospels begin with the preaching of the Baptist: Do penance. The second theme is detachment from the things of this world: "He is not worthy of me, that loves father or mother more" (Mt. 10, 37). Then he reaches the heart of the Christian life, the twofold commandment of loving God and loving other men. St. Basil links the first intimately with obedi-

---

1. See *The Ascetical Works of St. Basil*. Translated with Notes and Introduction by W. K. L. Clarke, London, S.P.C.K. 1925.

ence: "The man who loves me is the man who keeps [my] commandments" (Jn. 14, 21); "You will live on in my love, if you keep my commandments" (Jn. 15, 10); "Who will separate us from the love of Christ?" (Rom. 8, 35). The second he takes from the standard texts: love your enemies, etc., and, "The mark by which all men will know you for my disciples will be the love you bear one another" (Jn. 13, 35).

Then follow many teachings including being baptized, going to receive the body of the Lord, not lying, doing good works; then the injunction to be poor, which he derives from Luke, 6, 20 & 24 and 2 Corinthians 8, 2: "Blessed are you who are poor; the kingdom of God is yours." — "Woe upon you who are rich; you have your comfort already." Then he treats of prayer. But of virginity and of obedience to human beings not a word. These *moralia* are simply a chain of quotations, something like the instruments of good works in the Holy Rule of St. Benedict collected together without too much order.

This is a confirmation that for St. Basil there was no absolute distinction, division, break between the monastic ideal and that of the zealous layman. He discovered in reading the Gospels and the rest of the New Testament a complex of commands and counsels which covered the whole of life. It was this whole that had to be followed. Is it possible that we in recent centuries have concentrated over much on the three vows? This is the thought that emerges from the above short examination of the *Moralia* of St. Basil.

(II)

Yet no religious Order is the same as any other. If we were only to go to the New Testament we might miss the point of each of them. Each Order is an attempt to live the perfect Christian life, but with special emphases on this or that. What then should be done?

One method could be to collect all the Scripture texts from the Rule and thus discover what were the passages that first stirred St. Benedict to move towards seeking God, which ones were the basis of his teaching. In fact, however, this is a little disappointing. For instance, on the subject of obedience two texts recur, "He who listens to you, listens to me" (Lk. 10 16), and "I came not to do my own will, but the will of him who sent me" (Jn. 6, 38). Besides, in the text of the Rule the Bible occurs more as submerged references, than as quotations on the surface. It is hard to keep track of them all.

Another method might be to determine the main themes of the Holy Rule and then compare those with the teaching on them in the Old and New Testaments. Or, before doing that, would it be best to take the three basic vows of poverty, chastity, and obedience and search the Scriptures for guidance on them? The objection to that inquiry as a starting point would be that monks in fact do not take these vows, but obedience, stability, and conversion of manners. At first this may appear as an obstacle to our inquiry; it is in fact a great liberation, opening up wide vistas. It will become plain when we realize what is meant by *"conversatio morum."*

Without going into the study of the meaning of *conversatio morum* in detail,[1] we may safely say it means vowed following of Christ. For a Christian this perfect life is to be found, taught, and exemplified in the Gospels and the rest of the New Testament. Perfection is living according to Christ's teaching as well as we can. This will be done primarily by practicing the virtues of faith, hope, and love; it is listening to the words of Christ himself. There is a vital order in the way-of-perfection based not so much on the rational connection as on the process of spiritual insight and growth within a Christian soul, not in a desultory sort of way, but rather in an eager and thorough and dogged way.

(III)

It would be easy to establish an order if we conformed to the Thomist-Aristotelian categories; and they are very useful. But neither the early monks nor the writers of the New Testament

1. See Abbot Justin McCann's *St. Benedict,* London, 1938.

did. We have then to attempt some other kind of order which seems to emerge out of those documents.

The headings below are an attempt to present what follows in some recognizable shape. They will have to be kept in mind as the text flits from idea to idea.

Conversion: call, flight, desert

Baptism: death, new birth, vow to give up devil

Imitation of Christ: commandments, counsels, Sermon on Mount, beatitudes, law of love; for example, virginity, poverty, humility, asceticism, charity

Conversion

Let us follow the clue given by some of the early writers: they wished to lead the *apostolic life.* This, apparently, did not mean the missionary life, but the life of those first men who followed Christ. The Apostles were first *called* by Jesus. Precisely, there was a conversion, a *conversio,* a turning to Christ. This is the first step: a movement of the soul, and it can be seen most vividly and dramatically in the conversion of St. Paul: a voice, a striking of him blind. The old world is blotted out; a command, a response; and, from an enemy of Christ, Paul becomes a devoted follower, the great saint. The same pattern is visible in the lives of others among the Apostles. Matthew leaves his money tables; James and John their nets. Andrew and another follow Jesus. Peter says, "To whom else can we go? You have the words of eternal life." In the Old Testament, the story is the same: an ordinary life, a call, a response, a turning towards God. Abraham, Moses hear a voice and there follows for both an abandonment of all. This is especially telling in the case of Abraham, who left a great city at the call of God to go out into a wilderness, a so-called promised land. But even more striking is the theme of the whole Old Testament as a prefiguring of the religious life.

Did not Adam and Eve sin by disobedience? And is not the covenant of Sinai a restoration of obedience to the command of God? But as a start, the People of God have to leave the city where they were slaves to their foreign masters and march out into the desert; there God tried them for forty years, purified them, made them fit to enter the promised land. This is a symbol and was taken to be not only the type of the Church but also of the monastic life, a pilgrimage coming after a call, and one through desert places, where the pilgrim seems to be abandoned. The promised land is not here below but in heaven. No wonder that we find the cult of the desert at Qumrân, and in the case of John the Baptist. Christ himself went into the desert and Paul after him, the faithful disciple. It is not surprising either that the early monks penetrated into those forbidding solitudes of Egypt.

The life of the religious, the monk, must not be considered as a life distinct from that of the Christian, as something new, special, different, and, of course, better. This was the Protestant objection to monasticism as it was commonly understood at the Reformation. The impression given at the time of the Reformation was that only monks and nuns, friars and sisters were true Christians, the rest were second-class citizens at the best. But that is a false description. A religious is simply a Christian living one among many possible ways of the perfect Christian life.

Therefore, and this is of the utmost importance, we must first look at sacred Scripture to find out in general what is the perfect Christian life, and only later search out the specific peculiarities of religious life. Religious do not practice one set of virtues and the laity another. All are, first and foremost, Christians and practicing the Christian way of life. It begins with baptism.

Baptism

Exodus is the type of baptism. St. Paul wrote, "Let me remind you, brethren, of this. Our fathers were hidden, all of them, under the cloud, and found a path, all of them, through the sea; all alike, in the cloud and in the sea, *were baptized* into

65

Moses' fellowship. . . . It was we that were foreshadowed in these events" (1 Cor. 10, 1–2. 6).

In 1 Peter 1 and 2 there is a running comparison between the idea of baptism and the story of the Exodus. They are to gird their loins. Christians make up the new people of God who are torn from the bondage of Egypt (the world of sin— v. 18) by the blood of Christ the lamb (v. 19) in order to go to offer sacrifice to God while waiting to enter the kingdom of heaven (the Promised Land).

Note how Pharaoh objects to Moses and Aaron taking the people away from their *work:* the word has the overtone in Christian times of liturgy, sacrifice. Christ has delivered his people from the work of Satan (work of Pharaoh) in order to do his work (sacrifice with him).[1]

The baptismal rite has as its central theme: death to the old man and birth to the new. Immersion in water might not seem a suitable symbol to use for this. But St. Paul does. Of course, it has the sign of washing, but how that of death and rebirth? "You, by baptism, have been united with his burial"—the total immersion is like a burial—"united, too, with his resurrection" (Col. 2, 12). The coming of the water is likened to Christ's resurrection. This is crowned by a lovely baptismal hymn quoted by Paul near the end of Ephesians (5, 14). "Therefore it is said: Awake, thou that sleepest, and arise from the dead, and Christ shall give thee light."

Death was uppermost in the mind of Antony. He settled in a tomb, then he rose to seek God in the desert. Death to what? To the old man, to the world, in order to be born anew. Once again is apparent, as with conversion, the twofold nature of the monk's life—a turning away, a death; a conversion, a new life.

There we have another theme of Scripture dear to monasticism, to be *born anew*.

Of all the biblical ideas the one closest to the monastic idea, the one that explains it very well, is that of baptism. It is said

1. See Boismard, O.P., *Baptism in the New Testament,* p. 110.

that the earliest monks fled the cities and congregated in the wilderness in order to restore to the Church its primitive zeal, now grown lukewarm once the persecutions had ceased with the accession of Constantine to the imperial throne. The early Christians were spurred on by the witness of the martyrs. There were now none and all the Christians seemed to be sinking back into compromise with the world. The enthusiasm, the zeal, the dedication and sacrifice had slipped away from their lives. The vows of their baptism had been wholesome but were not heeded.

Monks speak of monastic vows. The baptized take vows; to renounce the devil and all his works. What is the relationship between these two sets of vows? The monastic vows are not another baptism, but a renewal of baptism, an intensification of effort, a re-dedication in the sense of the baptismal dedication, a fixed determination to carry through with the vows of baptism till death. The Eastern monks did not take vows, that is to say, in a sense did not repeat the vows of their baptism, but simply took their baptismal dedication seriously.

The Imitation of Christ

The fact of sharing Christ's life through faith in baptism led to the desire to imitate him. Our Lord's own words were an invitation. "I am the way, the truth, and the life."

The early monks thought of themselves and were thought of by other people as Christians who really tried *to imitate Christ perfectly*. They were not ones who took vows; vows, in our sense, came hundreds of years later.

Now, what does imitating Christ mean in the context of the Gospels? For an early Christian it meant picking up a New Testament or listening to it being read and then carrying out its advice. How lovingly the early monks did this: their only spiritual food was the word of God. They did not speed through the book, like sight-seers in their cars speeding through Yellowstone National Park, but stood still and learned it by heart.

67

For days they might ponder over one sentence until it had become part of their deepest being. This is what Pascal meant when he wrote about the "heart's reasons," not sentiment but the biblical heart, the inner man. A desert Father thought with his heart, which had reasons and insights the reason itself could not give him.

Of course we should not kill, nor commit adultery, steal, nor call anyone a liar. But Jesus wanted a more inward spirit than that in his followers; he said we should not lust after one another, we should not only not say hateful things, but should not in our hearts feel that way. He wanted an inward perfection. The following are three stages of holiness: first, the outward appearance; not to show anger or pride, or covetousness, not actually to steal, this is already something. But to have these desires within and to bottle them up ends in disaster. Therefore, the second is not only to appear to be but actually to *be* not angry, not to want to steal anything, not be boastful. Even that is not enough. The third stage is positively to be humble, to love, to be just. This threefold process of perfection, obviously, can be, must be applied to every sin and every virtue. One might spend ten years not showing any impatience or hatred with regard to a fellow man, yet nurse it in the heart, it eating one hollow, gnawing away like a canker. We must seize this inward thing and destroy it, then the outward manifestation will of itself vanish away. But how destroy? Here again a negative, destructive approach will end in frustration and with disaster. Love is the real answer, and once again, if love is introduced, the canker will be cured. "Where love is not, put love, and you will draw love out" (St. John of the Cross). Neither the Christian nor *a fortiori* the monastic life is genuine without love. The Christian God *is* love.

This is clearly the teaching of our Lord, particularly in the Sermon on the Mount.

"You have heard that it was said, 'Thou shalt love thy neighbor and hate thy enemy.' But I tell you, Love your enemies, do good to those who hate you, pray for those who persecute and insult you, . . . If you love those who love you, what title have you to a reward?" (Mt. 5, 43. 46).

The Beatitudes

The beatitudes are the summit of this climb towards perfection to which we are called. "But you are to be perfect, as your heavenly Father is perfect." (Mt. 5, 48). They express not merely the resisting of a vicious act, nor do they express simply a passive interior condition, but rather a positive interior and exterior disposition of love.

It is recorded in the first Greek *Life of St. Pachomius* that when he first set off on the work of founding his monastery "he paid great attention to the beatitudes in general."

It has been a modern simplification and impoverishment to reduce the religious life to the three vows. The very fact that the old Benedictine form of the vows was not these three should have given these moderns pause. When one reads a sentence like the one quoted above taken from the life of St. Pachomius, then the point of the earlier approach is plain. A monk was seeking to live the full life of the Christian in all its aspects to the highest degree towards which grace could lead him. This fullness of the Christian life includes the three vows but it is wider. It is above all expressed in the beatitudes of Christ our Lord in the Sermon on the Mount.

1. Take, for example, "Blessed are the poor in spirit, the kingdom of heaven is theirs"; the emphasis here is not that you can have all the money in the world and be poor in spirit all the same. Jesus was not necessarily speaking to the economically poor of the world but to the underdog, to the humble, to those who did not trust in themselves. Our Lord is here emphasizing the spirit of poverty, of dependence on God.

This is not enough for the monk; the spirit yes, but surely something more. The monk is not vowed merely to keeping the virtues, but to doing so to the limit. In technical terms this is called heroic virtue—but that sounds bombastic and so is best avoided. We may instead speak of the virtue and the counsel. The latter is the equivalent of practicing the virtue to the limit, not only in preparedness of heart but in fact; not only being ready to give up richness or one's own will, but in fact doing so.

So we can now proceed to examine the various beatitudes as pointers to this generous response of the Christian soul, to the teaching of Christ.

One might ask: What has all this to do with monasticism? This question is understandable in our present circumstances, but it denotes a shrinking of the idea of the monastic life. It seems to imply that monasticism is concerned with the vows and the beatitudes are for someone else. But we must press home in season and out of season that Christ taught the beatitudes or counsels rather than the vows. He taught many counsels and not only three. Therefore, in the renewal of monastic life we must keep in the forefront of our minds St. Benedict's teaching to his monks, that their way of life is a following of Christ, that it will be found in the Gospels, and that they are vowed to this wholehearted opening of their being to the mind of Christ. That mind was fully expressed in words in the Sermon on the Mount and in action during Christ's public life culminating in the cross.

2. "Blessed are the patient; they shall inherit the land." It is easy to be impatient, it feeds on itself; it relieves one's sense of self-importance: it drowns with its commotion self-criticism and that from others. At least we should control the display of impatience. But Jesus wants much more: an inward peace, an acceptance, a readiness to suffer injustice or calamity. This requires heroism, and as always in the life of the spirit, faith. Why should we be patient except that God allows these things, in a sense, wills this thing. The summit of patience is to see the hand of God in all and say, "I come to do your will, O Lord." — "Be you humbled under the mighty hand of God." It is easy to see the value of being patient in the little ups and downs

of human life. But in a wider and deeper sense, there has to be a profound struggle to reach the serenity of patience. Any great organization will suffer from stubborn conservatism; for example, the Church, the greatest of them all, suffers extremely from this malady. Since the purpose and nature of the Church are so infinitely more sublime than those of any other organization on this earth, it follows that any blow to its progress hurts more than in any other segment of human life. Here is needed the heroic patience of which Christ spoke. Faith is needed to hold on to the belief that, in spite of all, God guides the Church, God allows these benighted decisions. God allows men to use and misuse his greatest creation. We cannot understand, yet as the Spanish proverb has it, *"Dios sobre todo,"* God over all, and that is enough for us.

3. "Blessed are the afflicted for they will be consoled." The afflicted, the gentle and the patient, the poor, who are these but the "little ones" of the Old Testament, the humble of God, the *anawim,* the poor of Israel? They were promised the land: this is prophetic messianic terminology. "The land" is "the kingdom," in Christ's own heaven, and all that leads to it.

The monks, pondering these beatitudes and the others, thought that to strip themselves of all, was truly to be poor and humble, of no account. They stripped themselves of the world, its glamor and glory, its wealth and its pleasures. There may have been mixed with this a Platonic withdrawal from the material things because, so it was thought, they were bad. But the Church gradually corrected this excess, and St. Benedict was prudent in this matter as in everything else. He saw that the essence of poverty was humility and the key to humility obedience. To be humble is to admit complete dependence. In Hebrew, *anawim* is used indiscriminately for the poor or humble. But the most prized part of us is our free will. To give that up would truly subject us to God.

"Come to me, all you that labour and are burdened; I will give you rest. Take my yoke upon yourselves, and learn from

me; I am gentle and humble of heart; and you shall find rest
for your souls" (Mt. 11, 28–29).

Virginity

Both Christ and St. Paul treat of virginity. Both state clearly
that it is something that is not a command, but something of
great value nevertheless. Christ is laying down the rule of the
indissolubility of marriage and outlaws divorce. The disciples,
accustomed to the relaxing of this law by Moses, think this
is too hard and say, "If the case of a man with his wife is so,
it is not expedient to marry." Jesus does not encourage virginity
for this reason, but rather as an invitation of God. "That conclusion, he said, cannot be taken in by everybody"—namely,
of not marrying—"but only by those who have the gift" (Mt.
19, 11). "There are those who have made themselves so for
the sake of the kingdom of heaven"—that is, who have accepted virginity willingly and for God's sake. "Let him accept
it who can" (Mt. 19, 12).

St. Paul in 1 Corinthians 7, 25–27: "About virgins, I have
no command from the Lord; but I give you my opinion, as
one who is, under the Lord's mercy, a true counsellor. This,
then, I hold to be the best counsel in such times of stress,
that this is the best condition for man to be in. Art thou yoked
to a wife? Then, do not go about to free thyself. Art thou free
of wedlock? Then do not go about to find a wife." But he goes
on that it would not be a sin to get married! "I leave you your
freedom" (7, 28). But he foresees for those who do marry
"outward distress." A little later he explains his reasons for
preferring virginity: "He who is unmarried is concerned with
God's claim, asking how he is to please God" (7, 32).

The early monks—especially the Syrian ones—linked virginity with the life in heaven, remembering our Lord's words that
there, like the angels, we neither give nor take in marriage. So
we find monasticism equated with the heavenly and angelic
life. They went so far as to say, one could not be a true
Christian if one did marry—John Chrysostom in his early

period would be for sending all Christians into the desert: in all this one can see the influence of Manicheeism, and, that being the case, we should treat early monasticism with the utmost caution. Examples of its influence: utter contempt for the body, excessive mortification almost to suicide, no use of fire or cooked food. With Pascal let us remember, *"L'homme n'est ni ange ni bête et le malheur veut que qui se fait ange se fait bête."*

Poverty

The biblical ground for poverty for the early monks was the text that set Antony off on his great quest: "Go, sell all, give to the poor, and come, follow me." It was also the text in Acts describing how the early Christians had all in common, distributing the surplus to the poor. This poverty was also found in the very life of Christ who did not even have a place to lay his head; found in the simple life of Nazareth and in the manner of Christ's death. Poverty was linked with such teaching of the Lord as the one of being prepared to lose our life to gain it; found in the reaction of the Apostles who left their nets, their business, their father and mother, brother and sister. They were promised a hundred-fold even in this life—but, Mark drily adds, *"cum persecutionibus."*

The picture we get of poverty as a counsel in the New Testament is not only an interior detachment, but also an actual experience of poverty.

But poverty is not sought as an end in itself in the New Testament; nor is it a flight from things which are thought to be wicked in themselves. It is presented as a denuding ourselves of something attractive in order to be free to do something even more important, to follow Christ. The story of the rich young man is the classical text for an understanding of the meaning behind poverty. The rich young man is not condemned for refusing to give up his wealth. Christ is sad that he has not taken the opportunity, because in his case this would have led to his perfection. We are not led to understand that

73

the rich young man was damned for the failure of nerve. The position is left open. Christ does go on to explain, not that it is impossible for the rich to reach heaven, but that it is exceedingly difficult.

The reason for this is obvious: riches open the way to a divided heart. You cannot serve God and Mammon. Money is meant to serve us, but to serve it is an idolatry. That is always the danger of wealth.

Humility

Humility is everywhere in the New and Old Testaments. The expression of it that fits our new insights into the inward workings of man's psyche is Our Blessed Lady's *Magnificat*. Most of the *Magnificat* is praise of herself: "All generations shall call me blessed." She has clear vision that God has done great things in her. She does not deny the wonder of her being, she glories in it; at the same time she attributes it to the loving goodness of God.

The crushing weight of sin which Christ took upon himself, so that he could be humble as a sinner should be, is another aspect of humility which we find more difficult to emulate. But this, too, is liberating, because we all are in real fact guilty. To express and recognize this is also liberating; but it only can be for those who know there is a God and one, not a terrible Judge, but a merciful Father. The parable of the publican and the Pharisee is a clear expression of this side of humility.

The Syriac monks, described by Theodoret, in his *History of the Monks,* were galvanized into activity by two passages of St. Paul, one describing the Christian life as a combat, the other describing it as a *contest among athletes.* "You must wear all the weapons in God's armoury, if you would find strength to resist the cunning of the devil. . . . Stand fast, your loins girt with truth, the breastplate of justice fitted on . . . take up the shield of faith, with which you will be able to quench all the fire-tipped arrows of your wicked enemy; make the helmet of salvation your own, and the sword of the spirit,

God's word." (Eph. 6, 11. 14. 16–17). With these the ascetics went into the desert to fight in single combat Satan, the combat of the children of light against the children of darkness.

There was also the famous text of 1 Corinthians 9, 24–27: "You know well enough that when men run in a race, the race is for all, but the prize for one; run, then, for victory. Every athlete must keep all his appetites under control; . . . I buffet my own body, and make it my slave; or I, who have preached to others, may myself be rejected as worthless." So to the early monks there was no mortification too extreme or bizarre to daunt them. Each outdid the other.

Of obedience we treat elsewhere.

(IV)

Each generation must go back to the Gospel to receive the message at its source. Each individual man should do the same. We hear the message at many removes: the preacher who finds it in a book of notes for sermons, which is collected from a seminarian's theology textbook, itself drawn from the great manuals of Garrigou-Lagrange, Suarez, Cajetan, St. Thomas, who relied on the Fathers and on the Gospel. Each man must grasp his New Testament and read it himself. This is what Antony did and Benedict and Francis. That chapter on the instruments of good works is little more than a chain of quotations from the New Testament, the earliest rule of St. Francis is the same: great texts from the Gospel as guides to a Christ-like life. The *Imitation of Christ* also is little more than a well-ordered collection of biblical texts. Sacred Scripture has a peculiar and unique power of coming to life, emitting light for each age for each soul differently. Like a sacrament, the grace of it is the knocking at the door and all we have to do is open our minds and hearts to the message, but it will be Christ himself knowing our need. Is it possible to say what are the texts for our age? Some texts are for all ages, for example "Blessed are the poor," "Little children, love one another," "Take up your cross and follow me." The most telling for any generation are those which run counter to all the preconceived notions of the time, or those that sum up a new experience or insight. Of the latter perhaps this one, "He who takes up the sword will perish by the sword." Of the former, "I have come to bring not peace but the sword."

We are moving out of an over-introspective age in religion into a more God-centered and community oriented condition. Therefore, the passages that strike us in the Bible today are those which describe the People of God, with all the wealth of simile and metaphor and parable at the command of the inspired writers on the one hand and the personality of Christ on the other, as also an intense realization of the up to now hidden revelation of the Holy Spirit, all there in the Bible but scarcely explored.

Asceticism

As for mortification, we leave that to life, we say glibly. This certainly was not the reaction of the Fathers of the Desert. They took Christ's words on death to self almost literally. "A man cannot be my disciple unless he takes up his own cross, and follows after me" (Lk. 14, 27). A cross in Our Lord's day was no *"objet d'art"* but a hideous torture. Like Christ we must be reduced to nothing, who in the words of the prophet was a worm and no man. This is how Paul saw the matter: "God has chosen what the world holds base and contemptible, nay, *has chosen what is nothing,* so as to bring to nothing what is now in being . . ." (1 Cor. 1, 28). Later in his epistle to the Philippians (ch. 2) he equates this death to self with obedience, even to the ultimate of obedience, which is death and a death on a cross. His only desire for glory is to glory in the cross (see Gal. 6, 14). In the Gospel of St. John comes the same theme only with different imagery: "A grain of wheat must fall into the ground and die, or else it remains nothing more than a grain of wheat; but if it dies, then it yields rich fruit." Jesus was speaking of his own death which was soon to come about. But he goes on to generalize for all of his disciples: "He who loves his life will lose it; he who is an enemy to his own life in this world will keep it, so as to live eternally" (Jn. 12, 24–25).

It was these and similar passages which roused the saints to great feats of bodily asceticism, partly in simple imitation of their Saviour, partly in recognition that it was they who deserved the stripes that Isaiah spoke of, which the Servant of God took upon his shoulders for us all. Partly they did it to rid themselves of the evil desires that original sin and their own had left crowding in on their imagination and their mind. None practiced greater asceticism than those Fathers of the Desert, particularly an asceticism of the body with fasts and vigils.

In our chapter on the spirit of the Rule something will be said of St. Benedict's reactions to the tradition he inherited. Here let it be said that the teaching of the Scriptures remains firm and is our only way to God. We cannot live to Christ unless we die to self. Any half measures there keep Christ at arm's length and unable to take possession of our being. On the other hand, we now recognize that there are many ways, suited to many different types of Christians, of being rid of self. The monastic life itself, with its moderate asceticism, restrictions of obedience and of the other vows, with the patience and love required of community living, provides a very effective method for getting rid of "the old man" and putting on the New Man, Christ, *if only the opportunities are taken.* In this matter the spirit of St. Benedict and that of St. Francis de Sales come very close. But neither would teach anything less than the abandonment of self to reach Christ.

Asceticism is an expression of our unworthiness, our sinfulness, an attempt to love, to share, to take some of the burden of the cross, even if we know that our own efforts are vain, yet joined to Christ's they have virtue.

Even if we say that asceticism is praiseworthy, we still call out that we are unprofitable servants, and that all the good in our actions comes from the grace of God which antecedes all our acts. The early monks had the parables, just as we have—the publican in the temple who did not dare to raise his head, who "beat his breast, and said, God, be merciful to me; I am a sinner" (Lk. 18, 13). It was sinners Jesus loved. He came to save them; the others who claimed to be well did not need the physician. Peter, the greatest of the apostles, had said, "Depart from me, O Lord, for I am a sinful man." St. Paul wrote, "When a man becomes a new creature in Christ, his old life has disappeared, everything has become new about him. This, as always, is God's doing" (2 Cor. 5, 17–18).

What then is the use of all this asceticism, this obedience, this prayer? What indeed is the use of the imitation of Christ after conversion and baptism? We know, as the New Testament teaches, that religious actions are not worthy of themselves, but united to Christ, even man's good work acquires efficacy.

The ultimate point of them all—all the practices or works of the Christian life—is the same as the point of the whole of monastic life. They are expressions of love, in answer to the call of Christ. He did say, "Follow me." And if Christians and monks are faithfully following his life and teaching when they do not rely on their own efforts, so too do they follow his call when they embody their conversion to him in an express leaving of home and following of his way of the cross.

Love and asceticism, poverty and obedience, virginity and humility, silence and singing, are all ways of embodying a response to Christ. And though we assert truthfully that they are founded primarily on the call of Christ himself, they are still in accord with the needs of us men, —for who can have a deep personal conviction which is simply interior? What could a lover's affection mean if he showed no signs of it? So monasticism as a way of life and all the practices which are the elements of any Christian life have this point: They are gestures which embody our beliefs, in answer to the word of Christ which calls the Christian and teaches him, which dwells in him and is fruitful. Such "gestures," whether it be a life of virginity or an act of mercy, are traditionally and originally taught to be inefficacious of themselves, yet they are the saving will of God and holy when they emanate from our physical union with the body of Christ. When Christian works are actions of the living members of the body of Christ, they are made worthy by the spirit which animates that body.

Finally, but first as well as last, comes charity: the love of God in which we have to love him with our whole being as Christ taught, and then to love our neighbor as ourselves. The first is the source of all the prayer that has gone up before the throne of God from every monastery and convent throughout the ages, but also it is the source of that obedience without which love in words is only make-believe. The second, or love of neighbor, has been the source of all the apostolic work performed by monks and nuns throughout the centuries, in the missionary field, in the area of teaching, in gathering in the poor and the needy, in the writings of the Benedictines, in their preaching. But especially the love of neighbor is manifest in the mutual love also within each community, a form of love clearly most dear to the heart of St. Benedict: "Let monks, therefore, exercise this good zeal with most fervent love. Let them, that is, 'in honor prefer one another.' Let them bear with the greatest patience one another's infirmities, whether of body or character. Let them vie in paying obedience one to another. Let none follow what seems good for himself, but rather what is good for another. Let them practice fraternal charity with all purity" (ch. 72).

Surely there is no need here to give the Scripture teaching on love, to do so would require another book: God's love in creating and saving us; the images of this love in the Old Testament: the Shepherd, the husband of a wayward wife, the mother-like love for her child, the love of the lover for his beloved; [1] then in the New, Love incarnate who was crucified and died for love of us, who gave us teaching on our way to love both God and fellow men; St. Paul's hymn to love in the

1. See Origen, *Commentary on The Song of Songs.*

first epistle to the Corinthians (ch. 15); finally the little treatise on love which is St. John's first epistle.

(V)

In the succeeding hundreds of years, have there not been other insights which also are pertinent to monks and nuns?

To take only the most outstanding: "You, therefore, must go out, making disciples of all nations . . ." (Mt. 28, 19). That became an imperitive for a St. Boniface, whose action was as charismatic in leaving his monastery as was St. Antony's in going into the desert.

"When you did it to one of the least of my brethren here, you did it to me" (Mt. 25, 40). That has been the source of all of the works of mercy instigated by Christians.

"Jesus called the children to him, and said, Let them be, do not keep them back from me" (Lk. 18, 16), is surely the basis of the educational endeavor of Benedictine and countless religious Orders and others.

"Where two or three are gathered together in my name, I am there in the midst of them" (Mt. 18, 20). There, perhaps, we have the insight of today, that new realization of Christ's presence, not only in the Eucharist but in every encounter.

Of course, we know such texts as "This is my body" are the source of devotion to the Real Presence; the epistle to the Romans the origin of Luther's insight—which in this matter may not have been so wrong as was at one time believed. It would make an interesting study to see how certain texts are as it were brought to the attention of the faithful by the Holy Spirit in order to lead to new ways of understanding the Christian life to fit the needs of the times. That being so, there is no valid reason why Benedictines should not benefit by such insights; quite the contrary, they should. In so doing they may find that they will even modify the insight of earlier generations on certain other texts that have motivated certain reactions to the world around them. We must never suppose that we have reached the repose of perfect understanding. We are at the threshold of the Church's history, not at its end. We are perhaps at the end of the first great period of the Church, the age of Constantine as it is called. This is no reason to suppose that it is the end of the monastic age. But it would be, were there a failure to accept the new insights into Scripture that God grants his saints in every age.

(VI)

Biblical approaches to a Christ-way of living have not the tidiness of the textbook. We have imposed shapes on the teaching of Christ and so seen his words at one remove or even two. What we have to do is to accept the fact that revelation did not come to us in tidy packets, comprehensive systems, closed circuits. The Bible is open-ended. It is not a system but a number of insights. These do not necessarily fit into a scheme. They are concerned with matters partly far above our heads, and any scheme is bound to be inadequate and deceptive at a certain point, at that point where we are deceived into imagining that we understand the ways of God.

We would do far better to behave as the early monks and chew away at one short passage after another, not attempting syntheses, but attempting to grasp that thought thoroughly, aiming at this being one with that insight. Therefore, the chapter is simply a series of headings, guidelines, pointers which should encourage the reader to put it down and then simply look up the text of the Bible itself, and live by it.

Has it never been one's experience when reading a critic's book on a poet, to find that the odd line quoted here and there through the book—said to be superb by the critic—falls utterly flat when taken out of its context? So it is with the Bible—a chain of texts taken out of their contexts lacks substance and life, because though we know this is the word of God, it reads simply like a chain of quotations, and no more. The Spirit of God does speak to each individual soul and he does so specially when his Book is being read. Here is a direct communication

81

between the Christian and God. More of this when we consider *lectio divina.*

2. *Early Monasticism in the Eastern Church*

The asceticism of the third century not only continued in its previous form, but also provided the source of two new developments which were rich in consequences. . . . The baptismal spirituality and devotion to martyrdom of the second and third centuries, in conjunction with ascetical virginity, continued to exert influence as fundamental ideas of monasticism, and so proved their intense vitality. The vows taken by the monk were compared in value with a second baptism, and his life with a spiritual martyrdom which made him, like an actual martyr, an *athleta Christi,* while his continence ranked him in the company of those who are the brides of Christ. The ideal of virginity additionally prepared the way for the concept of priestly celibacy.[1]

Renewal requires a return to the spirit of one's Order. This means in practice a return to the writings and life of our founder, and provides no difficulty with modern Orders whose founder's or foundress's letters have all been edited and the definitive life lovingly written. For Benedictines there is no edition of the letters—none exist; and the "life" is too stylized to be reliable. That leaves the Holy Rule, and that is very short. St. Benedict himself refers us to Holy Scripture and particularly to St. Basil and Cassian; in other words, he points to the monastic tradition of the Eastern Church, to Cassian, and therefore specially to that of Egypt.

It follows that in the Benedictine renewal something needs to be said about the direct source of our "founder's" spirit, both because of its intrinsic importance and because of a scarcity of information on St. Benedict himself. Indeed, the reason for the anonymity of St. Benedict lies much in the nature of his contribution to the living to tradition of monasticism: he

1. Karl Baus, *Handbook of Church History,* vol. 1: "From the Apostolic Community to Constantine," New York and London, 1965, pp. 297–298.

did not make a clean break with the past and start fresh in the religious life, he adapted monasticism to a Western form, and did so by a lifetime of living it on inspiration from the East.

This chapter will consider Origen, St. Antony, the age of Enthusiasm, the great founders—St. Pachomius and St. Basil, then St. Augustine and finally Cassian. Among the questions that will arise are the influence of Manicheeism and of Evagrius.

What is the early history of monasticism? No one knows. Many have theories and there are few facts to support them; gaps abound, the story is a chain with links missing all down the line. Out of the darkness of the third century it seems to emerge ready-made into the fourth.

At the time of Christ, we now know, not far from the Dead Sea, there existed a monastery of zealous Jews, Essenes, with an organization much like a Christian monastic establishment. They recited prayers in common, they received novices, there was a hierarchy of authority within the group. They had their library and their refectory, etc. This perhaps was the "desert" that John the Baptist stepped out of to preach the imminence of the coming of the Messiah, the need for penance, the coming of the Kingdom. Did some of these Jewish monks become Christian and did they carry over into the Christian Church this mode of life? We simply do not know. We do know that wherever the Christian message penetrated, men and women were urged interiorly to imitate Christ by giving up all and practicing virginity.

In the half light of the third century we meet the gigantic figure of Origen. It is generally thought that in his life and writings are the germs of the later monasticism, just as there are the germs of much else in Christian life and thought during the succeeding centuries. But this influence was hidden because some of his theological views were condemned roundly at the fifth ecumenical council of the Church (Constantinople II, 553). Already the great abbot Pachomius was shying away from him. It is said in his *Life,* "Pachomius hated the very name of Origen . . . because, having heard that there were dangerous doctrines in his writings, he had considered him as a blasphemer. . . . Origen had indeed mingled the persuasively false propositions of the pagans with the true sentences of Scripture." [1]

Nevertheless it was Origen who lived in community with his disciples, though not, it is true, away from the world. They read Scripture in common. He praised marriage but praised virginity more—like many of his age he maintained that the marriage act could not be performed without sin. But for Origen separation from the world was far from necessary to the spirit of complete religious dedication. The spiritual man should keep away from secular life and from all fleshly desires, and this in order to go to God in contemplation. But he did not think that holy behavior had to be apart in a separate place. It was not from a place that one should seek holiness but in one's acts, one's life. As has been said, "His religious ideal was resolutely contemplative but his life was passionately active." [2]

Origen was born in Egypt in the year 185 and died in 254. He was the great teacher in the theological school of Alexandria. At one point he had a misunderstanding with the bishop and left Egypt for Palestine, and there was ordained priest.

His writings fall into three categories: scriptural, theological, and spiritual. It was his theological speculation which in part was too daring. It was, however, his disciple Evagrius who "hardened" his positions and led to the condemnation after his death.

As Urs von Balthasar describes it,[3] in spite of the condemnation there is an invisible omnipresence of Origen's thought throughout the patristic age—Cassian, for instance, is grounded on him for many matters, but never mentions him—and also throughout the medieval period. St. Benedict of Aniane, Wil-

1. A.-J. Festugière, *Les moines d'Orient,* vol. 4, Paris, 1963, p. 174.
2. *Théologie de la vie monastique,* Edited by Pierre Canivet, S.J., Paris, 1961, p. 18.
3. *Origène: Esprit et Feu, I. L'âme,* Paris, 1959, pp. 12–13.

liam of St. Thierry, and St. Bernard can all be shown to have read him.

While it cannot even be proved conclusively that he led a quasi-monastic life, nor that early monastic life derives therefore from him, it seems likely that the thought and life of Origen did exert an influence which finally led to the flowering of Eastern monasticism in the following century.

Whether Origen knew it or not, his theories on the ascetic life became the bases for the monasticism that followed. But on one point he was clear and his monastic followers, if such they can be called, took another route. He was surely set upon the ascetic way, on following Christ, and Christ crucified, and also on not following the ways of the world; but that did not mean for him that he should physically separate himself from the world as was to happen with the Fathers of the Desert and all monks of the succeeding centuries. He believed that he could both follow Christ and "leave the world" without being physically separated. His stand is expressed in a lapidary sentence, as it was translated into Latin: *"Segregari autem dicimus non locis sed actibus, nec regionibus sed conversationibus."* [1] — "I say that it is not physical but moral separation that counts, not a man's place but his way of life." We should note the use of the word *"conversatio,"* which of course is the word used by St. Benedict in his second vow, *"conversatio morum suorum."* There can be no doubt that in the Origen text the word means manners or way of life, behavior, actions, or ways; so too in St. Benedict, though the phrase is either clumsy or an idiom, it must mean way of life, and in this case monastic way of life.

Here at the very beginning of the history of asceticism is a clear analysis of the question of the relationship of the ascetic to the "world." It is not only an analysis but a position taken up. Origen recognizes that there is a wrong and a right behavior; he recognizes that it would be possible to practice right behavior by going away to another region of the earth, but he

1. "Lev. Hom. XI, 1," quoted by Owen Chadwick in his *John Cassian,* Cambridge, 1950, p. 82, note 2.

elects to stay where evil exists and to practice virtue there. For him there is no virtue in flight. This is true—we carry our temptations with us into the desert. He does not even recognize the usefulness of flight, though he had devotion to the saint of the desert, John the Baptist. It was Antony who added this dimension to the ascetic life by his spectacular withdrawals—to the tomb, the fort, the outer and the inner mountains.

ST. ANTONY, 251–356 A.D.

No account of primitive monasticism could begin without serious attention to St. Antony the Hermit, the moral founder of the desert movement. He was born in Egypt of Christian parents, who were well-to-do. They died when he was in his teens and he had a younger sister to care for. As he was going to church one day less than six months after their death, he was pondering over how the Apostles left all and followed Christ, also over how the early Christians in the Acts of the Apostles had sold all they had and put the proceeds at the feet of the Apostles. It so happened that the reading in church that day included the following: "If thou hast a mind to be perfect, go home and sell all that belongs to thee; give it to the poor, and so the treasure thou hast shall be in heaven; then come back and follow me" (Mt. 19, 21). That was enough. He first gave his property to the townspeople, sold all the rest except for a little he kept for his sister. But sometime later he heard in church the sentence, "Be not solicitous for the morrow," and gave away the little which had remained and put his sister in the care of "known and trusted virgins." Then he began to give himself up to the ascetic life.

We tend to think of Antony as the first monk. But at this very point in the story, Athanasius tells us indirectly that already there were monasteries. He writes that Antony lived near his own house, "for there were not yet so many monasteries in Egypt," [1] which implies that if there were not many, there were

1. Athanasius, *Life of Saint Antony,* Translated by Robert Meyer, Westminster, 1950, p. 20.

some. What was certainly unheard of was living in the desert.
"No monk even knows of the far-away desert." [1] This again
implies that when Antony began there were already monks;
his first action was to put himself under one of these ascetics
who lived in the next village. The latter was already old and
had been an ascetic from his youth—let us say fifty years. It is
generally agreed that Antony himself took up the ascetic life
c. 270—so the other man had been practicing it since c. 220.

The next step in Antony's life was his withdrawal to a tomb
some way from the village—a tomb was a little mausoleum, a
one-roomed house for the dead. He remained locked up there
in a vault until he was 35 years old, that is, for approximately
fifteen years. The symbolism of the tomb should not be lost.
In baptism the Christian dies to the old man in order to rise
with Christ in the new life. Monasticism is a burial with Christ.
All during this time a friend of Antony's would bring him
bread at regular intervals and, one supposes, though it is not
mentioned, the "bread of heaven" too. This was something a
lay Christian could do at this time as a kindness to the sick.

From there Antony went to Pispir on the east side of the
Nile, at a place known as the outer mountain. Here he took up
his quarters in an old fort. Equally symbolic, the fort was the
place of Antony's battles with demons. This period lasted for
twenty years, so at the end of it Antony was 55, with another
fifty years to live. At this moment in his story, midway between birth and death, some friends went out to find him. They
broke down the door of his fort and implored him to allow
them to copy his form of life. This he allowed and taught them
his way. Many gathered around him. On one occasion he even
led a group back into civilization to Alexandria, hoping to share
the death of the martyrs in the latest persecution that had suddenly burst upon the Church; but neither he nor they received
that grace.

As his solitude was more and more reduced by the intrusion
of disciples, he once again fled. He made towards the Red Sea,
seeking solitude and God. He settled at the foot of the inner

1. *Ibid.*, p. 20.

87

mountain, from which point he could look out towards Mount Sinai. Having fought the demons, he now made his way up the spiritual ascent to the dwelling of God. At the inner mountain he died, but not before he had revisited Pispir and his disciples, bequeathed a few belongings to his friends, including his cloak to Bishop Athanasius. He was over a hundred years old.

Antony founded no Order. He was a pathfinder, a pioneer, a sign. His message was very simple, and it has been the goal of monks ever since, to seek God and nothing else whatever. He had no need to preach, his life was a vivid enough sermon. He had left all, and his search in the desert on the slope of the mountain was for God.

There followed an episode in the history of the Church of enthusiasm on a gigantic scale. Not a handful, not hundreds, but thousands of men fled into the desert parts of Egypt in order to follow the example of Antony. His life seems extreme to us; it was certainly of a prophetic quality. But his extremes were nothing to what followed. The excesses of his successors outdid anything he attempted. It was, at times, asceticism run riot.

The extreme asceticism and rejection of the world of the early monks of the desert have represented for some the ideal of monastic life. For others these have seemed incompatible with biblical teaching. It is true that we have the famous passage in the Epistle to the Hebrews: "And others experienced mockery and scourging, chains, too, and imprisonment; they were stoned, they were cut in pieces, they were tortured, they were put to the sword; they wandered about, dressed in sheepskins and goatskins, amidst want, and destress, and ill-usage; men whom the world was unworthy to contain, living a hunted life in the deserts and on mountain sides, in rock-fastnesses and caverns underground" (11, 36–38). But they did not do these things to themselves; it was others who chained them, who hunted them so that they had to live in the caverns and mountains. They were suffering a major persecution. The early monks' sufferings were self-inflicted.

88

Pierre Canivet, describing the Syrian ascetics, writes as follows:

The ascetic fled his family and even his country, withdrew all alone to be in the company only of wild beasts, deep in the mountains, in clefts in the rocks, in holes in the ground. He ate nothing except what sprang spontaneously from the soil and which he had not tilled. Some went as far as to expose themselves to fire and snakes. These austerities, which went far beyond anything that might be suggested by examples from the Old Testament, *probably derived from Manicheeism,* which may well have stamped the beginnings of monasticism in Syria with its dualistic spirit, persuading it to destroy everything that could remind it of civilized life, persuading it to renounce the use of fire, to condemn manual labor as something evil, to be content with a vegetarian diet and push asceticism almost to the point of self-destruction and suicide.[1]

Arthur Vööbus, in his great work on asceticism in the Syriac Church,[2] quotes the contemporary St. Ephraem, the famous Syriac Doctor of the Church, as saying that monks had given up work, roamed about the desert like wild beasts, eating only grass and roots. They were matted with filth and dirt; they even killed themselves by their severe fasting, by delivering themselves over to wild animals, snakes, and even to the flames.

Vööbus points out that this is not reasonably derived from Christian Scriptures, and maintains like Père Canivet that it is closely related to Manichean thought. The Manichees believed that all physical existence was the work of the devil, not of God. Therefore, they aimed at destroying all earthly ties within the family and the nation, to destroy the desire to plant or sow. Manual labor was damned as a sin. The use of fire was forbidden, and any food eaten was to remain uncooked. The body was no better than dirt and to be treated accordingly.

1. Canivet, *Théologie de la vie monastique,* p. 251.
2. *History of Asceticism in the Syrian Orient,* "Corpus Scriptorum Christianorum Orientalium," 2 vols., Louvain, 1958, 1960.

In Mesopotamia at this time in the fourth century, the Mani-chees, the followers of Marcion and the Valentinians, were the majority of those who called themselves Christian. The Manichees, we must remember, considered that they were the genuine fulfillment of the Christian revelation. The orthodox Christians were a minority. The Manichees, as part of their eclectic principles, assumed Christian terminology, adapting their doctrines to Christian ways of thinking.

The Manichean influence had also spread to Egypt and North Africa. According to Jean Doresse, writing on the newly discovered Gnostic library from the Fayum, this find makes it evident that Manichean doctrine was largely dependent on Gnostic literature. "Mani acquired his doctrine . . . , for the greatest and most important part, from direct acquaintance with Gnostic thought." [1]

W. H. C. Frend sums it up as follows: "In Egypt we find two religious movements, both non-Greco-Roman in character, gaining ground in the countryside at the same time, namely, monasticism and Manicheeism. Though their adherents hated each other, they had much in common." [2] He describes how the disciples of Mani had penetrated as far as Upper Egypt. One Hieracas, a Copt, "at the same time that Antony was living in the desert, . . . was teaching the ascetic groups he founded the typical encratic precepts of abstinence from marriage, wine, and animal food, together with a denial of the resurrection of the body." [3]

We know that the great Augustine himself had been entangled in this religion. He wrote voluminously against it after his conversion to Christianity. In his *The Customs of the Catholic Church* he made a point of praising the anchorites of the East in order "to hold up to the Manichees the marvellous powers of self-denial which these Christians displayed, for the Mani-

1. *The Secret Books of the Egyptian Gnostics,* New York, 1960, pp. 312–315 and p. 98.
2. *Martyrdom and Persecution in the Early Church,* London, 1965, p. 453.
3. Frend, *ibid.,* p. 254.

chees were immensely proud of their own practice of these virtues."[1]

So it is not surprising if we find in the accounts of the monks of Egypt something of the same excesses that we have already noted among the monks of Syria and Mesopotamia. Every now and then those typically Manichean elements emerge: avoidance of washing, refusal to use fire, eating of uncooked food, vegetarianism, tendency to self-destruction by excessive penance. These early Egyptian monks and hermits were often competitors in hardship. Palladius in the foreword to his work, *The Lausiac History,* uses the term "athletes" four times in his description of them. They are contestants in the arena. Dorotheus, Palladius's first guide in the ways of asceticism, to the question "What are you doing, Father—killing your body in such heat?", replied, "It kills me, I will kill it."[2]

A good example of this competitive spirit is the story of Macarius of Alexandria, told by Palladius.

Macarius had a practice that whenever he heard of any form of asceticism, he would practice it himself and to perfection. On one occasion he heard that the monks of Pachomius's monastery at Tabennesi ate their food uncooked throughout Lent. So he made up his mind to eat *no* food that had come in contact with fire. For seven years he ate nothing but raw vegetables.[3] On another occasion his austerities so enraged the monks at Tabennesi that these went to their abbot and said, "Either he goes, or we do,"—a story which throws a vivid and strange light on the spirit in which penance was practiced in those days even in St. Pachomius's monastery.[4] But before going on to examine the great innovations of this great founder of monasticism we should draw some conclusions.

Our purpose is not merely to describe the monastic situation

1. Quoted by F. Van der Meer in *Augustine the Bishop,* New York and London, 1961, p. 208.

2. *The Lausiac History of Palladius,* Translated by R. T. Meyer, "Ancient Christian Writers," vol. 34, Westminster, 1965, p. 33.

3. *Ibid.,* p. 58.

4. *Ibid.,* p. 62.

in the fourth century, but to glean from the description the essential elements of its monastic spirit. They are: (1) a seeking of God through the asceticism or stripping of one's desire for property, one's marital desire, one's own will, subjecting it and one's body to mortification; (2) a tendency to separation from the world, either by complete flight from the town or cutting oneself off from normal human intercourse. The ascetic side should not be misunderstood; better than "stripping" oneself of one's desires and will, we should say the training or "exercise" of them towards God; such an activity, while not natural in the sense of ordinary, is not inhuman.

But these two essential elements of early monasticism were attended by certain misunderstandings and exaggerations: (1) We must admit that the tremendous experiment in solitude which St. Antony's example gave rise to, proved on the whole unwise, as it led to much individualistic asceticism of an extreme sort. In fact, as we shall see, it gave way to a more orderly and stable life in community. (2) We have to admit also that there was a strain in this early monasticism which can only be described as gnostic and Manichean, for their motive for being separated from ordinary society was that it was intrinsically bad. There was also a tendency, as in Gnosticism, to seek God not so much in love as in knowledge. Asceticism, flight from the world, contemplation—all these things needed clarification and distinguishing from neighboring ideas, so like but so different. (3) It must be noted, too, that early Egyptian monasticism had a limited goal, concentrated much on self. The second commandment and the practices which flow from it were rarely prominent. (4) Lastly, the impression one gets is that the monastic life of those multitudes who fled the world was viewed as the only perfect life, that everyone else was leading a life which was coming to terms with the world, particularly those who married. Once again this seems to have been due to the overpowering influence of Gnostic thought, particularly as organized in the Manichean religion. This problem has remained with the Christian Church ever since, and while it must have been clear that marriage is a noble Christian thing, not until our own day has a clear understanding of the various ways of Christian life been worked out.

ST. PACHOMIUS

Of the three great law-givers of monasticism, Pachomius is the earliest in time. He was born in *c.* 290 and died in 346, that is, ten years before Antony passed to his reward. But unlike Antony, Pachomius was born of pagan parents in Upper Egypt in the Thebaid. His life was written very soon after his death in Coptic and perhaps in Greek. The Greek version begins somewhat as follows:

While a crowd of martyrs, after all manner of tortures, were put to death at Alexandria (A.D. 311), faith in Christ increased beyond measure throughout the land. It was as a result of this that hermitages and places where asceticism was practiced sprang up, inhabited by persons known for their chastity and their abandonment of riches. When the converts from paganism to monasticism had witnessed the combats and patience of the martyrs, they undertook to reform their lives, living according to the words of the Epistle to the Hebrews, "plunged in want, in anguish and affliction, wandering in the deserts, mountains, caves and caverns of the earth" (See Heb. 11, 37 ff.). The atmosphere in the first quarter of the fourth century was one of great exaltation and there were many converts in Egypt.

When Constantine came to the imperial throne the persecution ceased but not the wars. Constantine sent word that he needed soldiers and gave orders that many should be pressed into service. Pachomius, then about twenty years old, was among those taken. As the conscripts were floating down the Nile, the soldiers guarding them disembarked them at Thebes, where they were kept prisoner. When evening fell, kindly Christians, who had heard about the plight of the conscripts, brought them food and drink and other necessities, seeing their affliction. Pachomius, on making inquiry about all this, found out that the Christians did not only practice acts of mercy on strangers but on all men. So he asked what a Christian was and they replied, "They are people who bear the name of Christ, the only Son of God, and who do all good works towards all, hoping in him who has created heaven and earth and us men."

Pachomius then and there vowed to God that if he came out of the present predicament he would be "the slave of God's will all the days of his life." As it happened, still traveling down the Nile, news came that the Emperor's war was over and won, and that he no longer needed these men. They were informed that they could return home. Pachomius did not return home but calling in at Chenoboskion received baptism. Wanting to become a monk, he was advised to put himself under a holy anchorite, Palamon. In great austerity he lived with him for some years. But one day, having penetrated into the neighboring desert, he prayed and a voice told him to stay and build a monastery. Palamon gave his permission and by slow degrees it came about. The first steps towards the creation of the cenobitic life are described beautifully in *The Life of St. Pachomius* as follows:

One day as he and his brother were cutting reeds on an island for making mats and when he had gone aside to watch and to pray in order to know the full will of God, an angel appeared to him coming from the Lord . . . who said, "The will of God is that you should serve the human race in order to reconcile them completely to Him." Having repeated that three times, the angel disappeared. As he was pondering over the words that he had heard, and was convinced on the point, he began to receive those who came to him. And thus, after having rightly proved their dispositions and those of their parents, he dressed them in the monastic habit and led them forward slowly in the monastic life, teaching them principally to renounce the world, their family, and themselves, and so follow the Lord himself in his teaching: for that is the carrying of the cross. . . . As they saw that not only was he worn out by mortifications but had taken upon himself almost all the business of running the monastery, they were stupefied. For it was he who prepared the table for meal time; who likewise sowed the vegetables and watered them; who answered when someone knocked at the door. And if any of the brothers was ill, it was he who hurried to help him and looked after him at night. . . . He was establishing for the novices a total absence of worry. "The purpose of your vocation is what you should work at," he told them. "Study the psalms and the teaching from the other parts of the Bible, but especially the Gospels. As for me, it is by making myself God's slave and yours that I find rest."

Even though Pachomius was not a cleric—nor was there a priest among his disciples—he practiced the missionary life as far as he could. "He put all his energy to rebuilding a church in a deserted village for the shepherds of the neighborhood who were in fairly large numbers. The aim was that they should congregate on Sundays and Saturdays to hear the word of God. This he did under instructions from Bishop Serapion of Tentyra. So he would go to the church with the brothers, and he would read the passages at the time of Mass, for there was no lector. He took charge of the expenses of the offerings for them and for strangers until a priest was stationed there." [1] On the right bank of the Nile at Tabennesi he had a great monastery of 1300 monks; on the opposite bank his sister founded one for nuns. It is recorded in the Greek biography that when the sisters had a death, the corpse would be laid out for burial by the nuns, then placed on the bank of the river. The brethren would then ferry across and, having wrapped it in palm leaves and olive branches, would bring the body over and bury it in the common cemetery.

Soon Pachomius had to found other monasteries. By the time of his death there were already nine of these, each with about two or three hundred monks; there were also two more convents.

Here is some account of the way his monasteries were organized, taken from the Greek life. It makes an instructive comparison with the life of St. Benedict.

In the presence of old people or the infirm or of children, he was moved to tenderness and looked after their lives in all respects. If some of the brothers were progressing in virtue, their faith flourishing, he would rejoice: in fact, they all outdid one another in well-doing. In addition, he appointed certain assistants to keep the lives of the monks safe and sound: one as administrator of all the

1. See *Les moines d'Orient,* vol. 4. pp. 170 f.

95

material affairs of the monastery, another under his orders to help him. He appointed also a head for each house and a second to help him too. The first house is that of the minor bursars (or housekeepers), preparing the tables of the monks and with the job of preparing the dishes to be handed out to them. Now the monks were very different in disposition; and if one of them wished to return to total abstinence, he could practice it zealously without any impediment. After that he established another house of bursars [*économes*], whose business was to nurse back to health all the sick brothers by vigilant care, according to the rules of the community; and he put at their head a house leader and his assistant. At the gates of the monastery he set circumspect doorkeepers who were strict and hospitable, with orders to receive the visitors each according to his rank, and to keep them with the future monks, instructing these in the ways of salvation until he gave them the habit. Likewise, he appointed other steady monks distinguished by their piety to sell the work of the brothers and buy the necessary tools. . . . Other houses were also set up by him with their house chiefs and the seconds for working at the various crafts and for making mats as well as to respond to any order, but without fixing the will of their hearts on any single thing, so as to bear fruit for God.

Pachomius established himself at his first foundation, Pbow, only a few miles away from Tabennesi, from where he ruled much like the general of any modern Order. The other monasteries were ruled over by an *"economus."* It has struck the present writer that the description of the *cellararius* in the Rule of St. Benedict derives much of its spirit from just these officials who had to be at once cellarers and fathers of the community. In the Rule of St. Benedict, where the *cellararius* is in the same monastery as the abbot, there would seem to be a duplication of functions.

Historians of the beginnings of monasticism had got into the habit of considering the Pachomian institution as an intermediary and transitory stage between Antony and Basil and so on to Benedict. This was an understandable position so long as the only source was the Rule of Pachomius, and that in the Latin translation by Jerome. But since we now have, especially owing to the indefagitable researches of L.-Th. Lefort, an extensive Pachomian corpus, among which are included the writings of his first disciples, such a position is no longer tenable. The more we study this "Pachomian dossier," the more we are forced to the conclusion that this man was of exceptional stature and that an intense influence emanated from him during his lifetime. Not without reason his disciples compared him to the great legislator of the Old Testament, Moses.[1]

The reasons Bacht gives are that Pachomius grounded his monastic theory firmly on sacred Scripture, the Rule is as up-to-date as it was when it was first written, and it has a form of monastic piety which "is not under the stifling influence of the ascetico-mystical doctrine of Evagrius of Pontus and which, therefore, is not exposed to the dangerous unilateralism of Hellenic spirituality." [2] He could scarcely have been under that influence, because Evagrius did not reach Scete until forty years after Pachomius's death. Even the latter's favorite disciple Theodore, had died in 365, and Evagrius did not arrive until 382.

According to the anonymous writer of *The Life of St. Pachomius,* Antony the hermit himself, when visited by some of the monks from St. Pachomius's monastery, once stressed the great significance of Pachomius's creation. This is how it happened:

Now it happened that on the occasion of Archbishop Athanasius's return from the imperial court (346), the brothers who had gone to Alexandria by boat learned by hearsay that blessed Antony was at the outer mountain [Pispir]. They disembarked from their boat, climbed the mountain to see him and receive his blessing, for he was a man of God. On his side, when he had heard that the brothers were arriving, he rose up, with great difficulty—for he was extremely old—came out at their approach, and welcomed them. Then he asked, "How is Abbot Pachomius?" As they were weeping, he understood that he had died. Then he said to them, "Don't cry. You have become like Abbot Pachomius. I tell you, it was a great service he undertook in gathering together such a large number of

1. Heinrich Bacht, S.J., in *Théologie de la vie monastique,* p. 38.
2. *Ibid.,* p. 41.

brothers, and he walks in the way of the apostles." Abbot Zacchaius then spoke: "Rather it is you, father, who are the light of this whole world. Your fame has reached as far as the Emperors, and they glorify God on your account." Antony replied, "I am going to show that you are wrong, Zacchaius. At the beginning, when I became a monk, there were no monasteries [coenobia] for the instruction of other souls. Each of the ancient monks, after the persecution, practiced asceticism by himself. Then your father, by the inspiration of the Lord, created that beautiful establishment. There was certainly one before him called Aotas, who wished to take upon himself this service; but as he did not give his whole heart to it, he did not succeed. As for your father, I have often heard people speak about his good conduct, according to the Scriptures. In fact, I have often wanted to see him in the flesh; perhaps I was not worthy of that honor. Be that as it may, in the kingdom of heaven, by the grace of God, we shall see one another, we shall see all the holy fathers, and above all Him who is our master and our God, Jesus Christ. Have confidence then, be strong and become perfect. Tell me, whom has he designated as his successor?" [1]

Once again we ask the question of value: What contribution did St. Pachomius make to our understanding of the sound tradition of monasticism?

He recognized that monks needed some guidelines, a Rule, to limit their ascetical fervor. In other words, asceticism was not the more perfect the further it reached to the limits of human endurance. Ascetical practices were only means to the love of God.

He saw that an ordered life in community was good for the monastic soul. He organized his monks so that they should all have some useful work to do. In this he was far from following the example of his predecessors who sometimes despised useful work.

By his example, he showed the way to the life of service

1. Festugière, op. cit., p. 225. See Les vies coptes de St. Pachôme et de ses premiers successeurs, Translated into French by L.-Th. Lefort, Louvain, 1966. I give this at some length because it is only recently available and in French.

within the monastery: he looked after the sick and the strangers; though not a cleric, he preached in the neighboring villages. This is an outstanding example in the literature of early monasticism of the love of God growing fruitful in love of one's neighbor.

Today we might be inclined to deplore the immense size of his monasteries, and the centralization of his congregation, where nine monasteries of more than 300 monks each were ruled by a kind of abbot-general from one of these monasteries.

We are indeed a far cry from the beginning where each monk lived, as his name implies, in utter solitude. Here we have a thriving "town" with all that was needed for civilized life, as known then. Nor were the monks averse to going out into the neighboring countryside at harvest time to work for a wage and come back with enough to keep them alive for the greater part of the year.

Our comment on this must be that monasticism has become, and legitimately, for the sake of the end it pursued, an organized life of celibates, possessing all in common, living by a common rule of moderate asceticism—by the standards of the time—in order to be able to seek God in prayer. Though much larger than the usual family life of contemporary monasteries, Pachomius's *coenobia* were nonetheless real monastic communities in which the search for God could be undertaken by all.

ST. BASIL

The second outstanding legislator for monks was St. Basil the Great. He was born *c.* 330 in Cappadocia of a cultured and Christian family. His studies were extensive, he went to Constantinople and even as far as Athens, and after his studies were completed he taught for a year. But then, with a brilliant career before him, he abandoned all and became an anchorite under his friend Eustachius, Bishop of Sebaste. He was dissatisfied with the monastic situation; even a journey to the Egyptian and Palestinian monasteries or laura did not resolve his doubts.

So he decided to find the answer from the Bible itself, especially the New Testament; there he discovered what the perfect Christian life should be.

On this subject St. Basil wrote two major works and a number of letters. The major works are the *Little Asceticon* and the *Great Asceticon*. These are in no sense a Rule—though often called so. They begin with a number of principles of the ascetic life, which are followed by questions and Basil's answers to them. It appears that the *Great Asceticon* is simply an expansion of the *Little Asceticon*. The latter was written before 370 and the *Great Asceticon* after that date, which was the time he was created bishop. There are some notable developments from the earlier to the later document. In the earlier penance comes first on the list of priorities and love of one's neighbor no. 162. In the later one, love of God comes first and love of neighbor second; penance is some way down the list.

There is another interesting and important shift of emphasis. In the later work it is clear he is not trying to found a religious Order. He is trying to show that the perfect life is for all Christians, each according to his capacities, desires, and grace. St. Basil's ascetics, or philosophers, therefore do not live away from other people but in the city. They are part of the people of God. They are away from the "world" insofar as the "world" is sinful, but primarily they do this in intention. As one commentator describes his "monks," they were "a mixture of the Christian life in the world and Egyptian monachism." [1]

Basil built a great hospital next to his monastery where the monks could fulfill their neighborly love by caring for the sick and the lepers; in the same complex of buildings was a hostelry for the indigent, for the old and for orphans. There was a school for oblates and for poor children. There were workshops too where the monks could do manual labor and where the poor who were out of work could find employment. It would be hard to find anything less like the desert concept of the monk than this. Yet it was St. Basil's ideal that appealed to St. Benedict,

1. Jean Gribomant, in *Théologie de la vie monastique,* p. 113.

and this we should not forget when the glamor of the desert appeals to us.

The world and St. Basil. We know that at Caesarea he established a huge hospital and had his monks undertake all kinds of social work. But it would be inaccurate to conclude that he did not believe that the monk should be away from the world. His position seems to have been something as follows, and it is important because of our present-day attitudes to the world. St. Basil really wanted all Christians to live the perfect life; he inherited this from his friend Eustachius. But he realized that in the world this was exceedingly difficult, though certainly not impossible. Therefore, the leaving of the world was more a practical decision than a theoretical one. On the other hand, as far as the inward man was concerned, there was no perfection for any Christian whether in the world or out of it except by an abandonment of it. Here is his thought from the sixth rule of the *Great Asceticon:*

The Necessity of Retirement

A retired habitation is a help to the soul in avoiding distraction. For to have one's life always mixed up in those who are fearlessly and scornfully disposed towards the exact observances of the commandments is shown to be harmful by the words of Solomon who teaches us: "Be not a companion to the angry man. . . ." Accordingly, our first step is to seek a retired habitation, lest through eyes or ears we receive incitements to sin and imperceptibly become accustomed to it. . . .

To deny oneself means a complete forgetfulness of the past and retirement from one's own will, in which it is very hard, almost impossible, for a man to succeed when he lives in promiscuous intercourse.[1]

If one thought only of loving God it was easier to take the plunge into the desert and leave all men behind. But St. Basil in his search through Scripture was forced to recognize that the second commandment was to love our fellow men, and that the second should normally flow from the first. It was this that

1. *The Ascetical Works of St. Basil,* pp. 162 f.

drew him and his monks back into or at least near the world and immerse them in good works.

"Now the solitary life has one aim: the service of the needs of the individual. But this is plainly in conflict with the law of love, which the apostle fulfilled when he sought not his own advantage but that of the many, that they might be saved." [1] Basil ends by quoting the famous description of the early Christians at Jerusalem, "of one heart and soul" (Acts 4, 32).

The significance of St. Basil for our inquiry into the essence of monasticism is of course great. Yet even he, no more than anyone else in those days, did not really recognize the equal status of the married and monastic life. Like his first master, Eustachius, he was near to thinking that the perfect life included the abandonment of the idea of marriage, and that the latter was a very second-class condition for the baptized. We have already noted the possible origin of this imbalance.

But St. Basil has many positive contributions to a true understanding of monasticism. He saw it as a way of following perfectly the Gospel, that is, chastity and poverty. He was convinced that obedience was more important than great asceticism. He was equally convinced that the monk was not excused from love of neighbor in any practical way that was needed in the locality. This led him, as we saw, to associate good works with his monastery.

It also led him not to be concerned that his monastery was in a town where these good works could be performed. But he was convinced that the monk should live a retired life.

It will be seen that this is a much more nuanced concept of monasticism than the simple outlook of an Antony or a Simon Stylites. He is taking into consideration many aspects of human nature: the need for work, the duty to help others, the need for obedience, like Pachomius. These are all practical judgments and perhaps all we are able to discover is this: granted that monasticism is a search for God without the worldly dedication required by marriage and money, the way that this situation can best be managed will vary from time to time, and from

1. *Ibid.*, p. 163.

102

person to person: one will be led, by the Spirit, to absolute solitude, another to a community; one to almost continuous prayer, another to good works.

As time goes on, this multiplicity will receive names. Thus those who propose to be absolutely solitary will be hermits; those who wish for community life which is almost entirely dedicated to prayer, Cistercians; those who wish prayer and some active and apostolic work, but subordinate to prayer, Benedictines; those who wish to make still more of the active life, make it in fact the chief element in their dedication to God, will not be monks at all, but, say, friars.

ST. AUGUSTINE

St. Augustine requires no introduction. His writings were known to St. Benedict and the Rule bears witness that the influence of his thought was considerable. St. Augustine created yet another kind of monasticism, different from that of Pachomius or Basil. His was, like Basil's, a city monasticism and one linked closely with himself as the bishop and superior. But while Basil's monks were not priests, many of Augustine's were. St. Augustine always considered himself a monk. Even as a layman before his conversion he had retired to a kind of Platonic haven with his friends. This had failed because the women folk of the party were not interested in the idea. But, from the time of his return to Africa after his conversion, his one aim was the perfect life. He did not, however, withdraw into the desert, he remained in his native town, and when he became a bishop he simply repeated the pattern at Hippo. He did not force his priests to join the monastic community, but he strongly urged them.

Thus, long before St. Benedict and before St. Gregory, the pattern of the priestly community already existed, and under the wing of the most revered figure of the Western Church.

This ideal included three elements of considerable importance: first, the very fact of it being in a city; second, that it consisted mostly of priests with parochial duties; third, that this arrangement required intellectual training and intellectual interests to cope with the situations as they arose.

We know that St. Benedict himself, though perhaps not even a priest, preached like Pachomius to the neighboring farming people around Cassino. So when St. Gregory established basilican monasteries in Rome, this was neither revolutionary nor contrary to the spirit of monasticism or of St. Benedict.

Repeatedly through the history of Western monasticism up to our own day there have been reforms and returns to the primitive ideal. Sometimes this return has been the return to the ideal of the desert. There has been great austerity, immense weight of prayers, a return to purely agricultural labors, and flight from the priesthood, from culture and scholarship. All these ideals are excellent and most suited to certain souls, but it is clear from history that these "returns" are not returns so much to St. Benedict or the Benedictine traditions as to some Eastern monasticism which St. Basil, St. Augustine, and St. Benedict very considerably modified in the direction of moderation and of having links with the world around.

CASSIAN

No one really knows where Cassian was born, and it is not important. It may have been the Balkans. What is important is his being a monk from early youth in Bethlehem and then getting permission from his superiors to go off with a companion to Egypt in order to inspect the monastic establishments there. He may have been born in 360 and he died between 433–435. He made two trips to Egypt and spent in all about ten years there, round the turn of the century; and it is sure he met Evagrius—of whom more later. It seems likely he got involved in the Origenist troubles, was linked with St. John Chrysostom in Constantinople after a possibly hasty withdrawal from Egypt, and then had to leave Constantinople when his protector St. John could no longer protect himself, let alone Cassian. It was then that he withdrew to Provence and there in a monastery near Marseilles became the teacher of spirituality to the

West: and his greatest pupil in the next century was Benedict of Nursia.

Cassian is famous for two books, the *Institutions* and the *Conferences*. The former were supposed to be for beginners in the monastic life, the latter for those well advanced. In fact, Cassian, being an unorderly person, mixed all the teaching up, so that in the second work he still keeps the beginners in mind.

These books are supposed to be verbatim accounts of his conversations with the Fathers of the Egyptian deserts. While he probably did his best to remember what had been said to him about a quarter of a century earlier during his visits there, in fact these conversation pieces are a framework for him to enclose the spiritual teaching he imbibed from one source mainly—that is, Evagrius from Pontus, who died in Egypt as a monk in 399.[1]

What is this teaching? Evagrius had said that the first stage of the spiritual life was the active, which meant the effort to reach *apatheia,* or the complete quieting of all the passions. This completely negative approach to the passions and emotions was more stoical, even Buddhist, than Christian. Cassian, perhaps more by accident than design, translated *apatheia* into Latin as "purity of heart" and "tranquility," and by so doing gave it a positive connotation. He recognized that the spiritual life would always be a battle. This shift was most important as he did not aim at annihiliating the body, the flesh, but at control. Consequently, his advice was moderation in mortification, in sleep, in food; the amount was to be decided by the results. Too little sleep or food could make the spiritual life harder, not easier. He enumerates the deadly vices, eight of them, which Evagrius had examined before him. These became later in Western Christian morality the seven deadly sins. But all this was only in order to free the soul for contemplation of God. As Chadwick observes, the important saying of Christ, "Thou shalt love thy neighbor as thyself," never gets even a

1. See *Dictionnaire d'Histoire et de Géographie ecclésiastiques,* Edited by A. Baudrillart, Z. de Meyer, and E. Van Cauwenbergh, Paris, 1909–, art. "Evagre."

mention. True, there are examples of fraternal love but they are given more as ways of reaching God rather than an overflow of love.[1]

For Evagrius, in the highest moment of contemplative prayer the mind goes out of action, it is prayer without thought, it is beyond thought. For Cassian, the mind reaches a simplicity of sight but it is not negated. Chadwick shows also that, although Cassian seems to be describing an almost non-Christian experience in his description of contemplation, this is not really so. And he quotes a fine passage from Conference 1, 15:

> In many ways we contemplate God. For God is known not only in the worship of his incomprehensible essence, a worship promised, but in this life hidden; he is seen in the immensity of his creation, in meditating on justice, in the daily bestowal of his grace; or when with pure minds we consider what he has done through his saints . . . : how he so brought us into the world that he gave us grace . . . and how in the end he was incarnate for our salvation and bestowed the wonder of his sacraments upon all nations.[2]

Throughout, there is a tinge of Pelagianism, as though it were possible to achieve this contemplation by the ascetic life without grace. St. Benedict took a more pedestrian view of human nature; he scarcely speaks of contemplation, as we shall see, and considers it sufficient to refer the more advanced monks to the works of Cassian.

Cassian's legacy to the Western Church and in the first place to St. Benedict was a more or less clear ascetic framework and a discretion in mortification which St. Benedict made his own. He extolled corporate worship. In a number of matters he was not followed by St. Benedict, but more from difference of objective. St. Benedict was writing for beginners and did not see the eremetical life as a likely denouement; he had a lower esteem for human nature and did not expect everyone to reach beyond the beginner stage. But without the careful analysis of the "active life" and of contemplation, the West

1. *John Cassian*, p. 107.
2. *Ibid.*, p. 164.

would have been without tools of thought to deal with the monastic and spiritual developments that came with its early and medieval religious life.

The following are some preliminary reflections at this stage of the inquiry into monasticism.

1. It would seem that monasticism in these early days is *one form* of the ascetic life which the early Church expected of those baptized. It was the first great division of the Christian life, not into *perfecti* and *audientes*—the Manichean distinction between those who aimed at perfection and those who did not —but between two ways of perfection: those who gave up marriage and property and those who did not.

2. The essential distinction was chastity and poverty; this was already a distinction in pre-monastic Christianity; but the monks took these ideas to their way of life.

3. At this point there is a further distinction, this time within the monastic genus itself, namely, between those who lived alone and those who lived in community. They all practiced the same kind of life, except that some did so in a community.

4. Another and less clear distinction within the genus *monk* was that between those who lived right away from the world, and those who were rather near or in the world. The former were such as those living in the deserts of Egypt and Syria, the latter were either those who lived on the outskirts of towns and villages, such as the monk who trained Antony in the first years of his monastic career, or those who lived in community within the towns themselves, such as the monks of Eusebius, Ambrose, Augustine, and Basil.

5. The aim of all, and of course of all Christians, was love of God and love of neighbor. But the latter was less evident in the hermits than in the Pachomian, Basilian, and Benedictine monasteries. Some came back into the world in order to help people materially or spiritually.

6. Practices: all aimed at contemplation, communion with God, and specifically by prayer and mortification and solitude

107

—this last more or less, as the case might be. The main prayer was always the psalter and the Book, the Bible.

7. Obedience was part even of the earliest form to the extent that one obeyed one's spiritual guide. But Pachomius, Basil, and Benedict made obedience to a superior the central pillar of the structure of their monasticism. St. Benedict gave it a deep spiritual as well as an ascetical significance.

8. Whether you were a priest or not was of little importance. It was useful to have a priest in the community to minister at the Sacrifice.

9. There is no doubt that the essential object was union with God and that all occupations were expected to be subordinated to that, even in the city monasteries.

We may say, then, that the earliest monks seem to presume that the monastic life was the only perfect Christian life: flight from the world, great austerity, chastity. With St. Pachomius we have the first restraining influence, implying that great austerity was not necessarily the only way; he introduced a strong community life, this being more in tune with fraternal charity as taught in the New Testament and sanctioned by his vision. St. Basil made a step forward towards a clear understanding of the relationship between the Christian and the monastic life. He recognized that all were called to the life of perfection. He did not resolve how the laity were going to do so; he recognized that the monastic life did lend itself to it. (It may almost be said that the resolution of this problem did not come till the twentieth century, when it was recognized that there are many counsels besides the monastic, and that the laity can reach to holiness by those others. The slur that hung over marriage for so many centuries—as in the thought of St. Augustine—is part of the unconsciously inherited Manichean bias.) St. Basil also made two other modifications, the first that he did not believe some contact with the world was against monastic life; and second, he was strongly of the opinion that monks had to perform the corporal and spiritual works of mercy as signs of love. The presence of Gnostic, Encratic, and Manichean thought throughout this period should make us wary of the attitude to

108

marriage, flight from the world, and asceticism generally. St. Basil's insight, which came to him from his master Eustachius, that all Christians in all walks of life are called through baptism to a life of perfection, makes the monastic way simply one means. Now a means is something of which we may have more or less, depending on all the circumstances of character and life which encompass us. The monastic means—solitude, obedience, discipline, self-denial, humility, prayer—may play some part in any one's life. Their enshrinement in a set of vows and a monastery is only a complete expression of a will to make these means the chief act of one's life.

3. The Spirit of St. Benedict's Rule

After the magisterial work of the great modern commentators, de Latte, Butler, Marmion, to say nothing of more ancient authors, it may seem presumptuous to venture into this subject. To attempt an over-all survey would be useless and impossible. The plan is simply to pick out certain elements which seem to be of particular concern to monasticism today. Certain other aspects have been treated elsewhere in this book: conversion, contemplation, poverty, and obedience. Here we shall treat of: moderation; prayer; interiorization of spirituality, with special reference to obedience; human relations; *conversio morum* or the wide aspect of Benedictine spirituality; concern for the individual; and end with some thoughts on humility, for there is truly the beginning and end of St. Benedict's spirituality, whether we understand it or not.

The question of the originality, or unoriginality, of the Rule of St. Benedict need not be considered here. The question would have seemed absurd to Benedict, and is in fact an insoluble one at the present time. We do not in fact know for certain—even if it is possible to make a good guess—whether Benedict borrowed from the Master or vice versa, or whether Benedict may even have written both rules. Whichever rule came first, in the Rule of St. Benedict are found large areas which the Master does not touch on; even more important, there is an almost miraculous pruning of rhetoric in Benedict's Rule, a new emphasis on fraternal charity, and a tempering of harshness. But again, the concern here is not with what is original but what is characteristic in St. Benedict's Rule.

On certain matters St. Benedict's spirituality may be the same or similar to, say, that of St. Basil. Well and good. St. Benedict would have been all the more reassured. He was happy to take good wherever he found it and make it his own. One could apply to Benedict the words of Pascal: "No one should argue that I have said nothing new; my disposition of the subject matter is new. When you play tennis it is the same ball for both players, but one player plays it better."

There are, however, certain aspects of St. Benedict's spirituality which are particularly relevant to our time of *aggiornamento*. Once we are aware that pre-Benedictine monasticism was tropically abundant in its profusion and variety, we naturally are anxious to examine which plants Benedict chose for his garden and which he did not. To say that pre-Benedictine monasticism was like a jungle is not exaggeration. There were literally tens of thousands of monks in the Egyptian and Syrian deserts; there were hermits in every nook and cranny of Western Europe: in the mountains of Italy, in the German forests, in the expanses of Gaul, on the high plateau of Spain. But the numbers of monks were no more astonishing than their variety. They ranged from the isolated hermit to the highly complex and ordered cenobia; from the isolated rural monastery to the urban one; from a life of agriculture to one of culture, and so on.

Moderation. When seen against this background of monastic overgrowth, the most striking characteristic of St. Benedict's Rule is its moderation. It is a moderation which is all pervasive, touching every aspect of the life.

1. St. Benedict is remarkably moderate on the subject of mortification. If the desert ascetic might not eat for a week, St. Benedict tells his monks to eat what is given. They are to

have plenty of bread and even wine. It is true that meat is forbidden, and that for long periods of the year the first meal is in the evening. But these austerities were hardly more than were the lot of the local agricultural workers. Even today in Europe, these workers often enough have their first solid meal of the day only on their return from working in the fields. What was St. Benedict after? We surely can assume that he was not trying to be as permissible as possible in the matter of food and drink. He says that the monks should be given more when they are working hard. Finally, he leaves the whole matter in the hands of the abbot. One can only conclude that he was aiming at moderation.

2. There is no mention whatsoever in the Rule of artificial mortification. In Syria monks might chain themselves to a particular spot, live on top of pillars, wear rags, or even wear nothing at all. Even for Lent Benedict does not recommend any very strenuous asceticism. He suggests a little reduction of food and drink, a little addition of time for prayer, a special book for the season. Even these things are to be carried out under the prudent scrutiny of the abbot. Permission must be obtained, for a very significant reason: because, he says, without obedience even these little self-denials could be worthless.

3. As for early rising, that was, and continues to be, an ascetical practice which is difficult. But St. Benedict's prescriptions are nothing compared to the practices of the Eastern monks. Even the cautious Pachomius disapproved of lying down on a bed. His monks slept sitting up. This item of the Pachomian Rule was quickly dropped. St. Benedict's Rule prescribes a bed and a mattress for each monk. He explicitly states that he is not trying to establish a way of life which is harsh. Indeed, his stated aim is to write a little rule for beginners. When one compares the life described in the Rule with the life of monks before Benedict's time, it is clear that he means what he says.

Prayer. Prayer, especially liturgical prayer, is obviously the food of monks. St. Benedict admits that his monks cannot

111

compete with the Desert Fathers, who recited the entire psalter each day. Benedict expected his followers to recite the 150 psalms each week.

It is difficult to put together a clear picture of the liturgical life of the early Eastern monks. It seems likely that most of those 150 daily psalms were sung by each monk in his own cell. Only twice a day, for instance, did the Pachomian monks gather for common prayer, apart from their gathering for Mass on Sundays and perhaps one other day. St. Benedict legislates for the whole of the *opus Dei* to be performed in common. Perhaps he did this to ensure that the entire office was recited by all; perhaps because there was only one, or few copies of the necessary books: the Bible, Ambrose, Augustine.

The Desert Fathers had a tradition of "continuous prayer," doubtless derived from the phrase of St. Paul, that we should "pray without ceasing" (1 Thess. 5, 17). St. Basil had moved away from that. Benedict regulated what a monk had to do during the day: now prayer, now work, now reading. In addition to the eight specified times for communal prayer, seven in the day, one at night, St. Benedict prescribed four hours each morning for *lectio divina*. *Lectio divina* is a vague term that includes a number of elements. Essentially it involved a slow, ruminative reading which would lead the spirit of the monk into prayer. Here was the time for private prayer, but it was hardly a fixed time. What is most significant is that the remainder of the day, except for time given to eating and sleeping, was given explicitly to manual labor. This would seem a conscious admission that monks could not be expected to pray all day. We shall come back later to St. Benedict's thoughts on work. The really astonishing thing about his teaching on prayer is that he has given us no treatise in any formal sense. However, what random fragments he does give in the Rule are rich in doctrine and implication, and should not be passed over lightly. His whole rule is impregnated with the sense of God's presence in the life of the monk. God is present to the monk at all times, but particularly at times of prayer. A simple thought, one might say, but of such simple thoughts saints have been fashioned. Another of the prayer-themes is that of *custodia cordis,* purity of heart. The monk should free his heart from any attachment other than to God. Another theme is the constant attitude of humility: the monk should begin each work with prayer; he should attribute all good to God and none to himself.

All this, however, remains meager fare. Had Benedict been in the tradition of an Antony or some of the more primitive anchorites, this reticence on prayer would be more intelligible. Their approach to prayer had been simple enough: the pondering of Scripture, of the redemptive life of Christ. It might have involved a spiritual combat with demons. Benedict, however, was not unsophisticated. He had at his elbow the works of Cassian; he knew Augustine. It is possible that the works of Origen and Evagrius were not known to him directly, as neither is quoted in the Rule. But Cassian was a conscious if discreet carrier of their ascetical tradition, even if he found it impolitic to mention either of them by name in his own works.

As the orthodoxy of Origen and Evagrius was suspect even in Benedict's day, it is possible that he considered it wise to omit from the Rule any theorizing about prayer. Whatever the reason, it is a pity he did not do so. He gives us little to go on: let prayer be short; monks are reminded that they pray always in the presence of God's angels; they are encouraged to pray in the solitude of their cells.

The modern reader of the Rule, perhaps looking for some guidance in the matter of prayer, may be disappointed when he finds no careful analyses of the various states of prayer. There is no mention of the three ways, what to do about dryness, ecstasies, and so forth. It is true that the Desert Fathers already knew something of the purgative, illuminative, and unitive ways. But to expect any sort of analytical discussion in the Rule would be to take Benedict out of the sixth century and place him in the sixteenth, a contemporary of John of the Cross. Benedict's teaching on prayer is no organized theory, but is scattered throughout the Rule. If we wish to discover his mind on prayer, we must collect all that he wrote on the majesty and justice of God, as well as the love and mercy manifest in his Son. We must consider all he has to say, especially in the Prologue, on the monk's dependence on God's grace. The whole chapter on humility legitimately can be said to be a treatise on prayer. So too, the chapter on obedience. The creaturely position of subjection to God, and his readiness to obey are truly attitudes of prayer. One might go so far as to say that the degree of the monk's intimacy with God is in exact proportion to the degree of humility and obedience. If prayer is more an attitude of mind than a rush of words, more a recognition of our littleness as we stand before God's majesty, then in Chapter 7 of the Rule Benedict has said almost all there is to be said about prayer. If to pray is to be humbly responsible to God, ready to follow his call wherever it may lead, then St. Benedict's teaching on obedience is a little treatise on prayer as well.

It may be a gauge of one's own involvement in a post-Tridentine spirit that a discussion of Benedict's teaching on prayer should have progressed this far without mentioning the fact that for Benedict the Divine Office is the primary form of prayer. The Office is Benedict's peculiar care; he legislates for it with the minutest precision, putting every psalm in its place, prescribing the exact times, both for summer and winter. For Benedict the supreme prayer was the communal prayer, that of the Church. The psychological reactions of the monk were not in the same realm of importance. To praise God was the important thing. But while he is precise about the organization of the Office, Benedict gives little help as to how it is to be said. He had plenty of masters to turn to, not least St. Augustine with his teaching on the Mystical Body sharing in the prayer of Christ its head. He wanted "the heart to echo the words," another aspect of obedience.

Was there any time set aside for meditation? Dom Jean Leclerc has shown that *lectio divina* is the natural place for a monk to find the setting for meditation. But Abbot Cuthbert Butler, in *Benedictine Monachism*—a book that has lost little of its relevance—concludes from the *Dialogues* of St. Gregory

114

that St. Benedict had an immense devotion to private prayer. For example: according to the *Dialogues* Benedict had a tower to which he would withdraw for prayer. Then there is the story of the monk at Subiaco who regularly skipped his mental prayer in order to do something else. This prayer would seem to have been of some duration, and to have been of obligation, else Benedict would not have considered it important enough to administer a reprimand.

Interiorization. The outstanding characteristic of the Rule, apart from its moderation, is its interiorization of the spiritual life. Externals concern Benedict very little. For him it is clearly more important to be a saint than to seem one. The primary degrees of humility are the inward ones. The outward manifestations will flow naturally from them. It is reasonable to claim that, by his emphasis on humility, Benedict is reversing a trend towards extreme ascetical practices and concentrating on an absolute trust in God's mercy. He certainly cannot be accused of Pelagianism. The primacy of grace and God's mercy is never in question. To place humility as the foundation of religious life, rather than austerity and battling against demons, or solitude, or even silence, is to dig to the heart of religion. God is placed first and the human being is at his feet.

Obedience. In the chapter on obedience and in the references to it scattered throughout the Rule, Benedict may not appear to be particularly original. St. Basil and St. Pachomius, as well as the Master, had placed obedience at the center of their spiritual teaching. However, a careful examination of Benedict's spirituality reveals that in the Rule obedience is even more central and fundamental than in any of the rules of his predecessors.

One's impression of Pachomian obedience is this: Pachomius was determined to create order out of chaos. There were hundreds and hundreds of monks in the desert, solitary or in

115

groups of twos and threes, unsure what road to take. Pachomius established a regular way of life with a certain measure of flexibility in ascetical practices. But for Benedict, obedience really *was* his ascetic practice, a very different thing. He abandoned the competitive asceticism of the Desert Fathers; the immense fasts, all-night vigils, cave dwelling, constant prayer, wanderings, and flagellations. He saw the source of sin in the waywardness of the human will. That is what he purposed to redress, with God's help. In the Rule are the seeds of a profoundly simple spirituality, based on obedience and humility: the putting off of selfishness and the steady growth in love of God through obedience.

Benedict's regime is, then, one of sobriety and interiority rather than one of austerity. There must be asceticism. However, it is possible to practice severe mortification without giving up one's own will. In his Prologue, Benedict sets out the principle of his asceticism: What separated Adam and all succeeding men from God was disobedience, so only by obedience shall men be reunited to him. Benedict knows this spirit of obedience will itself be a gift of God, but he likes the military metaphor: "Our hearts and bodies must be ready to fight under the holy obedience of his commands." At the beginning there must be strict discipline, but as we progress "we shall run with unspeakable sweetness of love in the way of God's commandments."

When examining the various types of monks, Benedict makes obedience the touchstone. The first type is those who live in monasteries under rule and an abbot. The second group are the anchorites or hermits, who have been so well trained in obedience that they can go forth to single combat. As for the third and fourth groups: "their law is their own good pleasure" (the Sarabaites); or they are wanderers "given up to their own wills" (gyrovagues).

In Chapter 4 of the Rule, "The Tools of Good Works," there are only two "tools" which refer directly to obedience: "To hate one's own will," followed by "To obey in all things the commands of the abbot, even though he himself (which

God forbid) should act otherwise." In chapter five, "Of Obedience," Benedict provides four reasons for obeying: (1) for
the love of Christ—"this becomes those who hold nothing
dearer to them than Christ"; (2) the fact that the monk is
vowed to obey—"because of the holy service which they have
professed"; (3) for fear of hell; and (4) for the reward of
heaven—"the desire of attaining eternal life."

The emphasis throughout the chapter is the willingness, the
ungrudging preparedness to obey: "immediately abandoning
what they are doing; swift obedience, almost in the same instance . . . in the swiftness of the fear of the Lord . . . not
timorously, tardily, tepidly . . . but cheerfully."

The Scripture texts are ever the same and the same as the
Master's: "He who listens to you, listens to me" (Lk. 10, 16)—
twice; and "I came not to do my own will, but the will of him
who sent me" (Jn. 6, 38), and "God loves a cheerful giver"
(2 Cor. 9, 7).

Obedience is seen as the summit of humility and of perfection. The third and fourth degrees of humility give the essence of Benedictine teaching on obedience. "A man for the
love of God subjects himself to his superior in all obedience,
imitating the Lord, of whom the apostle says: 'He was made
obedient even unto death' (Phil. 2, 8)." This text is more
significant for our subject than sometimes we realize. We obey
the Church in the person of our ecclesiastical superior (the
abbot) and we are prepared to obey the Church *because the
Church and Christ are one,* He the Head, the Church his body.
The Church has a supernatural duty to perform in guiding
souls towards God. But we know that in this same supernatural order the way to God is the way of the cross, of death
to self, of abandoning one life to find another. This text is the
one that reminds us of this: he was made obedient even to
death. Consequently, sooner or later in our obedience to Christ
through his Church—that is, through its teachers, including the
abbot—we will be asked to sacrifice our wills, not against the
moral law, but undoubtedly against our wishes and even
against our judgment, as Christ was unjustly put to death, but

117

he did not raise his voice or use all the power at his command to prevent it.[1]

Human Relations

It has been pointed out that only once in the *Rule of the Master* is there even a reference to fraternal charity, in Chapter 3, concerning the spiritual skill (*ars sancta*) that the abbot has to teach his monks. Here is the sentence: *"Omnibus bonis ex toto corde obedire":* to obey with all one's heart all those who are good. De Vogüé remarks: "a unique comment in the *Rule of the Master* in which otherwise obedience to the superior is the only one envisaged." [2]

It must be admitted that in the same chapter—in part almost word for word the same as St. Benedict's chapter on the instruments of good works—are cited biblical axioms: Not to kill, to feed the hungry, not to render evil for evil; then one of his own making, "to love one's enemies more than one's friends." [3] But all the rest of the *Rule of the Master* is given over to the relationship between abbot or superior and monks. This attitude of remoteness from one's brethren might be acceptable and natural in a set-up where the monks were almost anchorites living together yet apart. One might expect it in some early Egyptian monastery where the cenobitical life was only just burgeoning. In the *Rule of the Master,* so close to St. Benedict in time and space, we are surprised, unless we accept that the Master is prior to Benedict's Rule, in which case the latter is a perfecting of the former.

In the Rule of St. Benedict the horizontal as well as the vertical relationships are plentiful, relationships between monks as well as those between monks and the abbot. Perhaps the clearest expression is to say that there is the atmosphere of a family. Some squirm these days at the family image; it brings

1. See A. de Bois, S.J., "Obéissance et liberté," in *Nouvelle revue théologique,* March, 1965.
2. *La Règle du Maître,* Edited by A. de Vogüé, 3 vols., Paris, 1964; vol. 1, p. 371.
3. *Ibid.,* p. 367.

up the picture of two grown persons, the father and the mother, and all the rest immature children. But an analogy or metaphor is never perfect, otherwise it would be comparing the same thing to the same thing, the thing itself. An analogy falls down at certain points. So this one falls down on the point that all members of a community are supposed to be adult, mature, capable of mature judgments, whereas in a family most of the members are under age, incapable of making a prudent judgment.

Nevertheless the analogy is valuable. A family is small, it is of human proportions. So should a monastery be. The relationships between all the members should be intimate, not that between a general and the privates in his army. St. Benedict was not competing with the mammoth organizations of Pachomius, with hundreds of monks in every monastery. Perhaps in the Subiaco days this was beginning to emerge as the pattern, with sub-monasteries and deans. He may well have been glad to start again on Monte Cassino to found a monastery which was a thing in itself, family-like, with its abbot who would know all his monks and be a kind of father to them with a spiritual paternity. He would lead them to God. While some would be in the position of authority and others in that of obedience, neither the authority nor the obedience—any more than it is in a family—would be military, mechanical, inhuman, but personal, warm, and understanding.

In St. Benedict's monastery before a plan is decided upon there has to be discussion, not between a select few but with the whole community, the young being specially mentioned by him. This is extraordinarily in tune with the Church of the Vatican Council. The abbot is not a policeman who is there to see that at any cost the rule is observed. He is the servant of the community. He must lead, not drive. Temperaments have to be taken into account, the simple, the lazy, the proud, the wayward. With one, admonition is enough, with another stern reproof, but to all the abbot must show love, hating only the sin. His aim is not to destroy but to restore.

In fact, apart from calling the superior Father and so implying a family, St. Benedict does not make use of the analogy in any other place. So we should not over-strain it. The way he describes the relationship of the members of the community is through the scriptural symbolism of the mystical body, of which each is a member. We are all one in Christ (Rule of St. Benedict, Chapter 2). That the monks should see Christ in their superior is a spiritual commonplace today. But St. Benedict saw Christ in everyone else also, in the guest who must be received as Christ; in the poor and the pilgrim because in these Christ is specially welcomed; particularly too in the sick, who have to be most lovingly cared for, as Christ is indeed in them. For St. Benedict, Christ is everywhere in a community, in the abbot, the brethren, the sick, the guests, and in this he fulfills a saying of Christ which has been preserved only by Tertullian: *"Vidisti fratrem tuum, vidisti Dominum tuum."* [1]

Conversio Morum (or) Conversatio Morum

This phrase was so obscure that many Benedictine congregations, including the English, abandoned it as one of the three vows the monks took and substituted poverty, chastity, and obedience. During the last eighty to one hundred years scholars have grappled with the problem and come to some general agreement. This is far more important than we might think at first sight. The religious life in the Tridentine Church has concentrated its thought and practice on the three vows, particularized in the three concepts above. But the monastic life is far broader than that, and hidden in the meaning of *conversatio morum* is the key to the monastic attitude to its own spiritual life.

Conversatio comes from *conversari* and means conduct, manner of life, ascetical life; it translates the Greek *askesis* monastic life. What about *conversatio morum suorum?*

Dom Philibert Schmitz and Miss Mohrmann: conversion of

1. Tertullian, "De Orat. 26," in the chapter "Medulla Doctrinae S. Benedicti," in Abbot Cuthbert Butler, *Sancti Benedicti Regula Monachorum,* Freiburg, 1912.

life. Their ground is that when in the ninth-century *conversatio* was changed to *conversio* the scribes knew they meant the same.

Abbot Cuthbert Butler:	conduct of life
Abbot Chapman:	monasticity of conduct
D. Steidle:	monastic behavior and striving for virtue
D. Lottin:	life in community
Abbot Justin McCann:	self-discipline

Abbot Justin McCann has given the most thorough account in English of the above. The following is his general conclusion in his book *St. Benedict:* "Taking the word *'conversatio'* at its lowest level we must translate 'moral conduct'. But considering St. Benedict's use of the word and the implications of the context we may reasonably take it in its further sense of disciplined conduct. It is clear in fact that he is thinking of a moral ascesis, a discipline of character and life. We may go further than that and say that he intended the special monastic discipline. May one be more precise still and specify some of the elements of this discipline?" [1] He goes on by giving as his translation of the three vows: "Stability, self-discipline, and obedience." It will be noted that Abbot McCann began his description with moral conduct, but ended it with self-discipline, the one more positive, the other rather negative. In another place he notes that *fides et observatio morum,* which occurs in the Prologue, is very close to *conversatio morum suorum,* which he translates: virtuous observance. But he does not stick to this positive attitude. This is a pity, because as said earlier this is the key to the true understanding of monastic life, neither a negative ascesis nor a concentration on the three modern vows of poverty, chastity, and obedience, *but rather an embracing of the whole spiritual life.* We have so concentrated on the negative aspects that we have not bothered to work out more important matters like the relationship between virtue and beatitude, between the gifts of the Holy Spirit and heroic

1. Dom Justin McCann, *Saint Benedict,* London, 1938. See also Claude J. Peifer, *Monastic Spirituality,* New York, 1966, pp. 303–306.

virtue, the counsels and the virtues, or how many counsels there are, and so on.

Once we see the second vow as a short expression of the desire to lead the virtuous life fully, then the religious life becomes rich indeed. All Christians are bound by their baptism to seek God, to follow Christ, to take the necessary means. But the monk has vowed to do this unremittently, not merely to follow the counsels if required, but seeking them out.

The perfect Christian life is grasping the Gospels and attempting to follow all Christ's teaching, precept and counsel. Pre-eminent among the counsels are those which have been the backbone of religious life. When one reads modern works on the religious life these three loom large as the very essence. The paradox that St. Benedict only mentions one of them and that monks only vow themselves to one of them should give us pause. The fact is that the ancient attitude to the spiritual life was different; a monk was vowed to lead the whole Christian life as perfectly as possible. This would include chastity and poverty, but not exclusively. We are vowed to faith and hope and charity, patience and all the others, not in a minimal way—all Christians are bound to that—but to a maximum degree.

Light was shed on this conundrum by a remarkable "intervention" at the Second Vatican Council. The Bishop of Arras, Gérard Huyghe, made the point that every Christian is called to holiness—there are no second-class citizens in the Church. Holiness does not only include keeping the commandments but also the beatitudes or counsels. "The perfect and complete teaching of the Gospel embraces both commandments and counsels, which are part of every Christian's vocation to holiness in the Church." [1]

It follows from the above that the difference between religious and laity is not in the keeping of the counsels, but (1) in the special emphasis on certain of them, and (2) in vowing to keep them. So the difference between the laity and the reli-

1. In *Council Speeches of Vatican II*, Edited by Hans Kung, Yves Congar, O.P., and Daniel O'Hanlon, S.J., Glen Rock, 1964, p. 93.

gious is not between two groups, one seeking perfection and the other a lesser goal, but between two ways of seeking the same end; the religious commits himself solemnly to seek perfection in certain ways. The lay person is already committed by baptism but does not commit himself to a particular way. The second vow, then, *conversatio morum,* aims at seeking perfection according to the monastic way, none other than the perfect following of Christ with special reference to certain of the counsels, but not excluding any.

The Prologue could be called a commentary on this vow of *conversatio morum,* an appeal to a virtuous life. Chapter 4, the tools of monastic life, now makes more sense, because it does cover the ground of the virtuous life, not merely confining itself to teaching on poverty and obedience, but treating every virtue—and every vice to be avoided. At first one is surprised, almost shocked; the monk is advised not to steal, not to commit murder or adultery. Has not the monk left those things far behind? No, he is still keeping the commandments, still loving his neighbor, respecting his rights. As our Lord said, it is possible to commit adultery in the heart, no word said, or action done. Benedict saw the monk's life simply as the following of Christ. What Cardinal Léger said at the Second Vatican Council as applying to all Christians applies to monks and nuns too. "Since one must speak to all Christians about the evangelical counsels, let it be with the full spirituality of the Sermon on the Mount. What we call the evangelical counsels also include justice, humility, gentleness, mercy." [1]

St. Thomas calls the perfection of charity the counsel of that virtue.[2] We are not concerned here with the almost revolutionary implications this teaching will have for the spirituality of the laity, but simply with the implications for religious, specifically monks and nuns. Monks are vowed by the second vow to seek perfection with all their hearts, therefore, to the counsels of all the virtues which are suitable to their state of life. So the second vow, which sounds so vague, is the most precise

1. In *ibid.,* p. 90.
2. *Summa Theol.,* II II, 44, art. 4, ad 3.

of them all and the most all-embracing, the one that guides to the fullness of likeness to Christ. The Rule itself often enough becomes the exposition of this vow. Unlike many a modern Rule, which is little more than an application of Canon Law to a particular set of circumstances, the Rule of St. Benedict is an ascetic treatise. Take the example of Chapter 72 concerning fraternal charity; this is no piece of routine rules about times of office or the manner of eating, but about practicing the counsel of the virtue of fraternal charity. Monks, being vowed to the Holy Rule, are vowed to that. St. Benedict does not expound each and every virtue and its counsel. Instead he refers his readers, his disciples, to the Rule of Rules, namely, the Gospel itself.

This is something we still have to do, to extract from the Gospels the complete way of life. This is the spirit of the Holy Rule, and the desire of St. Benedict. He tells his followers to return continually to the Bible. Too long we have done it at second or third remove, through text books and works of writers who themselves have been brought up on these text books. Back to the source is our chief aim today. We must learn to see life through biblical eyes, in a biblical framework. Not that Aristotle is useless, but he must remain always subordinate.

The virtue of faith should not be given as a dissertation on the various kinds of knowledge such as we find in Aristotle, even such as we find in Newman, but a return to the biblical notion which we find in the story of Abraham, Isaac, and Jacob and summed up in the Epistle to the Hebrews; a return to the notion of faith in the Gospels, the awakening of the faith, for example, in the Apostles, that personal commitment to Christ.

The virtue of humility should not be given as a Jungian dissertation on the dependence of the creature on the creator so much as a return to the fundamental ideas of the poor of Yahweh in the Old Testament and of the servant of Yahweh in the New, as it is in the Holy Rule. Charity is not best explained as a careful sorting out of the relative values of those to be loved, but a return to the Johannine teaching in the epistle and a study of Christ's love during his life, a study of the meaning of the indwelling of the Spirit of Christ in his Church.

Sensitivity

Sensitivity to the needs of the individual monks is yet another characteristic of the Rule; St. Benedict is always giving away with one hand what he seems to be holding on fast to with the other. Monks of course must be frugal and abstemious; but— and there is always a "but" if you wait long enough—as some monks cannot these days do without their wine, let those who want it have it, but in moderation. Here is a wide-sweeping principle.

For St. Benedict the Rule was devised for people, not people for the Rule. Like language, which came before grammar and is more subtle than any grammar, so too monks and sisters come before the Rule and are more complex than any Rule one could devise. Therefore, the Rule should bend to the needs of those who keep it, not vice versa.

This is a subtle distinction and liable to misinterpretation. It is not an all-clear signal to modify the Rule for *all* because of the clamor of a few; rather it is a recognition that in par- ticular circumstances—even over a long period of time—a particular rule would have to be waived. This is the principle underlying St. Benedict's own ruling about drinking wine. He is not encouraging all to drink wine; rather he says, it is more becoming for monks not to drink it, but since some monks cannot be so persuaded, let *them* be allowed to have some. No more, but notice, he makes it a part of his Rule. This case was for a group of monks, but we presume he would have been equally tolerant for an individual. Thus the Rule remains, it is not changed: both those who keep it and those who are excused from it are keeping the Rule.

For every work in the establishment a monk is made re- sponsible. But St. Benedict is continuously on the watch in case there is overstrain. The waiters may have a snack before serving at table. We can readily imagine some enterprising young monks taking a snack before it was allowed and in so doing breaking the rule of eating between meals. St. Benedict does not reiterate the hard and fast rule in more forceful terms. He recognizes the exception, and makes it a rule too.

The guest master, the infirmarian, the cooks, the cellarer may have assistants if the work becomes heavy. Children and old people must have special attention, and the sick also. If a brother has been justly but severely punished by the superior, he is not to be cast off, but without his knowing about it the superior will send two wise monks to cheer him up and commiserate, console, and restore.

Humility

There are two elements to be safeguarded when speaking of humility. The first is the recognition of our worth, both in the natural order, the gifts that we have of mind and body and will, that lovely voice, that keen intellect, that capacity to get things done; these are facts. Then in the supernatural order also, the fact of grace and the virtues that we must practice, of charity, of patience, of courage, and so forth. It would be the sin of lying to deny their existence and also a big one of ingratitude not to thank God for them.

This the moderns rightly plead is an essential foundation for the building up of a human personality; he must love himself, and he cannot do so unless there is something lovable there. He cannot love others unless he already loves himself; we must love others as ourselves. Humility cannot come before this initial, fundamental recognition. But this self-confidence usually comes from a recognition that God has loved us first. It is only people whose childhood has been deprived, where they have been treated with contempt or been abandoned, that this requires building up in the grown-up stage of their development.

The second element to remember is that humility is not a second stage which attempts to knock down all that carefully previously established self-confidence. Humility has a threefold aspect.

126

1. It recognizes all these gifts and in the same breath recognizes where they come from: God.

2. It recognizes also that we have not lived up to the possibilities of these gifts that God has given us. Hence the tears.

3. Lastly, humility should never be dissociated from hope or trust. We only bow down before God in humility to recognize that he can lift us up again and that we can cooperate with him.

Perhaps the Rule of St. Benedict weights the scales rather heavily on the side of the recognition of our nothingness and it does not build up enough the realization of the marvellous works of God in our souls and high destiny each has; but this picture is chiefly the result of most of the material on humility being solidly in one place, and the other side of the picture dispersed throughout the Rule. It would not be lacking in reverence for the Rule if we were to emphasize in our day more the spirit of the constitution on the Church, how we are the People of God, the redeemed, children of the Most High. Moreover, St. Benedict shared this spirit, as we see from the Prologue where he wrote:

> Such men as these, fearing the Lord, are not puffed up on account of their good works, but judging that they can do no good of themselves and that all cometh from God, they magnify the Lord's work in them . . .[1]

But, just as it is a truth that men have been gifted in many ways, so it is a truth that these are gifts and they come from God, also that they have not always been used well. To say anything else would also be a lie. Men should stand in the middle way of the redeemed.

4. According to the Sound Tradition: General

The Fathers of the Second Vatican Council admonished religious to renew their spiritual lives according to the sound tradition of their respective Orders. This implies: first, to know

1. *Rule of St. Benedict,* Translated by Dom Justin McCann, Stanbrook Abbey Press, 1937, p. 3.

what the history of the Order has been; second, to be discerning enough to seize the good and reject the bad; third, to apply all that to our own day.

It was not possible in the past to assess the history of the Benedictine Order for the reason that no one had ever grasped it in all its vast extent—so much of the source material had to be critically examined. In our age, some great work on this mass of material has been done and a few great scholars have even ventured to give an over-all picture: David Knowles for England, Philibert Schmitz and Stephan Hilpisch, Patrice Cousin and Justo Pérez de Urbel for the whole of monastic history. Jean Leclercq has been examining with laudable industry the Benedictine medieval heritage in great detail. Nothing in this area can ever be definitive, but we are in a better position today to make value judgments and to respond to the call of the Vatican Council as a result of these labors.

The history of the Benedictines is long, complicated, and often obscure; but we may divide it into three parts, by an (inevitably) arbitrary system:

1. From St. Benedict up to the founding of Cluny: 547–910.

2. From the founding of Cluny to the Council of Constance: 910–1418.

3. From the Council of Constance to the present day: 1418– c. 1900.

Why do we choose these divisions? The answer is that our first period of Benedictine monasticism was its growth within a world still pagan; the second was its life in a Christian society; the third its life in a world becoming more and more secular. The first period saw dispersed efforts, the second more concentrated ones, the third world-wide but sparsely distributed ones.

THE FIRST PERIOD: 547–910

To begin with there was no recorded history: the Rule simply circulated, was read, was used, was passed on, but was by no means the only monastic document to be so used. It shared a place of honor with, for instance, the Rule of St. Columbanus. Perhaps St. Wilfrid in his monastery at Ripon, England, was the first to use it exclusively (*c.* 700).

Charlemagne's efforts to make the Rule of St. Benedict supreme in the monasteries of his empire may have been done on advice from his Anglo-Saxon monk-aides, Alcuin in particular. However, from the death of Gregory the Great (604), disorder was almost universal on the continent of Europe and monastic life was no sooner established than some calamity destroyed it, if only the calamity of lay control. This was the time of invasions from every direction. Once again after the death of Charlemagne the empire did not survive long; the second dark age was worse than the first, but shorter. The collapse of monasticism and of much else was halted by the founding of Cluny.

Having given a general picture of the gloomy centuries (600–900), we might see what the monks succeeded in doing in spite of it all.

The monks survived—no small achievement. This was partly the result of their autonomy, each being a self-contained unit, not looking for orders or for survival from anywhere beyond their monastic enclosure. The second reason was undoubtedly their faith. They were not daunted by difficulties, and around them would gather after the storms the remnant of the local population. These they taught to farm, to build; meanwhile within the monasteries the work of prayer went on, the work of transcribing the manuscripts: commentaries on the Bible, especially those of Bede, Augustine, and Gregory; the Bible itself; even a few pagan authors—Cicero, Virgil, Horace, Tacitus. As pointed out elsewhere, schools were started in every part of Christian Europe, not big ones but places where boys were taught the trivium and quadrivium— the arts of reading and writing and music, particularly singing: basic monastic skills for their liturgical life.

How did all this come about, this staggering persistence, this European relief work during all these centuries, the Benedictine centuries? This is a period in the Benedictine tradition worthy of careful study.

Three elements contributed to and helped create a genuine monastic tradition. The first was the arrival of the Rule in a city—the city of Rome. Monte Cassino and Subiaco were both remote monasteries, away from civilization. The monasteries in Rome were the opposite, which fact had immense consequences for monasticism in the West. No one now claims that the monasteries at the basilicas in Rome must have followed only St. Benedict's Rule. Tradition has it that Gregory welcomed the refugee monks from Monte Cassino into one of his palaces; we do know that it was to St. Andrew's—Gregory's old home converted into a monastery by him—that Wilfrid went to find an authentic copy of the Benedictine Rule to take back home to Yorkshire. We do know that Gregory wrote a life of Benedict and extolled him especially for living a life such as he had described in his Rule. So in Rome, slowly perhaps, the Benedictine form of the monastic idea merged with the other kind of monasticism, of St. Basil and St. Augustine. St. Gregory was, after all, a monk. But an urban monastery meant a clerical monastery: some of the monks were priests, for example, at Hippo.

The second element which makes this period important for the Benedictine follows from the first: monks, who are likely to become priests, required intellectual training. These city monasteries were places in which the young clerics would be taught the humanities and sacred Scripture. In any case, a strong tradition of study already existed in the monastery which Cassiodorun had founded at Vivarium. According to Abbot Chapman, Cassiodorus used the Rule of St. Benedict when writing his own; other scholars—Décarreaux and Cousin—do not agree and would grant him only a nodding acquaintance with the Rule. Nevertheless Cassiodorus is important in this period, not because his monastery was a great success—it faded with its founder—but because it carried an idea; it represents an influential strand of the Western monastic tradition at its source, in a form not foreign to the contemporary "Benedictine" observance.

In 555, Cassiodorus, the distinguished retired civil servant of the court of Theodoric, founded his monastery of Vivarium in the toe of Italy. He was about 70 at the time. It was his objective, as it had already been that of Boethius, to arrange a marriage between the Greco-Roman culture and Christianity. Now that his political dreams were at an end—in 555 the Gothic rule at Ravenna was finally crushed—he turned to prayer and the contemplative life; but unlike Benedict—now of course already dead seven or eight years—he did not turn his back on learning. His monastery was to be a place where one would not be ashamed to read the pagan classics—or at least some of them.

This was a great step forward. What would Jerome have thought, and said, and written? It was a revolution far greater than we realize. This was a change of direction for monks and it would be followed right up to our own day.

Before the monks of succeeding generations would be able to take advantage of this "tolerance" and read these pagan works, or any works for that matter, someone had to establish a systematic way of transcribing them. It was Cassiodorus who made sure that this copying of manuscripts was properly and methodically done. He set up a scriptorium at Vivarium; and this work took the place in many cases of the monks' manual labor. In this book-factory, Cassiodorus engaged not only monks but professional copyists and translators. Of couse, a bindery too was needed: he had one. All these books needed housing: a library was built. Over all Cassiodorus kept a close personal watch. His objectives were accuracy and beauty.[1]

But what use was a library full of books unless the monks could read and relish them? The third legacy of Cassiodorus to the coming medieval world was a complete if narrow system

1. See *Dictionnaire d'Histoire et de Géographique ecclésiastique,* Edited by A. Baudrillart, Z. de Meyer, and E. Van Cauwenbergh, Paris, 1909–; art. "Cassiodore."

of education which he salvaged from the Roman culture; it was the one of the ancient world put to Christian use. All this he carefully explained in his book, the *Institutions*. In the trivium, the students would learn grammar, rhetoric, and dialectic. In the quadrivium, they would learn mathematics, music, geometry, and astronomy.

Having been trained in these disciplines, the monks of Vivarium could, so Cassiodorus thought, approach the Bible with deeper understanding. It might be truer to say, then, that not Benedict but Cassiodorus was the school master of Europe. But here again the Rule of St. Benedict was ample enough and flexible enough to allow something which Benedict himself had not envisaged to be introduced into it.

But Vivarium did not survive the death of its founder at the ripe age of 100 years—which is perhaps a symbolic number to indicate the patriarchal wisdom of Cassiodorus. But though the place ceased to exist, his idea continued on, and the Benedictine tradition was thereafter enriched by yet another element, a providential example of growth which, leaving the essentials intact, was a true development.

The third element which flowed into the Benedictine stream, and one almost inevitably following on monks' being priests, was the missionary activities of monks, especially those of the Anglo-Saxons. The movement began with St. Gregory, who sent Augustine and his companions to England (597). As today the Benedictines are once again experiencing the missionary urge in their blood, this first step in that direction is important and should be examined at leisure. That handful of monks from Italy, fearful as they were of the barbarians across the Channel, were the first in a movement within the Church that in fact civilized and evangelized Western, Central, and Northern Europe.

The characteristics of the Anglo-Saxon monastic Church were (1) their eagerness for a civilized Christianity. Bede stands out as a saint, but also as a humanist. In his autobiographical note at the end of the *Ecclesiastical History of the English Nation,* he wrote that "learning, writing, teaching have always been sweet to me." Among his writings are treatises on chronology, on grammar, on meter, on orthography, besides his commentaries on Scripture (which Boniface in Germany was so eager to lay his hands on) and his historical works—the *Ecclesiastical History of The English Nation,* the lives of Cuthbert and Wilfrid and the Three Abbots. The scholarly aspects of this period have been treated elsewhere. But we must at least mention St. Aldhelm. What Bede was for the north of England, Aldhelm was for the south. The pupil of an Irish monk, though himself an Anglo-Saxon, he also sat at the feet of Abbot Adrian in the famed school of Canterbury. It is said that he was the first to free his countrymen of a scruple about reading the ancient classics. He enjoyed Virgil and Horace, Ovid and Lucan, Terence, Persius and Juvenal. He himself wrote, when he overcame his self-consciousness, in an easy, limpid style. But when he took great pains over his prose, his style became turgid, abstruse, and ugly—unlike his contemporary Bede whose writing reflected the simplicity and peace of his soul. Aldhelm died in 709.[1]

(2) In this age of reconstruction, or simply of construction, of creating a civilized life, there was also need of the pioneer spirit, exemplified in two friends, Wilfrid and Benet Biscop. They both went across Europe several times, not only as pilgrims but as collectors: of saints' relics (which were the passion of that age), of books, of images, and of workers in glass and stone. Wilfrid, we know, built his first stone building—his little minster at Ripon—of old Roman stones already masoned, salvaged from the ruins left behind by the conquerors.

None of these, for all their activities and energy, ceased to be monks. But it was a new sort of monk, in the service of the Church, unknown in the East where the purely contemplative prevailed. There is a kinship between the pioneer Anglo-Saxon monks and those of the Middle West in the nineteenth and twentieth centuries and those French monks of today in Africa. Their framework was monastic—the family, the liturgy, the vows—but in their work they adapted themselves to

1. For Cassiodorus and Aldhelm, see the excellent pages in Décarreaux.

the needs of their times. It is this flexibility in grasping the work that needed to be done which proved the key to monastic growth or stagnation.

(3) The third important work of the Anglo-Saxon monks was missionary. Their leaders were Willibrord, Wilfrid, and Boniface, to say nothing of the nameless others, both monks and nuns, who joined the bands of missionaries. For a century and a half, they and their successors spread through western and northern Europe. It was a national effort. Many letters were written by Boniface to his friends in England imploring the despatch of more laborers in the vineyard, for books, for all that was necessary to divine service. Monks and nuns crossed the Channel to join him. He and they trudged the roads and tracks in the forests of Germany; they founded monasteries, convents, centers from which to operate. Sturm, Boniface's disciple, was sent to Monte Cassino to learn the ways of the Holy Rule at the very source. What use was this unless they proposed to live the monastic life? Sturm became Abbot of Fulda. The missionary work also attracted women. Leoba (which means Loved One), a nun of Wimborne, was abbess of Bischofsheim and had care of all the other convents of the new church. When Boniface was approaching his end, he ordained that he should be buried at Fulda and that she, who had been so great a support in all his labors, upon her death should be buried in his grave—"reaffirming his wish that after his death her bones should be placed next to his in the tomb . . . so that they should await together the day of resurrection." In fact, when she died, a great procession formed and she was taken to Fulda, but the monks did not dare open Boniface's grave, and she was buried on the north side of the altar.

This evangelizing work was methodical, permanent, and orderly; it was under the direct control of the Holy See. Boniface established dioceses wherever he went with bishops and parishes and churches. For the instruction of the neophytes he set up monasteries. Repeatedly he himself went to Rome to insure that everything should be done in due form.

So, once again we find monks setting up their way of life but adapting it to the needs of the time. One can imagine Boniface in his young monastic years in his English monastery carrying out his monastic obediences, teaching the children Latin and the Christian truths, writing his grammar for them; practicing the monastic asceticism, the common round of prayer, reading, and study. But as a result of this earnest faithfulness to his vows and as a call in his prayers, he conceives an urgent desire to leave his native land and evangelize the peoples of Germany. This was in tune with the spirit of the English monastic tradition. Had not the Anglo-Saxons themselves been given the gift of faith by the labors of earlier monastic missionaries? Gregory has sent Augustine, Boniface could follow that example.

Today monasticism is faced with a similar opportunity: in Africa, in South America, in parts of Asia, the hundreds of millions of men and women who have never really heard of Christ are waiting. Few go to their assistance; and every year we delay, the opportunity shrinks. Just as the eighth-century monk and nun missionaries founded monasteries at the same time as being preachers of the word, so too must the twentieth-century followers of Boniface and Leoba.

St. Bede died in 735 and St. Boniface was martyred in 754. Monasticism in the West fell upon evil times, chiefly because of the political instability under which the monasteries lived and the rapacity of the kings and nobles. The lands were taken over by nobles and the abbacies became the gift of the king to bishops or even to laymen.

Charlemagne at the turn of the ninth century, c. 800, was eager to restore monasticism in his kingdom, chiefly as an instrument of his educational plans. Alcuin, a monk of York, became his "minister of education." Schools were established everywhere; the Rule of St. Benedict became the only Rule for monks. But neither Charlemagne nor his successors were prepared to free the monasteries from lay control and even from lay appointment of abbots.

However, a reaction set in, which though it did not last,

became the pattern for the great monastery that set off the second great period of monasticism. The reaction was led by Benedict of Aniane (*c.* 750–821) and the monastery which a hundred years later took up his ideas was Cluny (founded 910).

Son of a Visigothic noble from the Mediterranean coast of Gaul, Witiza—later Benedict—became a monk at Saint Seine in Burgundy in 773. Dissatisfied with the form of monasticism he found there, he returned home to Aniane on the Mediterranean and turned his home into a monastery, building a fine monastery, church, and library. He began austerely, first following the Rule of St. Pachomius; finding that too severe, he changed to that of St. Basil; and finally turned to the Rule of St. Benedict. Soon three hundred monks joined him. Charlemagne asked him to restore and reform the monasteries of Provence. This he did by sending out a team of twenty which moved from monastery to monastery. He soon found that you can bring a monk to the water of reform but you cannot make him drink it. So he turned to persuasion. His *Capitulare Monasticum* was a commentary on the Rule in great detail; then his *Codex Regularum* was a collection of all the great Rules for monks; in the *Concordia Regularum,* when commenting on the Rule of St. Benedict he attempted to show how much it surpassed in wisdom all the other Rules. He founded a monastery at the imperial city of Aachen. He was supported by Charlemagne's successor, Louis the Pious.

The reforms did not last, chiefly because of the onslaught of the second Dark Age, which consisted of one sweeping invasion after the other. The Saracens were always menacing in the south, the Magyars were pressing in from the east—they even reached the Atlantic coast in one raid—but worst of all, the Norsemen were coming down the Channel, destroying all Christian life and all monasteries on the east coast of England and Ireland, pushing up the great rivers, the Seine, the Loire, the Garonne. But, though the buildings were destroyed and the monks killed or dispersed, the ideas of Benedict of Aniane survived, and it is because of their survival that we must examine them in detail before moving on to the Cluniac revival, which took up where the second Benedict left off.

Benedict of Aniane set up a kind of Congregation in the modern sense, with himself as chief abbot equipped with fairly wide powers. What was the extent of these powers? Scholars disagree. Abbot Cuthbert Butler and others say that Benedict of Aniane destroyed one of the essential ingredients of Benedict of Nursia's plan, namely, the autonomy of each monastery, thus destroying the wise and fruitful relationship between the abbot and his monks—that of father and sons, master and disciples. The local abbot simply became the overseer, an appointee from outside, whom the monks themselves had not chosen. Dom Patrice Cousin, in his excellent book *Précis d'histoire monastique* categorically denies this. "The supervision [*intendance*] of a general nature over the abbeys, granted him [Benedict] by the Emperor, aimed simply at introducing the Benedictine Rule there and seeing that it was faithfully carried out." [1]

On the other hand, Dom Cousin admits that only certain royal abbeys, selected by the monarch, had the right to elect their abbots; for the remainder it was the sovereign himself to choose whom he willed.

Benedict of Aniane did not increase the choir office; he added a great number of prayers to be said privately. Another of his reforms was to keep oblates and lay school boys from the monastic school. According again to Dom Cousin he had no objection to an outside lay school existing as well as the internal school for the young monks.

Whatever be the truth of a number of disputed matters concerning Benedict's reforms, this valiant effort came to nothing, as Benedict himself died and no successor of his caliber could be found to succeed him. Besides, the political climate, as already mentioned, deteriorated into ruin; and the fatal mistake of allowing the secular arm to appoint the abbots insured the ruin of the Anianian reform itself. All, however, was not to be lost because in 910, about ninety years after the reformer's

1. Belgium, 1956, p. 220.

death, Cluny carried on where he had left off, with some improvements and some exaggerations.

THE SECOND PERIOD: 910–1418

Cluny began with the help of a great noble but one who "knew his place," William of Aquitaine. He did not want to control his foundation; he handed it over to St. Peter and the Holy See. The lesson had only recently been learned the hard way. So the Abbey of Sts. Peter and Paul of Cluny was made by its first abbot Bernon a fief of Rome.

In fact, the greatness of Cluny only began with its second abbot, St. Odo (927–942), and reached its peak of power and importance under the fifth, St. Hugh (1049–1109)—perhaps the longest ruling abbot in history.

Cluny gave over most of the day and most of the night to the celebration of the liturgy and its peculiar version of the liturgy at that. For instance, 138 psalms were sung—yes, sung —every day. Over and above this there were two conventual Masses of great splendor daily, as well as a number of supplementary offices and *"preces."*

Its constitution also was peculiar to itself. We are at the entrance to the feudal age. All the subject monasteries—and they went into the hundreds—were considered just an extension of Cluny, so that all the monks, wherever they were, were monks of Cluny; while the superiors were feudal subjects of the liege lord, the abbot of Cluny.

The spread of the Cluniac reforms either by Cluny itself founding a monastery in which the superior was appointed by the abbot of Cluny; or by Cluny being presented with an already existing monastery, perhaps by the monks themselves or by the local lord or king who claimed some jurisdiction over the place—here again the abbot was appointed by Cluny; or lastly by a monastery taking over the ways of Cluny. Among this last group were many of the greatest houses of Europe, such as Monte Cassino and Farfa. These did not wish to lose their independence—and the relationship was respectful but more distant.

Over the story of Cluny hangs a mystery. Why did this splendid reform concentrate almost exclusively on the liturgy? There was so much else to do: studying and writing, teaching, missionary work, the revival of agriculture. Such an enormous quantity of hours was devoted to the reciting of psalms, Offices of Our Lady, of the Dead, celebration of Masses, that there was no time left for anything else. So, from Cluny the future generations have inherited almost no writers, no tradition of manuscript copying. Sculpture, yes, and architecture. It is said that these monks felt it their business in the feudal world in which they lived, where everyone had a fixed work to perform in society, to do the world's praying; and they did it with all the solemnity they could muster.

Looking back on it with hindsight, one cannot help wondering whether this, without denying the primacy of prayer, was not the beginning of the end of monastic influence upon the world around. Had the monks looked out over the walls of their gardens they might have seen things that needed desperately to be done for that infant society. Apostolic work of many kinds was waiting to be done.

Cluny did not fail nine hundred years later, at the French Revolution, because of any great scandal—there was none: it failed from lukewarmness induced by wealth. Nothing fails so surely in monastic matter as material success. But nine hundred years is a respectable history.

But those who sought poverty and obscurity went elsewhere. They found Cîteaux. Before, however, looking at Cîteaux from the point of view of renewal, there is another revival worthy of examination and which came between the founding of Cluny and that of Cîteaux; it is that of Chaise-Dieu.

Chaise-Dieu, even more remote than Cluny, in the central massif of France, was founded by a St. Robert, who like so many other founders began as a hermit. He did not, on deciding to found a monastery, straightway pick the Rule of St. Bene-

139

dict. The austerity of his life, the genuineness of it attracted followers. The part of France where Chaise-Dieu is situated is by the river Dore, about thirty-five miles north-northwest of Le Puy. This is wild mountainous country and, though there were many other monasteries west of there and further north, in its own chosen area it was alone. The eleventh century was not only the century of Cluniac influence; other monasteries in France, Germany, Italy, and the Low Countries were radiating a reforming influence. These were all old foundations that, after the shock of destruction or sack either by Saracens or Hungarians or Normans, had almost miraculously freed themselves from the barbarous feudal ties of the period and re-established monastic ways; they were founded almost always somewhat on the model of St. Benedict of Aniane. Such were the abbeys of la Cava in Italy, Gorze in Lorraine, Marmoutier in the West, St. Victor at Marseilles, and so on. Like these, Chaise-Dieu owed its rise to the initiative of one saint; unlike these it never took to the ideas of Benedict of Aniane. Chaise-Dieu was independent of that revival, not only "politically" but also ideologically.

Robert of Turlande must have been born about the year 1000. He was put under the care of the canons of Brioude. When ordained, he himself became one of these canons. His life at this time was evangelical in its simplicity and in its good works. But he was closely linked with the abbot of Cluny, perhaps his uncle Odilon. He was tempted to throw in his lot with Cluny; the canons implored him to remain; he became ill. He stayed. But still he was torn between the love of contemplation and the love of his neighbor. Cluny was too near the world in its many monasteries, but also not involved enough. He saw the pope, he journeyed on to Monte Cassino, to discover the true tradition, "to study the Rule of St. Benedict and gather the sound monastic tradition." [1] He, now clear as to his plan, together with two companions, established their first hermitage at Chaise-Dieu in 1043. His companions were not clerics but

1. Pierre-Roger Gaussin, *L'Abbaye de Chaise-Dieu (1043–1518)* Paris, 1962, p. 100.

laymen, a typical sign of the times when the reformers were turning away from clericalized monasticism. Their second essential trait was their poverty, again typical of those turning away from the comfortable wealth of the great monasteries following the Cluniac revival. The third element was solitude, flight from the world, as the best condition for contemplative life. To quote Gaussin:

> It seems that, at first, Robert was strongly drawn towards the eremitical life. He did not, however, persevere in that form of life. Fairly soon he controlled that tendency. Instead of being a simple hermit in some Livradois solitude, he became a monk-apostle, drawn by the human problems in the Livradois, and understanding that the great need in a region of that kind was the conversion and evangelizing of the populations which had remained on the edge of the Christian world.
>
> We see, then, the erstwhile canon, the hermit of yesterday, travelling the Livradois and the other regions of the Auvergne, especially the more mountainous parts, everywhere preaching, curing, casting out the devil.[1]

St. Robert thought he could follow St. Benedict of Nursia in having hermitages near the monastery for those monks who were already tried in the spiritual life by long years in the monastery. Once again this was in the air at the time—the Camaldolese (1012), Vallombrosa (c. 1036). But Robert saw no division between contemplation and action, and in c. 1050 he became abbot; the abbey church was erected and by then 300 monks had joined him. For a period of twenty-five years St. Robert's apostolic labors continued, chiefly founding small priories, sometimes of six or seven monks, sometimes of only one or two!, and chiefly in that cold austere highland of the Auvergne. Round these priories gathered the local people to form parishes. He must have made about fifty such foundations. At the same time he established a convent at St. André de Comps. Now the foundations from Chaise-Dieu began to extend beyond the Auvernais. Robert died at his abbey April 17, 1067.

1. *Ibid.,* p. 105.

He was succeeded by other saintly abbots; but success brought with it wealth and lands and the interest of nobles. However, because of its remoteness and the austere tradition of its founder, it continued to the French Revolution if not in the first flush of spiritual endeavor at least a worthy Benedictine house.[1] But we may well ask whether Robert's solution of the problem contemplation versus activity was a truly Benedictine solution. This multiplication of very small communities, where the monks could not live a life much different from the secular clergy, scarcely fulfilled the ideal. On the other hand, the needs of the time forced his hand, and which should take precedence, the Rule or the times?

Cîteaux did not take that path. She and her daughter houses kept to their solitude. No need to repeat what all know, the origins of Cîteaux, the founding of Clairvaux; the coming of Bernard; the spread of the reform throughout Europe; the splendid quarrel between the two saints, Peter of Cluny and Bernard of Clairvaux. Who has not read the sonnet of Words-worth on the ruins of Tintern Abbey, or heard of the glories of Rievaulx and Fountains? Sts. Robert, Stephen, Bernard, Ailred are household words in monastic circles. These men and the thousands who followed them into the wilderness in France, Spain, Portugal, Italy, Germany, England, and the cold lands in the North, were seeking God and God alone. Of that there could be no doubt in the minds of their contemporaries. They wore the rough habit and lived in simple cells, their churches were austere, they ate no meat, they rose in the middle of the night to praise the Lord, performed the liturgy not in costly vestments but in simple chasuble. By the work of their hands and that of the lay brothers the wilderness began to flower, to become cultivated and beautiful. Rich and poor, mighty and lowly flocked to put themselves under the guidance of a saintly Cistercian abbot. More than 700 monks lived at Clairvaux; Rievaulx and Byland were not far behind. It was an austere life. The book was the Bible; silence the rule; secular studies,

1. In 1518 the abbot became lay. The *"in commendam"* took hold. It was suppressed in 1790.

especially the new wave of Scholasticism and artistic concerns, were, at least at first, considered inconsistent with the life of the monk.

The Cistercian Order is one of the greatest monastic religious families in the Church and stands, today as it did at its birth, as a sign to the world of the importance of prayer, penance, and silence. Nothing that follows can contradict that judgment.

It is a firm conviction, nevertheless, that while the letter of the Cistercian Rule is Benedictine; the spirit is nearer the monasticism of the Egyptian desert.

1. Its austerity is outstanding: the remote locale, the spare food, the rough clothes, the unheated buildings, the common dormitory, the almost perpetual silence. All these can be justified from the Benedictine Rule; but St. Benedict himself was not aiming at establishing the most austere discipline in the Church, he was legislating for beginners, for men who could not even do without their bottle of wine a day. Transplant his Rule to the twentieth century, taking only the positive regulations and omitting the mitigations and the spirit of the mitigations, and you are left not with a Rule for Everyman, but for giants.

Once again, this is not criticism of the Cistercian but praise, with however, a distinction. Their life is stricter than St. Benedict meant it to be.

To show that this is not simply a personal, erratic view, here are some weighty judgments by a scholar of no mean renown. Dom Wilmart, writing of the famous quarrel between Cîteaux and Cluny in the persons of Bernard and Peter the Venerable, sums up as follows:

> If one dare make a judgment on the essence of the quarrel, one must admit that Cîteaux, heroic Cîteaux and all it represents, proposed a return to the sublime and dangerous life of the Fathers of the Desert, and by the same token, was foreign to the specific thinking of St. Benedict.[1]

2. By turning their back on culture and beauty—of course,

1. Quoted by Dom Philibert Schmitz, O.S.B., *Histoire de l'ordre de Saint-Benoît,* 7 vols., Maredsous, 1942–; vol. 3, p. 35.

it could not be kept out—the Cistercians also give the impression of being against civilization much as the Desert Fathers did in Syria and Egypt. This extreme renunciation is so strikingly similar that it crosses the mind: could the same pervading thread of Manicheeism have been present in the twelfth century as it had been in the fourth? The austerities and unworldliness of the Manichees in the fourth century had helped create an extreme unworldliness in the zealous members of the Church, the monks; was the Cistercian phenomenon likewise a too extreme effort at unworldliness, partly the effect of the infiltration of the Manichean—now called Albigensian—spirit through Western Europe at this time? Cathars by their austerity and otherworldliness exposed by contrast the laxity of the twelfth-century Church.

True or half true, it remains a fact that the Cistercian attitude had most important effects on the whole monastic world at that time and the following century, a turning point in the cultural history of Europe. The Cistercian ideal veered monasticism away from the new Christian world which was growing up all round, forcing the monks in on their own lives, away from the towns, away from the new thought, from the new universities springing up everywhere. For all the splendor of Cluny and Cîteaux, monasticism now became a backwater in the life of the West; others would come forward to create new links between Christ and his People. The monks with a characteristic sign had turned their backs on the world, retired into the solitudes of valley and hill. St. Bernard had attacked and defeated the champion of the new Scholasticism, Abelard; the monks had withdrawn from schools; they no longer evangelized. They were emulating the Fathers of the Desert, rather than a Bede or a Boniface. It was left to a Francis and a Dominic to find ways of keeping the monastic spirit in touch with the world though not of it.

The preceding paragraphs may give the impression that the author disapproves the Cistercian way of life. This is far from the truth. It is one of the greatest expressions in the Church of the idea of *fuga mundi,* flight from the world. But it is of vital importance that in our times we recognize that there are *many* ways of following the monastic life. The Benedictine way is also authentic. It was the failure to recognize this in the past that led writers to denigrate the Mixed Life, such as the Benedictines have led and still lead. Each soul has his way of following Christ, each Order is a presentation of some facets of the almost infinite manifestation of the divine in Christ's humanity. We must praise the Lord for this wonderful variety, and each go on his own way rejoicing.

One remembers wistfully the life of St. Anselm of Bec and Canterbury. A young Italian from Acosta sought out the greatest teacher of his age, Lanfranc of Bec, put himself under his discipline. Lanfranc became abbot and then archbishop of Canterbury. Anselm succeeded him in these offices. The latter was born in 1033 and died in 1109. P. J. de Ghellinck writes of him in his great work *Le mouvement théologique du xii siècle* that he *"dépassa complètement son époque."* [1] By which he meant that his thought was so far in advance of his own generation that he remains like a lonely promontory in that century. He was a genius and therefore not to be explained by his own surroundings.

Anselm approached and illumined most of the great themes of theology and philosophy. He reintroduced metaphysics into theological thought; in his *cur deus homo* he opened new fields of understanding of the Incarnation and the Redemption. He studied the freedom of the will, the relationship between reason and faith, the nature of God himself and of the human soul. He died searching for the origin of the latter.

The school of Bec after his withdrawal to England to become primate lost its lustre. In those days a school was the master. But one cannot help wondering whether the tradition of learning, both philosophical and theological, might not have taken a different turn, perhaps less analytical, more contemplative, had Anselm remained at Bec and founded a school of masters. Perhaps, too, when the great universities began, the Benedictines instead of enclosing themselves in their monas-

1. Bruxelles, 1948, pp. 80–81.

teries might have taken part in the first formative years. History of course is what happened. But we may learn also for the future from what might have happened had history taken another turn.

There have been two deep wells from which monasticism has drawn the waters of its life, the well of poverty in its broadest sense and the well of learning. It is rare that these two have been present at the same time in the history of the Order, but among those times was that of Lanfranc and Anselm at Bec. The first without the second lets the monk sink into a morass of ignorance. The second without the first leads to pride and self-seeking.

For the time being the future of monasticism was with the Cistercians. They understood the meaning of poverty, but the lead of Anselm they did not take.

Dom Philibert Schmitz sums it up as follows:

Up to the twelfth century the work of the monks, one of the primordial elements in the Benedictine life, had been determined by the times and the localities where they were situated. Monasticism had in consequence evolved as a result of and in intimate connection with those needs. During the high Middle Ages it had responded to two great social missions: it had propagated the Gospel throughout Europe, it had presided over the early education and instruction of its peoples. This double task was completed, it can be said, by the twelfth century. Other opportunities of social dedication were presenting themselves to the monks. These they did not grasp. They withdrew into themselves.

By this withdrawal, the abbeys more and more let slip their influence upon the world. The Order of Cluny and all those inspired by its spirit abandoned schools; many monasteries refused to give themselves to the care of souls. Many there were which broke off all contact with intellectual culture, though it was tense with life at that period, just when it was being reborn. Thus the monks isolated themselves from society; society no longer sought them out, it turned instead to other institutions! [1]

The Benedictines of the thirteenth and fourteenth centuries have little about them to arouse our interest. They were settling down into the feudal system, administering their lands, per-

1. Schmitz, *op. cit.,* vol. 3, pp. 4–5.

forming their allotted function of public prayer. They grew rich and mediocre. Perhaps as good a picture as we are likely to find for the thirteenth century is that of the Register made by Eudes, Archbishop of Rouen, on his rounds. The monks had their own money boxes and keys thereto; they were not very regular about saying Mass or confessing. They ate meat even though this was against not only the Rule but the statutes of recent popes. What they did apart from prayer is not recorded. The same kind of picture is seen in reading the very human but uninspiring chronicle of Jocelyn of Brakeland when he describes his abbey of Bury St. Edmunds. But evidently it is impossible to generalize for two centuries and over the whole of Europe. All one can say is that history does not record anything outstanding within the Benedictine Order during that period which saw the growth and rise to influence first of the Cistercians and then of the friars, Dominican and Franciscan.

Yet all was not grey. Gertrude, nun of Helfta in Thuringia, illumined the mid-thirteenth century with her holiness and her writings. What is of particular significance, her piety was entirely liturgical and sacramental—if these two can be really separated. Her experiences of God usually took place during Mass or the Divine Office, and the texture of her imagery and the structure of her thought are made of a true grasp of the images of baptism and the Eucharist, of the doctrine of the Holy Spirit, the Incarnation, and grace. How many more, like her, but not so articulate there were during this long period, we simply do not know.

What shook the whole fabric was the sudden disaster of the Black Death, 1348. Houses that had room for a hundred or more monks or nuns were reduced to twenty; smaller ones were reduced to a handful, and not always by any means those survived who were most fitted to shoulder the crushing burden of restoring life to the shattered community. The smaller houses fell into a decline; the larger ones like Glastonbury, Westminster, and St. Alban's survived. But some new plan, some renewal of ideals was needed. The popes kept up a steady stream of decrees, laying down reforms, but little happened.

The turning point was the Council of Constance in 1418. In medieval times as many abbots attended these councils as did bishops. Many abbots were present at the great reforming Council of Constance. We may date the reformation of the Benedictine Order from that date.

THE THIRD PERIOD: 1418–1900

The story of these early reforms has a particular relevance to our own day when at another great Council many abbots were also gathered. What did the monastic reformers of 1418 set out to do? To what extent did they succeed and in the areas where they failed, why was it so?

The first signs of reform in fact preceded the Council. Louis Barbo, a native of Venice and early commendatory abbot of St. George in Alga, together with his brother formed a pious association. In 1409 the Pope Gregory XII told him to reform the Benedictine abbey of St. Justina of Padua. He was clothed, made his profession, and created abbot in February of that year. Within a couple of years postulants began to flood in, twenty at a time. He was able to spread out in the work of reform. Their first aim was to abolish the *in commendam*—the very thing that Barbo himself had been given—which usually meant a layman or some worldly ecclesiastic was sucking the revenues of the monastery and at the same time being an absent superior. The monks themselves did not benefit from the great wealth of the monasteries; but each of them had an obedienciary which meant a job in the monastery associated with funds which each administered. The less intelligent members of the community and the young kept the choir going.

Barbo's answer to this situation was reminiscent of Cluny, but not entirely. All the monks in the monasteries of the congregation took their vows to the congregation, much as the Cluniac monks had taken theirs to the abbot of Cluny no matter in which monastery they lived. But Barbo was afraid of the life abbot; so he was elected only for a year and the supreme authority was firmly held by the general chapter. This may have been a brilliant idea but it was not entirely Benedictine.

Once an abbot always an abbot, and consequently the retired abbots moved from one abbey to another each year, or lived in their own house as titular abbots. The control was firmly in the hands of the general chapter and visitors that it selected each year. The reform soon extended to the whole of Italy and was, in fact, instrumental in the reform of other Orders and of monks in other countries.

The reform collapsed but not before inspiring the German, Spanish, and English monks to search for reform themselves. Of the German reforms the most lasting was that started at Bursfeld. That abbey and its fifty dependent monasteries survived until the Reformation when they were dissolved. In this case the houses and their abbots preserved their autonomy, with the abbot of Bursfeld the perpetual president.

When the Reformation broke it was the spark from St. Justina of Padua (now called the Cassinese Congregation) which set aflame the reform in Belgium and at St. Vanne. From there came the revival of the French monasteries, which formed themselves into the Congregation of St. Maur.[1]

Except for the French and Spanish houses and two or three English ones, wars and the Reformation between them crippled and nearly killed the Benedictine tradition in Europe. The French Revolution did the rest, leaving only a remnant and sending the English houses on the continent scurrying back to their home country to learn slowly how to be monks once again and not hunted priests in recusant homes.

The nineteenth century and the first half of this century are part of our present situation and will be treated in a separate section.

Post-French Revolution Monasticism

Monasteries revived after the conflagration of the Napoleonic Wars as they had done in earlier centuries after similar disasters. On this occasion there were many different strands.

The old English Congregations that had four or five houses

1. See Cousin, *loc. cit.*, p. 424.

on the continent before the Revolution, Douai, Dieuleward, Paris, and so on, now found themselves homeless. So they returned to their native island and slowly, very slowly, re-established monastic life in all its fullness at Downside, Ampleforth, and Douai, there being a pull away into the parishes that had once been mission stations in persecution times. In the present century these re-established abbeys have grown in importance and have large schools attached.

France had seen the obliteration of her monastic life. The revival came with the Romantic revival *c.* 1830. Dom Guéranger had been a parish priest. He now conceived the idea of a return to medieval monastic tradition, to a splendid liturgical life, and to unexcelled devotion to the Holy See. He and his monks restored Solesmes (1833); they became the spearhead of the liturgical revival within monasteries—it was not until Dom Beauduin appeared that it dawned on anyone that the liturgy, which had been captured by the monks in the Middle Ages, was meant for the laity too. The scholarly work of preparing the texts from the ancient plain-song manuscripts done by the monks at Solesmes was a powerful contributory cause of the liturgical revival. But Solesmes had a fascination by its claim to be the authentic form of monasticism, which almost prevented other monasteries seeking their salvation in other directions. This is even more true of the nuns who tended to become more and more withdrawn.

The Swiss simply and with no fuss could return to their monasteries—Napoleon himself had granted them the right to re-establish two—and they carried on in their own traditional way: pilgrim monasteries with efficient schools attached. But the German ones had been badly mauled by the wars. Much in spirit like the French revival of Solesmes, the start came through King Louis of Bavaria who put Metten back on its feet with the help of Austrian monks and some Bavarian secular priests (1830). Thirty years later D. Maur Wolter, a secular priest from the Rhineland, having become a monk in Rome, returned to Germany and founded Beuron.

This revival was so powerful that it spread to other old

foundations in Germany, such as Maria Laach, and even into Austria and Belgium. Maredsous, in Belgium, at first associated with Beuron, became after the First World War independent and the center of a Belgian Benedictine Congregation of which St. André near Bruges and Mont César in Louvain became members, they being Maredsous' daughter houses.

Metten, founded by King Louis of Bavaria, was to become the source of the greatest expansion of the Benedictine way of life in modern times. A secular priest, who took the name of Boniface, Boniface Wimmer, was a member of that house and conceived a great desire to evangelize the great Middle West of North America. This was the origin of St. Vincent's near Latrobe in Pennsylvania, and of St. John's in Minnesota, and all the daughter houses, not only in the United States but as far afield as the Bahamas and Japan.

When the monks came out to the Middle West, the nuns followed. These came from Eichstadt. Their greatest center became St. Benedict's not far from St. John's, Collegeville, and what the monks did, the nuns did too, schools, colleges, work on the Indian missions; while the monks ran parishes, the sisters ran hospitals. It would be difficult to find a more heroic venture than that of those early sisters from that old-fashioned enclosed convent of Eichstadt, setting off into the wilds in the rough Middle West. They felt they were emulating the missionary work of a Boniface and a Leola, and indeed they were. If numbers of vocations through the years are any indication of the blessing of God, then without a doubt the American Benedictines, both monk and sister, have been blessed by and have the approval of God whom they serve.

The conditions which prevailed in mid-nineteenth century are not those of today, and therefore we must not have a fixation over the way of life, the work of those days. The world moves on, new needs, new aspirations, and we have to be conscious of these, as the Spirit inspires us. If Benedictines listen, they will be made aware of which way the voice of the Spirit is beckoning. *Ausculta!* Be attentive to the voice of the Master.

5. *According to a Sound Tradition: Schools*

Some spiritual writers give the impression that to have a school is unmonastic or un-Benedictine. They place such a strong emphasis on the contemplative life—though the phrase is absent from the Rule of St. Benedict—that scholastic activities, and especially schools, are thought to be in some way against the spirit of the Holy Rule. No Benedictine scholar has yet provided us with a complete study of the whole matter of convent or monastic schools through the ages.[1] But it is such an important matter, particularly in our time of renewal, and for Benedictines, that it must be separately examined here.

Schools are attested to throughout the history of the Benedictine Order. When we read in the Rule of *infantes, pueri, adolescentes,* and *juvenes* (children, boys, adolescents, and young men), there is no reason to suppose that they were anything more than oblates, presented by their parents with the hope that they would become monks in due course. The same is true of the convents, as far as we know. St. Gregory mentions in the *Dialogues* that Maurus and Placid were presented by their fathers, Roman patricians. But they, too, must have been oblates. St. Benedict probably never thought of a monastery as anything else than a school of divine service, and boys were simply in the preparatory stage for this. But if there were boys in his monastery—and we have seen that there were—then they had to be taught, they had to be kept in order, they had to be given recreation. All this required the care and supervision of monks.

St. Benedict had witnessed vice in the school he attended in Rome and so, thinking it better for himself to remain wisely unwise, he fled from his school to Subiaco. This is a paradox which surely needs some explanation: the founder of an Order who apparently is not interested in education, but whose followers become among the greatest teaching Orders in the

1. Pages 322–326 in Abbot Cuthbert Butler's *Benedictine Monachism* are still the best pages in English for this subject.

whole history of the Church, and known for their love of learning. Can this change, this modification or development of the original idea, be the supreme example of what the Second Vatican Council Fathers meant when they spoke of renewal as being sought for in the following of a "sound tradition"? Can schools be one of those elements in the history of the Benedictine tradition which developed out of the very nature of the thing, even if it was not in existence at the start? Or is it one of those sprouts to be uprooted as destructive of the original tree? At least we are in no doubt that, on the one hand, schools in the ordinary sense were not part of St. Benedict's conscious plan for a monastic way of life, and that, on the other hand, schools have been ubiquitous throughout the whole fourteen centuries of Benedictine history. This remains true even though, at certain times and in certain parts of the order, they have either been consciously excluded, for example, Cîteaux, or squeezed out as at Cluny.

We shall proceed to study this question historically and then as it could concern Benedictines today.

There were two decisive and forceful people who caused monks to have schools. The first was St. Gregory. According to an early tradition he founded a clerical monastery out of the refugee monks of Monte Cassino to serve a Roman basilica; and to serve it meant to be clerically educated. The second was Cassiodorus. He founded his Christian humanist monastery at Vivarium in the life time of St. Benedict. He believed that the profane sciences were not to be despised by monks. The divine science was the object and aim of the monk, but the profane sciences helped him to understand the former better. This was a revolutionary step, going counter to the trend set by St. Jerome and St. Augustine in his more pessimistic moments.[1]

When the Empire collapsed, its pagan schools collapsed with it. If the schools could not be Christian schools, the horror and the fear of them would cease. St. Benedict came just too early to see that this could happen.

1. The whole question among the early monks is described by Festugière in vol. 1 of his *Les moines d'Orient.*

153

It is clear from the early history of Benedictine monasticism in every country of Europe that there were boys, *"infantes,"* and oblates; we know that the monks read for many hours a day. It follows that these boys had to be taught to read and write in order to read the manuscripts and to copy them. The early monasteries had schools at least for their prospective monks. These monasteries trained their monks for the clerical state and so, from giving very elementary instruction, these schools soon became centers of ecclesiastical learning. It was natural that youths aiming to be secular priests should join these schools.

During the seventh and eighth centuries, there is not one mention of public schools, as there had been in the fourth. Only episcopal and monastic schools existed. Wherever the missionary monks went they opened schools. The earliest examples we know of were in England. At Canterbury a saint, Bishop Theodore, another saint, Benet Biscop, and Adrian created a school which became famous. Bede says all the pupils spoke Latin and Greek like their native language.[1] There were other notable centers, Beverley, Worcester, Rochester, all originating from the school at Canterbury; there was Jarrow with the Venerable Bede, York with Egbert and Alcuin, and several others, All these were monastic schools.

Later Charlemagne met Alcuin and was so impressed by him that he commissioned him to rejuvenate the educational system of his empire. Charlemagne issued an edict—a capitulary to this effect: Let each monastery keep up a school where the children can learn the psalter, that is, reading and writing, the chant, arithmetic (to compute) and grammar, that is, Latin (I, 60). Schmitz mentions among others the following monasteries which complied with the decree: Aniane, Tours, St. Wandrille, Fleury, Ferrières, St. Aignan of Orleans, St. Riquier, Murbach, Reichenau.

Then came the reforming activities of St. Benedict of Aniane (a monastery on the Mediterranean coast of southern Gaul)

---

1. *Ecclesiastical History of the English Nation,* Edited by Charles Plummer, New York and London, 1896; vol. 1, bk. 4, ch. 2, p. 205.

and his friend, the Emperor Louis the Pious. Between them they decided to reform the monastic order. At a synod held at Aix-la-Chapelle in 817—one of the most fateful dates for Benedictines—they persuaded the assembled abbots to decree that there be no other school in a monastery than that for oblates! *"Ut scola in monasterio non habeatur, nisi eorum cui oblati sunt."* [1]

It need scarcely be pointed out that decrees are not enacted against something unless that something is prevalent. Therefore, we conclude that schools for non-monk boys were prevalent. The importance of this decree was not apparent immediately. Historians are divided as to its meaning. Did it intend that extern students should not be admitted within the enclosure to share with the oblates in their school, but yet have a school outside the enclosure? Or did it mean to eliminate nonclerical students completely? Schmitz leans to the latter view when he writes that "from the period when the new Carolingian system of schools was being organized, many monasteries showed reluctance to accept secular scholars in the community." [2] Dom Patrice Cousin, a strong defender of St. Benedict of Aniane, writes, "Was he [Benedict of Aniane] an enemy of studies? Certainly not. If he kept the claustral school for oblates only, following the Rule, and refused to admit—as Charlemagne wanted—children of nobles or future clerics [clerks], the reason was that he did not wish to have future monks continually in contact with children destined to live in the world. . . . besides, it was always permissible to set up a school for lay people outside the monastic enclosure, as was done at Fleury-sur-Loire." [3]

Whatever this decree meant, it did not stop many monasteries throughout Europe from having schools even within the cloister, for example Bec, Gorze, Reichenau, St. Trond. "In the ninth century this evolution was frankly accepted and

1. Quoted by Schmitz, *Histoire de l'ordre de Saint-Benoît,* vol. 2, p. 57.
2. *Ibid.,* p. 58.
3. Cousin, *op. cit.,* pp. 222–223.

schools were opened everywhere." [1] In the words of Schmitz, "The tenth and eleventh centuries were the golden age for Benedictine schools." [2] "We can hold as certain that the greatest number of monastic lay schools whose origins are prior to the tenth century go right back to the time of Charlemagne and even beyond." [3]

Sometimes the lay schools, as at Fleury-sur-Loire and at St. Gall in Switzerland, were extra-claustral schools, as were also, for instance, the ones at Gellone, St. Germain d'Auxerre, St. Riquier, St. Vaast (d'Arras), Lobbes, St. Amand, St. Hubert, Hautmont, Granfel: these were all in France. In England there were extra-claustral schools at Canterbury, York, Glastonbury, Abingdon, and elsewhere.

To quote Dom David Knowles, "From the disappearance of the Roman tradition of secular education beneath the advance of the new northern nations until the intellectual adolescence of those nations shortly after the millenium, the only permanent depositories of the resources of culture were the monasteries, and the part which they played in educating Europe has been generously appreciated and assessed by modern scholarship." [4] Describing the revival under Dunstan and Ethelwold, he writes: "Everything we know of their lives and activities suggests that they desired to use the educational resources at their command so as to influence the greatest possible number, though indeed in the England of 970–1066 the number outside the monasteries who would desire to make use of these resources must always have been small." [5] Dom Jean Leclercq several times stresses that these schools were small and he is right, "When considering the number of students we must beware of exaggerating them under the influence

1. Berlière, *L'ordre monastique*, p. 116; quoted in Dom David Knowles, *The Monastic Order in England*, New York and London, 1963, p. 488, note 3.
2. *Ibid.*, p. 58.
3. *Ibid.*
4. *The Monastic Order in England*, p. 487.
5. *Ibid.*, p. 488.

of present day ideas." [1] The reasons for the small numbers are many, among them the few who wished to learn; learning only led to the clerical state or the law. There were very few books and the life of the school boy almost intolerable. It is not possible to be certain how many students were in these schools. At St. Gall, there were eight class rooms. At St. Riquier in Carolingian times there were 100 pupils. The monks wrote the textbooks on both secular and religious subjects. Among them were saints: Bede, Boniface, and Anselm, and other famous names such as Alcuin and Raban Maurus of Fulda.

It was the success of Cluny, "grandchild" of Aniane, that proved almost fatal to monastic schools. Cluny admitted no lay students to its school, and in its oblate school it admitted only six.[2] There could have been room for both liturgy and schools. Once Cluny had taken a hold on European monasticism the initiative in the educational life of the Middle Ages passed to other hands. Cluny's influence was immense but not uniform. Dom Cousin explains this influence in some detail. Those which fell under its spell, either by being ruled from Cluny or by accepting reforming priors or by copying its constitutions, tended to squeeze out time for schools or scholarship simply by the immense increase of public prayer sung by the monks. As Dom Cousin tersely remarks, "Intellectual activity [at Cluny] did not have the expansion that might be expected in an abbey that was both so powerful and so large. The reason: the monks were weighted down by the Divine Office." [3]

The influence of Cluny was sufficiently pervasive to leave monastic education without influence during the next stage in Western intellectual development, namely, the rise of the universities and Scholasticism. Some may think that this was right. Monasteries had schools to train youths before their entry into the monastic life proper—as Leclercq maintains—but no schools for the monk. "If there were studies in the monasteries,

1. *Los monjes y los estudios,* Poblet 1963, p. 114, note 1.
2. Schmitz, *op. cit.,* vol. 2, p. 62.
3. *Op. cit.,* p. 240.

they were a preamble to the monastic life, and in that sense were not at all 'monastic studies.' " [1] "There was a monastic culture, but there were no monastic studies." [2] "There were no organized studies for the monks." [3] Dom David Knowles maintains that from 1050 onwards education was increasingly in the hands of the cathedral schools in France.[4] Concerning England, after the Norman conquest, he writes, "There is no trace of a systemized lay or clerical education in the Normanized monasteries of England; the learning of Canterbury was famous, but it attracted only monks." [5] In England, too, schools became associated with the cathedrals rather than with the monasteries.

Dom Philibert Schmitz gives an interesting example of the withdrawal of the monks from the educational field: "In 1139 the abbey of Lobbes received as abbot, Leonius, a monk of Anchin where the Cluniac customary was in use. Leonius immediately closed the extern school to the deep chagrin of the chronicler, who was astonished that people should think the education of youth was repugnant to the monastic ideal." [6] He describes also how the school of *"canonici"* at St. Gall was also closed. As the monasteries half shut their doors, the episcopal and collegiate doors were opened wide. The cities themselves set up schools; universities came into being; the Dominicans and Franciscans were in the vanguard of the new advance. Only in those parts of Europe where Cluny had only a slight influence did the monastic schools continue to flourish, as for example in England, Austria, and Bavaria.[7]

During the later Middle Ages the repeated encouragement of the Holy See to the monasteries to have internal schools is perhaps a sign that things were not altogether as they should have been in this matter. Schmitz refers to the canons of the Lateran Council of 1179 and to those of the great Fourth Lat-

1. J. Leclercq, *op. cit.*, p. 117.
2. *Ibid.*, p. 115.
3. *Ibid.*, p. 115.
4. Knowles, *op. cit.*, p. 490.
5. *Ibid.*, p. 491.
6. Schmitz, *op. cit.*, vol. 5, p. 110.
7. *Ibid.*, pp. 110–114.

eran Council in 1215; the laws of Clement V, and to Benedict XII in his bull *Summa Magistri* of 1336. The popes also encourage schools for externs, but separated from those for the prospective monks.

It is impossible to generalize for so long a period and such varied situations. But the situation of the Spanish monastery in Valladolid at the end of the Middle Ages may give an indication of a trend.[1] "In the early days"—he is speaking of the second quarter of the fifteenth century onwards—"there reigned in the observant monasteries, on the subject of studies, a spirit of mingled contempt and suspicion. The following facts will suffice to prove this: In 1436 they petitioned and obtained a pontifical dispensation in the first place from sending monks to the universities to study—a thing the bull *Summi Magistri* had laid down. The reason they gave was that the monks of Valladolid and their imitators observed perpetual clausura at that time; in the second place they obtained a dispensation for each monastery from having a master *"in primitivis scientiis."* This was a thing likewise prescribed by Canon Law; and in 1438 they won a confirmation of these privileges, alleging in their request, beside their vow of perpetual clausura, the following very significant argument. They said that, in the monastic life [*religiones monasticas*], especially when the observance was strict, the monks must rather *"vacar"* ponder the study of their consciences than that of science. In this they were using a play on words dating back to St. Bernard." [2]

The ignorance of these monks must have been abysmal. It is not surprising that Rabelais fled from his first effort at the religious life if his Benedictine monastery was similar. At Valladolid the Constitutions of 1500 enjoined that at least one of the two monks in charge of the money box "should know how to read and count reasonably well." [3]

After the shock of the Reformation and in accord with the

1. See the essay by D. García M. Columbás, "Los Estudios en la Congregación de San Benito de Valladolid," in *Los Monjes y los estudios.*
2. *Op. cit.,* p. 340.
3. *Ibid.*

humanism of the times, the revived monastic congregations, those of Valladolid, of St. Vanne, the English in their small way, and finally St. Maur, not only gave serious attention to scholarship, but in several branches took the lead. What is not generally known is that St. Maur, beside its vast scholarly output, also maintained excellent schools for lay people. The only author who seems to think this worth mentioning is once again Schmitz. The Maurists had colleges, even military academies and many smaller and less significant schools. Their manifesto published by the General Chapter of 1636 ran as follows: "Wishing to walk in the footsteps of our forebears we are earnestly endeavoring to put back into its honoured place the ancient custom of our Order, brought back to its primitive and integral practice as much as circumstances allow, namely, to educate the children of distinguished parentage and principally of those from noble families. . . . A certain number would be educated free." [1] The first of these "colleges" was opened by Abbot Tarrisse (d. 1648). Schmitz gives a list of fourteen including the famous Sorèze. In 1776 they acquired five military academies from the government.

The total number of scholarly establishments served by the Maurists was 30. The boys studied the classics, modern languages, music, dancing, dramatic art, speech, and gymnastics.[2] Just before the Revolution Sorèze had 46 professors. The "regents" of the upper classes were monks, and monks taught special courses. There were many lay faculty: 8 for music, 3 for fencing. In 1767 there were 200 students; in 1789, 400 boarders alone, including 80 Americans. Sorèze survived the French Revolution.[3] Laplace was one of the 300 pupils at Beaumont. The Congregation of St. Vanne also had three colleges.

We have omitted all mention of the copying of manuscripts, the huge literary output through the centuries, the building up of great medieval and later libraries. All this was exemplified

1. Schmitz, *op. cit.,* vol. 5, pp. 115–116.
2. *Ibid.* p. 118.
3. *Ibid.,* p. 119.

in the Saxon tradition by Bede and others, in the French tradition by Mabillon and his fellow workers; the surge of scholarship in the Anglo-Saxon period, *c.* 650–750, and in the seventeenth and eighteenth centuries among the Maurists.

It is not necessary to describe the increase of schools among Benedictine communities during the nineteenth and twentieth centuries except to note that in every country where this invasion has taken place the monasteries and convents have flourished. One has only to think of the abbeys of St. André and Maredsous in Belgium, the great monastic schools in England and Scotland: Downside, Ampleforth, Douai, Ealing, Belmont, and Fort Augustus to mention only a few; the vast establishments in America, not least those of nuns: St. Scholastica's, Atchison, Kansas; St. Benedict's at St. Joseph's, Minnesota; the schools and colleges of the monks, St. John's, Collegeville; St. Leo's, Florida; the college of St. Benedict in Atchison, the oldest of them all, St. Vincent's, Latrobe. In all these places where for a hundred years vocations have been plentiful, there is food for thought on the subject of activism. In several of these monasteries steps have been or are being taken to control the colossus, and none too soon. For contemplation is a tender plant and in the rough and tumble of school activities could be trampled underfoot and die.

Now that we have traced the development of the Benedictine schools and scholarship, it is right to ask the searching question: Is all this monastic? The question is not a new one. It was asked by Benedict of Aniane and answered in the negative. But the bulk of the monasteries did not follow him. It was asked again by de Rancé, the founder of the Trappists, and once again answered negatively. But on this occasion there was a champion on the other side in Mabillon. Their controversy was long, involved, but courteous. At the end Mabillon went to La Trappe to speak peace. They made peace, edifying one another. But Mabillon did not venture on that occasion to speak on the debated point. The argument remains essentially the same today. On de Rancé's side are all the points that can be made

161

stressing the worldly and distracting nature of study and teaching. It is worldly wisdom; whereas all, in the contemplative life, should lead the mind to God.

On Mabillon's side is a twofold argument: that sound learning is a fine preparation for a worthy and profound understanding of the word of God; that a man cannot pray all the time, he needs a change, and study is better for modern monks than agriculture. This is even more true today when agriculture is not profitable even with free labor. If it is done so scientifically that the skill is greater than that required to be a school master, then it requires a good deal more concentration even than teaching.

No doubt some men may be able to concentrate on God for sixteen hours of the day. St. Benedict was not legislating for that type. He had in mind the ordinary man, one who tries, but who needs a change. In other words, we are saying: the division of the timetable in St. Benedict's time into sleeping, eating, praying, working (manual), and *lectio divina* was good for his time; it provided a suitable framework and rhythm for prayer for the people of the sixth century. Today we need more intellectual activity, less pure spiritual reading, less manual labor, and so more study.

A Benedictine monastery is made up of many types, not of pure contemplatives. These types are all more or less active, and this has never been more true than in the twentieth century. Are they going to be turned away from the monastic life because they do not conform to the style of the sixth, tenth, twelfth, eighteenth centuries? To do so would be utterly unrealistic; these men and women want a life with God, dedicated to prayer, but also a normal amount of activity, to give them a sense of sharing in the Church's apostolate, and to keep them sane.

Almost all those who present themselves in Western countries have had a high school education; many hold university degrees, and most, even if this has not yet been the case, could profitably go on to a university to obtain a degree. Study has been the setting of their lives, as agriculture was the setting for the vast majority before the discovery of printing, before the enlargement of science, and before mass education and the flight to the cities. The ideal work for them is not hours of heavy manual labor—now obsolete since the bulldozer can do in a day what it took a community months to achieve—but intellectual work. Now the question is: What kind of intellectual work is suitable? It might be thought that the writing of books and learned articles, the work of scholarship, historical or liturgical or theological or patristic research were ideally suited. The picture of a monk's head buried in great tomes, immersed in heaps of manuscripts in some ancient library is attractive. This is what we are led to expect from reading romantic accounts of monks. Very few monks or nuns, however, in an ordinary monastic house are capable of being scholars, writers, researchers. Scholarship is a very specialized vocation. It could even be argued that we have enough books to go on with and it is readers rather than writers that are required.

On the other hand, running a school fits the situation almost perfectly. (1) It is there on the premises. Scholars could spend, like the late Dom Henri Leclercq, their whole monastic life not in the monastery but affixed to a seat in the British Museum. In a school, the work comes to the monk or sister in the shape of a boy or girl; the monk or sister does not have to leave the monastery or convent. It is true that in their train the students bring all their bustle and noise, all their relations at times, their own problems and those of their parents. But this is a problem that has been well controlled in a number of twentieth-century monasteries. (2) A school requires not just one talent—as do scholarship or retreat giving—but as many talents as are available, from the artistic to the athletic, the scholarly, the counselling. A monk who is a linguist finds he can be useful; if he is an archeologist, or a bird enthusiast, or a gardener, he can use his talent for others. (3) Then everyone has a different capacity for work; sometimes one is inclined to call it a nervous energy reservoir which just has to be released. The amount of work, in a school, can reasonably vary from

163

one member of the community to another. On the other hand, some religious are moved to greater periods of prayer. It should be possible, in a monastery with a school, to provide a timetable of prayer and work to suit most temperaments.

Snags undoubtedly there are and they must be faced. The first and most dangerous is that of too much work piling up upon an individual or worse, upon the whole community. This can come about either through a real demand from the people outside, or through the misdirected energies of one or more of the inmates. In many countries Catholic education has been slow in keeping pace with the standard of instruction for the rest of the population, owing to poverty, persecution, or war. The bishops plead for help, the parents cry piteously that if their children cannot be accommodated they will have to be sent to the public school. The religious introduce a few more pupils each year, until almost imperceptibly the school has grown to unmanageable size. The very upkeep is no longer a monastic job, it requires teams of workers. The superior finds that very few, if any, of the monks are capable of new and difficult burdens which are not normal monastic ones. A solution to megalomania is to reduce drastically the size of the mammoth establishment, a difficult operation once it has reached its swollen condition. Another solution is perhaps in keeping with the thinking of today: to introduce lay people into many more places of authority, even as principal or president, into the procurator's office. This solution gives the lay Catholic opportunities he has been lacking and needs. It does, however, bring a further problem, a constitutional one. Monks should be under a monk, and nuns under a prioress or mother superior. It may be that the head mastership itself would have to remain in monastic hands.

A boarding school is very demanding of time. The students are present and must be looked after from rising time to late in the evening. For someone there is no respite. This arrangement, however, has notable advantages from the point of view of the students. They are free from the distractions of home and can concentrate on their work. The influence of the teachers too is likely to be more penetrating, thorough, and effective, because communication occurs not only in the formal and somewhat forbidding periods of class, but in the relaxed, friendly times of play and natural human intercourse, such as during a quiet friendly discussion after supper with the aid of nature's evening atmosphere of peace.

The monastic house, on the other hand, gains immeasurably if the school is only a day school, because then the students only appear after breakfast, after morning Office and morning prayer. They are gone at the latest at five, and once again quiet descends upon the place. This is a happy mixture. But some means has to be found for really strong links with the students.

When a school flourishes, a new danger presents itself: to be associated with the well-to-do could be harmful both to the spirit of poverty and to the actual practice of poverty. The children, we recognize, should have all those amenities which go with a good school and with the effort to make their school days as contented as the rigors of school life will allow. These same amenities are at hand for the monks and sisters. Should they have as much use of them as their pupils, or should there be considerable restraint? They become friends with the parents. The latter are eager to show their appreciation and to lavish presents and invitations upon the monks and sisters. It is not easy to refuse such kindness without seeming ungracious. Indeed, it is possible in this way for a community to lose its spirit and practice of unworldliness, recollection, and poverty. But a difficulty does not create a reason for holding back from a course of action which is in itself good; the right behavior would be to recognize the danger and to take the necessary precautions.

Should these schools and colleges be abandoned? The very poor are being left out in the cold. Should not the Benedictines go straightway to these same poor? The answer will not appeal to all. They should go on doing what they are doing, knowing it is a good work and what obedience has given them to do. If they have members of the house to spare, and it would be feasible to set up another monastic house which would remain truly monastic, to do this other work, then if they so decide, let them do it. But it should be borne in mind that there are ten thousand good works that need doing in the world. Now one, now another accumulates all the enthusiasm of the eager. They *all* need doing, for all people, rich or poor, have souls to save. Voltaire, who for all his lack of "religion" had some wise things to say, remarked at the end of his notorious novel, *Candide,* that each of us should cultivate his own garden. This is good advice, especially to monks and sisters. They have chosen a way of life and a work. It may not be particularly glamorous, nor the most heroic in physical endeavor, but it is the one to which God led them. Let them, as Voltaire advised, cultivate their patch of God's garden, and be content that God will send others into other parts of that same garden to deal with those other plants which need cultivating also.

Over a century earlier St. Francis de Sales had put the same point in his inimitable way when writing to St. Jeanne de Chantal in 1605: "It is remarkable, my Daughter, how set my mind is on this piece of advice: not to sow in our neighbor's field, no matter how good a plot of land it may be, so long as our own has need of care. To be divided in the core of our being is always dangerous, to have our heart in one place and our duty in another." [1]

The thorny problem of monks and schools has been approached here mainly from an historical point of view. There are, obviously, many other aspects of the question which would warrant attention in a more detailed study.

What, for instance, is to be said about monks and nuns managing large, complex educational establishments? Some think that such work is now outmoded. In response to this objection, it could have been shown that education remains one of the great and permanent ways of being of service to one's fellow men. Such work shares in the loving and selfless service of the young, which is the task of the family, the com-

1. *"Lettre* CCCXX," Novembre 30, 1605, de S. François de Sales à Ste. de Chantal, *Oeuvres,* Annecy, XIII, p. 123.

munity, and the Church. This service is never to be despised, especially if offered freely out of love for others in Jesus Christ.

It would have been interesting to have shown how none of the great disciplines: history, languages, Classics, science, or the arts is alien to Christ. Everything created by the word of God continues to bear his imprint. Contrary to much common opinion, science especially seems to have avoided the distortions of truth which often arise through the weakness and arrogance of the human intellect.

There is also the question whether monastic schools have any particular contribution to make to education. How, for instance, does a school taught by religious differ from a public school? In what way is a monastic school specifically different from either of these? These are questions which seem to need answers now, more than ever, when private schools are finding it increasingly difficult to finance themselves.

Closely related to this is another question: What is the value of our present educational commitments relative to the many other tasks which face the Church today? What other new work might monks engage in, without sacrificing their fundamental vocation? It is clear that present commitments cannot be lightly abandoned, but how can the monastic orders prepare for the future?

Finally, there is the large question which follows necessarily upon all of the above: that is, the question of the education of the monks themselves. How can be prevented that in-breeding which has so long plagued Catholic education in the United States and other countries? How can the monks relate themselves to the best secular universities without compromising their vocations? Is there any place for the monk, as student or even as teacher, on the secular campus?

For all these difficult problems, this chapter should end on a note of enthusiasm as well as on one of caution. It is true that there is a constant danger of overloading monks and nuns with work, to the point that their contemplative vocation is lost sight of. But the intellectual apostolate in all its phases is one of the long-established splendors of the Church's activity. Is this not especially true of our own age of the "knowledge explosion" an age so enamoured of knowing things? Not all this knowledge is sound, not all is worthy of man. But the vast amount of it is a truly noble achievement, whether it be in history, in science, in the arts, or in theology. The Benedictines, in keeping with their tradition, have the right to make this new knowledge their own and the duty to see it with the eyes of faith. They can share in the task of transmitting this new knowledge to coming generations in a way that accords with revelation, bringing forth both new things and old.

There is abroad today, and rightly so, an increasing concern over the relation of the Church to the poor, to those who are economically and socially deprived of the benefits of an affluent society. This concern, however important, must not obscure the immense importance of other apostolates, none of which can be abandoned without loss to the world and to the Church itself. One of these is the apostolate of learning and scholarship, and its necessary handmaid, education. While it is unfashionable, and rightly so, these days to give signs of triumphalism, it is a cause for joy and satisfaction to recognize the important contribution which the monks have made to the intellectual apostolate throughout the centuries. There is no reason why this contribution should not continue.

What, then, are our general conclusions? Schools are a significant part of the genuine tradition of monasticism. For monasteries with schools the danger is an over-active form of life; just as in monasteries with no clear work the danger is laziness. Monasteries must adapt themselves to the needs of the Church in each age, within the framework of their basic contemplative way of life. Where a school has grown too big, there are two paths open: reduction of its size, or handing over much of the management to lay people. In a setting where a school flourishes, it is vital for the monastic spirit of the place that the superior keeps ever before the minds and hearts of his monks and the prioress before her nuns that the essential for a Benedictine is the life of prayer, with separation from worldliness.

168

CHAPTER FOUR

OBEDIENCE

OBEDIENCE is no longer a tidy little subject with its Scripture texts, its understanding of "blind obedience" to the superior's will as automatically the will of God, its references to the acceptance of difficult obediences, to the immense value of the insignificant obediences, to the mortification of the will. Today almost all these points have become problems, from supporting Scripture texts to the mortifying of the will.

It is this problem which is turning young people from the religious life; it should not, but as obedience is not clearly stated in its true dimensions, this is not surprising.

Of course, among anchorites there was no obedience except to God; there was no one around to obey. It would be to misunderstand these anchorites to maintain that they had no obedience. The very fact of their being where they were—in the desert—was an expression of their obedience to the Gospel. "Go, and sell all that you have, and come follow me." That had been the call. This was their response, and heroic it was. Every truly Christian life, a following of Christ, is a life of obedience, a conforming of one's ways and thoughts and desires to the pattern Our Lord presented to us by his words and his example.

Very soon, as the crowds increased in the deserts of Egypt, the need for regulation was evident and it became, haphazard or at least by instinct, normal for the elders to have some kind of authority. It was chiefly a spiritual one, the authority of a leader or guide in the spiritual life, but also as organizers of the chaos. Many of the saintly hermits attracted disciples; at first the latter would go to one after the other of these holy ones and gather their holy *obiter dicta,* but in time one would stand out. Such a one was Pachomius, much as another, Benedict, came to be in the West.

This obedience included several elements, which should not be confused; the first was the purely practical need for regulations, such as the time for meals, and this could be considered a-spiritual. The second type of obedience was regulations of the religious side of the life, restraints of mortification, rules of silence, the establishing of a round of prayer, of work, of study, and finally the third, spiritual guidance, an interpretation of the New Testament teaching.

It is not without significance that the first book of the Bible is an account of God's gifts to man and of man's repeated flouting of God's law—Adam and Eve, Cain and Abel. The climax of the early part of the Old Testament is God giving his commandments to his chosen People through the person of Moses. The rest of the Old Testament is the piteous story of the disobedience of Israel, her forsaking the true God, idolatrous worship of false gods, refusal to listen to prophets sent by God; and then the sign of the wrath of God: the destruction of Samaria and Jerusalem, the exile and captivity of the Jewish people, the desecration of the Temple and the Holy of Holies. The Jews played out in their history once again the ancient story of Adam and Eve. They would not serve. When the greatest of the prophets came, the One whom all the others looked forward to—the Anointed One—him too many rejected.

Christ established his Church to perpetuate his teaching, protect it, and propagate it. The Church carries the message, the word, down the ages; the voice of the Church is the voice of the Spirit of Christ. If we should obey the authority of civil governments, how much more Church authority. (See Rom. 13, 1–2: "Every soul must be submissive to its lawful superiors; authority comes from God only, and all authorities that hold sway are of his ordinance. Thus the man who opposes authority is a rebel against the ordinance of God . . .")

The history of the Church is also full of man's failure and disobedience, God's punishment in divisions and persecutions. But God's promise to the Jews and to the Church still holds.

God's answer to men's disobedience was to send his only Son, in the form of a man, to do what men fail to do: to obey the will of the Father and then to be a light and guide, a way and life for all other men. The climax of Christ's redemptive life was to offer his death in obedience, even to the death of the cross. This obedience was not in his divine will, because he himself was the divine command, but it was in his human will, which was in fact under the rule of his Father.

Our Lord's teaching and life emphasize obedience to the Father. "Not everyone who says Lord, Lord, will be saved, but he who does the will of My Father." His brother and sister and mother is the one who does the will of the Father.

Christ's teaching on taking up our cross and on dying to self is at the heart of the spirit of obedience. For what is the chiefest self, if not self-will? The point is clear in St. John's Gospel. "Believe me when I tell you this; a grain of wheat must fall into the ground and die, or else it remains nothing more than a grain of wheat; but if it dies, then it yields rich fruit" (Jn 12, 24). "He who loves his life will lose it; he who is an enemy to his own life in this world will keep it, so as to live eternally" (12, 25). "If anyone is to be my servant, he must follow my way" (12, 26). And what is his way?: "Give up all, give to the poor, and come follow me." The way is the way of the cross, abandonment of self, not merely abandonment of things or people; it is becoming obedient, even unto death (see Phil. 2, 8). He was obedient to the Father, indeed, but it was by being subject to men who crucified him. He was led as a lamb to the slaughter.

Is there a mystery here? The giving up of our supreme gift, in so radical a way, cannot on the natural plane appear rational. On the supernatural plane we take a plunge, make a

171

great act of faith that *God is over all,* guiding all, guiding the leaders, teachers of the Church, popes, bishops, priests, abbots. They have the grace of state. Besides, we want to give back to God the best we have; we want to be at-one with the divine will, united in mind and will. How can we find God's mind and will? In what happens! In the teachings of the Bible and the Church, in the leadership of those appointed by the Church in the Church. And why? Because the Church is Christ. We should want to obey this Christ who in the Church is physically, visibly present, and conform ourselves to Him in all things.

At this point it might be well to summarize. There are three motives for obedience: the first is the practical, traffic-sign type of obedience that is necessary in any organization. The second is the obedience from ascetical motives, obedience to liberate the will from the thrall of passions, vanity, selfishness, and align it with the will of God. The third is a refinement of the second, namely, the seeing of God's will in all things and all people, but particularly in every wish of one's superior. This is reasonable in the world of faith. By faith we know that nothing happens except by the will or permissive will of God. Once we are fully aware of this tremendous truth we, as it were, swim in a sea of the divine will. It is in this way that those hard things superiors may tell us to do, or those hard happenings that befall us can be taken, if not at first with joy, at least with confidence and resolution and love.

Surely it must have been in this spirit that Christ our Lord himself faced the horror of the crucifixion, which was a barbarous act of injustice on the human and natural level, but which in the realm of the supernatural and in faith was part of the permissive plan of God. Is there any other way for religious, monks and nuns, to accept the harsh things that come upon them from authority or from their brethren or simply from life, except to see the underlying—and this only by faith —the divine wisdom, no matter how obscure that wisdom may appear to be?

There are then those three motives of obedience, but a

Christian person need not confine himself to the first in any particular situation, he could do most "obediences" for ascetical reasons, and all from desire to conform his will to the will of God, from love.

The *Rule of the Master,* thought by some to have been a source book for the Rule of St. Benedict, examines the theological position of the abbot more deeply than does the Holy Rule. Since St. Benedict is in the same tradition, it will be of value first to translate the relevant passage from the *Rule of the Master* and then to make a few comments.[1]

Now the Lord has established in his Church, on the analogy of the Trinity, three degrees of instruction: a first degree of prophets, a second of apostles, a third of teachers,[2] under whose rule and teaching the Churches and schools of Christ are to be governed. Thus like shepherds, they enclose in the sheepfold their holy sheep and teach them there, as the Lord said through Isaiah, "I will give you shepherds according to my own heart and they will feed you with discipline" [really from Jer. 3, 15]. The Lord himself said to Peter, "Simon, son of John, feed my sheep." "You will teach them to observe what I have laid down." "And behold, I am with you all days to the consummation of the world."

Therefore, all those who still have Folly for their mother, have good reason to want to be under the authority of a superior in order to walk according to the decisions of a teacher and to learn to put on one side, forget, ignore, the way of their own wills. Through the teacher, Christ himself is commanding us, because, as it was said above, he is with those teachers forever, "all days to the consummation of the world," obviously having no other purpose but to build us up through them, as the Lord himself said to his disciples who are our teachers: "He who listens to you, listens to me, and he who despises you, despises me" (Lk. 10, 16). Consequently, it follows that if we do what we hear those teachers tell us, we no longer are doing what we ourselves want to do; and so on the day of judgment, the devil will have nothing in us that he could claim as his own to take with him to hell, since the Lord will aways have

1. *La Règle du Maître,* 3 vols., Edited and Translated, with Notes and Introduction, by Adalbert de Vogüé. "Sources chrétiennes," Paris, 1964–1965.
2. See 1 Cor. 12, 28 and Eph. 4, 11.

brought about in us actions which he was to judge worthy of glory [I, 82].

There follows a chapter *"Qualis debeat esse abbas"* and it is very close to the Holy Rule. Now for a few comments upon the above text.

The Master bases the relationship of obedience to authority on the teaching authority of the Church established in sacred Scripture: the prophets, the apostles, the teachers or "doctors." The prophets, being put before the apostles, here refer to the prophets of the Old Testament. The apostles had authority while they lived, and the doctors or teachers are all those who have a teaching authority in the Church, chief of whom, of course, are the bishops.

It is a curious fact that the Master, at least subconsciously, is referring to—without quoting—a passage from Paul's First Epistle to the Corinthians (12, 28). "God has given us different positions in the Church; apostles first, then prophets, and thirdly teachers . . ." But note that the order is different: prophets come after apostles, and so in the text must refer to the prophetic office within the Church. Teachers remain in their place. And we read more fully in Ephesians 4, 11: "Some he [Christ] has appointed to be apostles, others to be prophets, others to be evangelists, or pastors or teachers. They are to order the lives of the faithful, minister to their needs, build up the frame of Christ's body. . . ."

De Vogüé says in his Introduction to the *Rule of the Master* that in an earlier book [1] he had considered the basis of the abbot's authority to be "some charism directly granted him by the Holy Spirit," but that now he sees it as in some way a sharing in the normal teaching authority of the bishop. De Vogüé says of the *doctors* in the text: they are in office since the disappearance of the apostles, whom they rightly succeed. They are the bishop and the abbot, each in his own domain (the church or the "school") assisted by their respective collaborators (priests, deacons, clerics, or provosts). "Doctor" or

---

1. *"La communite et l'abbé,"* p. 137, n. 1, p. 182, p. 360–361.

"teacher" signifies, then, simply successor of the apostles. In giving this title to the abbot, the Master puts him on a par with (*équipare*) the supreme pastor of the Church, with the bishop, just as he assimilates the monastery (or "school of Christ") to a church.

That assimilation, that approximation, poses, quite clearly, at first sight a fairly delicate theological problem: By what right is the abbot put in this way on the same footing as the bishop? Can one legitimately apply to him the promises made by Christ to the apostles and their successors? To feel the full force of these questions, we should remember that the abbot according to the *Rule of the Master* is a layman. He cannot therefore claim the character of "doctor" on the grounds of being in holy orders, a priest or a deacon. This claim belongs to him simply in virtue of his function as abbot.[1]

The abbot, however, is not an authority independent of the bishop, in the mind of the Master: he has received this authority from the bishop. This he makes very clear in Section 93 where the "ordination" of the abbot by the bishop is described.

1. The name of the abbot is solemnly inscribed on the diptych by the bishop himself.

2. The prayers of the rite, among them one which calls upon the Great High Priest to "bind" in the acts of heaven what you have received on earth.

This is a clear reference to the powers given by Christ to Peter over the Church (Mt. 18, 18). Vogüé concludes, "We have here then an ordination 'in the presence of the bishops,' even better an '*ordinatio sacerdotalis*,' an ordination whose minister is 'the bishop.' "[2] He calls the rite later "*quasi sacramental*" and says it provides the visible sign which permits all to recognize the authenticity of the "doctor," and that it is "the latter's right to claim" obedience from all, for it makes him a representative of Christ.[3]

This relationship of dependence on the bishop gives the

1. Vogüé, *op. cit.*, vol. 1, p. 111.
2. *Ibid.*, p. 112.
3. *Ibid.*, p. 114.

teaching of the Master on the position of the abbot greater stability than had the guides among the Desert Fathers. St. Benedict was to follow the Master in this.

There is a real danger in twentieth-century monasteries where membership gets beyond a hundred that the head of the house, the abbot or the prioress, loses human contact with the members of the community. If they do, then one of the chief activities of the abbot is nullified, that of spiritual father, leader of souls; and this would be utterly contrary to the whole monastic tradition from Antony and Pachomius onward. As we have already seen in St. Benedict and the Master, the abbot is the *doctor,* "learned in the law of God" (Rule of St. Benedict, ch. 64), and to listen to him is to listen to Christ. The abbot's "commands and teaching should be infused into the minds of his disciples like the leaven of divine justice" (ch. 2). St. Benedict goes on explaining how the abbot must adapt his approach to each of his monks according to the character of each; "adapting himself to many dispositions" (ch. 2). In this he would be acting with and in Christ. But if the monastic family becomes a crowd, this uniquely monastic personal and continuous relationship between superior and monk is in danger of being lost.

No one doubts we should obey God in all things. He knows what is best, even if we do not. It is reasonable to obey God even if the command appears unreasonable in our eyes. Obeying God is often accepting his will. It is not possible for us always to understand his reason: for instance, why he takes an only child to himself in death, why he allows a war. Everything comes under his divine providence. Hell we find difficult to recognize as reasonable. But we accept all these things, we obey them and him, because, in spite of their seeming unreasonable, we know by faith that he is all wise; and also let it be said—and it was said by Job's comforters *ad nauseum*— we are not all-wise, we know so very little.

We cannot conceive that any human being is always right in his decisions, even when he has consulted us—because even we might be wrong too. Do we obey a spiritual superior because his decision is the right one? or do we obey because, for us, the voice of the superior is the voice of God?

If we follow St. Benedict and the older writers, the abbot and the other superiors have the place of Christ (ch. 2, ch. 63). They ground this teaching on the fact that these persons are representatives of the Church. They are installed by the Church, the pope or the local bishop. Christ lives on in the Church. We are, therefore, obeying him in obeying them.

Do we really see this in all its full possible extent in every command of the superior? St. Benedict says we should obey even an unexpressed wish, and also our brethren (ch. 71).

What are the reasons? We could give practical reasons. There must be some kind of order in a crowd—and this was clearly one of the reasons for obedience in the very early days of community life in the Egyptian desert. Obedience is needed for the smooth running of any organization. But St. Benedict does not mention that. One could obey because the decision, the command, was the correct answer to a problem. St. Benedict does not mention that one either. As we have noted, in human affairs we cannot guarantee the right answer has always been chosen. And yet St. Benedict does say we should obey and for the love of God (ch. 7). But he also provides two outlets, and important ones. He calls upon the abbot to have meetings of the whole community to discuss any major matter, and his council for matters of less moment (ch. 3). He, St. Benedict, tells the abbot to let every one who wishes give his opinion—in all humility—because even the youngest may have the answer (ch. 3). However, at the end of it all he says is: "Let the abbot decide." He is not establishing a democracy. That type of government, in which we suppose that the majority is bound to be right, or at least less likely to be wrong, was not present to St. Benedict's mind when he wrote his Rule. So when all is said, St. Benedict does not ask obedience of his monks only if they have approved of the decision, nor simply on the ground that the majority has voted for a particular policy. He requires obedience because the abbot has decided.

Because the abbot represents the Church, does that give

him any infallibility? If it did, our problem would be solved. We would obey because he was infallibly right. But the superior is a very fallible man. He can easily be wrong. Of course, in matters of faith or morals, we do have an infallible guide, the Church, in her ordinary teaching power and in those occasional flashes of Councils or papal pronouncements. We may not be in the area of faith or morals but in the day-to-day decisions of life. If, however, we are in the area of morals or doctrine, it is one where all the alternatives are possible, within the framework of the faith. If this were not so, the subject, judging that a decision was immoral or heretical, would *have* to object and refuse to obey.

In two places St. Benedict faces up to the crisis for a monk who finds himself asked to do the impossible—in the fourth degree of humility and in Chapter 68. The fourth degree of humility is that, "meeting in this life with difficulties and contradictions and even injustice, the monk should with a silent mind hold fast to patience, and enduring, neither tire nor run away. . . ." In Chapter 68: "If it happen that anything hard or impossible be laid upon any brother, let him receive the command of his superiors with all docility and obedience, . . . If after his representations the superior still persists in his decision and command, let the subject know that it is expedient for him, and let him obey out of love, trusting in the assistance of God."

St. Benedict positively links obedience with the sin of disobedience of our first parents and with humility (Prologue). No one would deny that man must return to obedience to God, but why should that imply obedience to men? How does that redress the balance? His answer would be that in obeying men we are obeying God and that is our human way of a return to obeying God. "All authority comes from God," but especially that within the Church, which we must continually remember is Christ. To obey the Church and her representatives is to obey Christ.

We ourself venture to think that in the natural order no obedience to men is reasonable or right unless it is in accord with right reason. In the natural order all obedience, all laws, should be in accord with right reason. If they are not, that becomes a beginning of a justification for not obeying them. A human law is of God if it is according to the eternal law.

But on the supernatural plane another element comes in. We are trying to turn ourselves God-wards, we are trying to offer sacrifice, holocaust of ourselves, and this may make our attitude to obedience quite different. We are trying to hand over our wills to God, to be rid of self-will. We are obeying the reason of God.

This is a hard saying, and does it go counter to some of the treasured ideals of the modern age: self-expression, free discussion, personalism, commitment, and the rest? Are we not here suggesting the giving up of the supreme power of man, his free will? Yes. We must hate our own will (ch. 4). But this last must be understood.

"Hate our own will." How so? Is not the will the highest faculty of man? Is it not the will which distinguishes man from all other creatures on this earth? He can say, I shall or I shall not choose this or that, decide this, refuse that. How should he hate this supreme gift of God? To do so would seem ingratitude itself. No, man must not hate his will, but hate wilfulness, that will which seeks self rather than God. Like Pascal's *"le moi est haïssable"* this strong and hard saying has to be interpreted: *le moi pécheur.*

We have to be rid of the "old man," but the precious gift of freedom, this we cherish and offer back to God in sacrifice.

Let us compare this with the sacrifice in chastity. We are faced with a similar situation. Married life is the best human relationship, again in the natural order. By the vow or promise of chastity we give up that element of human perfection. One does not do this as an end in itself, but as a means to love someone else undividedly. It might be possible to do this in marriage. But the immediate objects of love are so engrossing and the concerns of married life so anxiously absorbing that God very easily is left way out in the background.

So in obedience we give up our wills. But we cannot destroy

179

our wills, or if we do, we cease to be human. To give up, to "hate" must be understood in a very special sense, because we only remain men and able to love God, able to merit, to give him glory, if we preserve our innate power of choice. The point is that we willingly give up the intention of ever following a way which we ourselves have chosen. We have, however, every day, every hour, to align our wills with the choice of another who takes for us the place of God, who is the channel of his providence. We do the same for the Rule itself.

It is true that every decision is a curtailment of our choices. For instance, to be an American citizen, one ceases to be a citizen of any other country; getting married to Ann cuts off the choice of Jane and commits one to a certain general pattern. In essence, of course, these two examples are curtailments as monastic obedience is. But they have immense areas of freedom which is their object, whereas monastic obedience is aimed at limiting it very much, or rather redirecting it.

All of us cannot help being free in one sense. Every human act is a commitment in one direction or another. The fact of making a vow of obedience in 1960 does not blot out all free acts from that date onwards. It simply directs every free act in a specific direction; that is, we have to cooperate with God's will. We do *not* become dead. Every act of our life, on the contrary, becomes meaningful, God-filled, God-directed.

An act can be spontaneous for two reasons, or in two ways. The first way it can be spontaneous is from the point of view of the thing done. Now if that is not obligatory, it is spontaneous or gratuitous. The other way is from the point of view of the doer of the act, the agent. That is when it is willed freely. Therefore, even if an act is done under obedience, if it is done with prompt, eager will, then it remains spontaneous, meritorious.[1]

What of the modern objections to obedience—there is something in them. Modern men have become very conscious of their own personality and its development. This includes the

1. See St. Thomas, *Summa Theologica*, II, II, q. 104, art. 1, ad 3.

use of freedom, self-expression; they are against all cramping conditions, irrational curtailments of their actions and desires. Rules seem like chains, restrictive, deadening, not liberating. What they crave is a few necessary guide lines and then consultation with a superior, who, finding what the desires of the subject were, would do all in his power to fit in with those desires; and if he did not, the subject would know that it was not from want of trying. Man, they say, is a developing being and this development comes from self-expression, and the liberty to unfold all his powers, intellectual, emotional, esthetic and the rest. Any cramping of this is positively harmful. We are then emerging from a monastic age, good in its way, but limited as all the past is, in comparison with the perpetual evolution of man towards the *omega* point. Monastic obedience is outdated and we must work out a new form of obedience more in conformity with our own needs, with the new psychological insights we have.

In monastic obedience the abbot is called father. This is not without significance, and his aim is to bring out all the best in the brethren. In the past the father image has been interpreted too much as a father of *children* and the subject not considered as a mature grown-up being, at the most as a child, at the worst like a piece on the chess board. In true monastic spirituality the relationship should be one of two grown-up persons. The abbot has the decision to make but he should do it in collaboration with the intelligent cooperation of his monks.

This idea is put very strongly by the Fathers of Vatican II.

Governing his subjects as God's own sons, and with regard to their human personality, a superior will make it easier for them to obey gladly. Therefore he must make a special point of leaving them appropriately free with respect to the sacrament of penance and direction of conscience. Let him give the kind of leadership which will encourage religious to bring an active and responsible obedience to the offices they shoulder and the activities they undertake. Therefore a superior should listen willingly to his subjects and encourage them to make a personal contribution to the welfare of

181

the community and of the Church. Not to be weakened, however, is the superior's authority to decide what must be done and to require the doing of it.

Let chapters and councils faithfully acquit themselves of the governing role given to them; each should express in its own way the fact that all members of the community have a share in the welfare of the whole community and a responsibility for it.[1]

This freedom of discussion makes the supernatural motive of obedience easily smothered in rationalizations. Difficulties, however, do not make a situation less valuable, but rather sometimes more valuable. The difficulty is that discussion may make the subject do the thing commanded because he sees it as right and omit the fact that it comes, in the first place, from God. It becomes his decision and he clings to his choosings. On the other hand, if he sees it as reasonable *and* God's will, then his whole being goes towards it with joy. If the decision still seems unreasonable, at least he has had his say. But now there is no natural joy, only a knowledge that for him this is the will of God and a knowledge that he has had an opportunity to express his opinion.

He unites, in each case, his free will to the decision, making a thoroughly human act. If, on the contrary, he revolts against the decision, which, without anyone knowing, he could do, then, while proving his innate freedom, he is losing the virtue of the act even though it is one of outward compliance.

The need for self-expression and for the development or use of this Western trait of man, the executive urge, need not be stifled in a monastic framework where monks exercise their various gifts. St. Benedict himself allows for the artistic talent. All the later history of the Order has shown the flexibility of work, from St. Boniface in the eighth century getting permission to go off to evangelize the Germans, to the Encalcat monks going off in the twentieth century to evangelize the Moslems in Morocco.

Should the rules be reasonable? Of course they should. The Holy Rule itself aims at being so; but they cannot always seem

1. *The Documents of Vatican II,* p. 477.

so in particular circumstances to the subject. It may be true that in the past religious superiors have taken a rather high-handed military line in their injunctions. In so doing they were wrong, even if the subject was most submissive. Their rule, like God's, should be full of discretion, considerateness, patience.

Obedience is due to authority because authority is expected to be the expression in this particular set of circumstances of God's providential plan—the eternal law in little. Therefore, it must be reasonable. This is St. Thomas's approach. In the natural order, when authority becomes utterly unreasonable and against the eternal law, the time has come for rebellion. In the supernatural order, too, conscience is supreme. But this only applies to matters of sin. In the day-to-day questions of policy, where there is plenty of room for differences of opinion, the superior in fact may be wrong, but after representations and all the constitutional safeguards have been brought into play, the subject goes ahead willingly.

Legalism has been the bane of the Western Church, inheriting as it did the Roman skill at law-making. But legalism is akin to Pharisaism, the kind condemned by Christ. We will not be saved by the keeping of the law. How surprised the Pharisees must have been at the hostility of Christ. Surely if there was any group deserving of commendation it was they. They had struggled for generations to keep the rules laid down. They were meticulous, unswerving in the adherence to the Law. They even added more of their own. Surely they would be saved. God had made a pact with the Jews: if they kept his law, they would be his People. But Christ saw it differently. They thought to be saved by their own action, but he knew and the Old Testament repeatedly taught that salvation is not of men, but of God. Besides, they had piled up laws of their own devising, unbearable for the common folk, who despaired. The Church is awake to this danger. For instance, the old fasting laws have been wisely modified, making only two days obligatory fasting. If we are legalistic we will instinctively say the Church has abolished fasting. No, it is the *law* that is abolished, and we must now decide to do penance of our own volition, freely, not by fear. No one denies it was possible to do so freely before. But there is plenty of evidence that fear of the consequences rather than love of God was the motive.

What this has to do with monastic obedience may appear remote. Legalism is supposed to be a relic of our medieval past, and monasticism the summit of that attitude of mind. Monasticism is riddled with legalisms, laws, and regulations, a kind of ritual life, utterly alien to the modern free-and-easy approach to everything including religion. We might then propose: Why then have monastic laws? Is not monastic obedience legalism? It could be, there is no doubt. We could do the right deed for the wrong reason, obey just because it is the law, not for the love of God; or obey because we like a superior, not because we love God; or obey because we think it reasonable.

The point of monastic obedience is this: that for those eager to serve God, obedience gives the knowledge that they are doing God's will. To obey because it is God's will is to obey from love. While obedience could be from many motives, it can be from love.

We must not equate love with feeling. Once we do, then obedience in matters that are against some instinct of ours will not seem to us love, because our feelings are roused against it. Is it possible that the uneasiness among the young religious over obedience as restrictive, killing, and crushing comes from this confusion? When a command is hard, unreasonable, certain sides of us rise in revolt. To obey goes against those elements in us: our sensibility, our imagination, our reason even. But this is not *against* the will. The will is free to go counter to any part of us, and obviously must. Nor is this a crushing of the will; it is, strange as this may seem, a liberating of the will from the thrall of sense and sensibility, from the limitedness of our own reason and placing it under the guidance, but freely, of the almighty and all wise God.

To sum up. The monk takes his vow of obedience to the Benedictine way of life, which is the Rule; and this itself is a way, a special way, of following Christ according to the Gos-

pels. St Benedict himself tells us to go continuously to the
Gospel. The abbot is the interpreter of the Rule. He stands,
and all our brethren stand in the place of Christ for us. The
Church is Love, it is the life of Christ. Therefore, as the life
of a monk proceeds, he finds more and more that obedience,
which at first was hard, becomes love, a giving of one's whole
self to others in the person of the abbot and the brethren.
Christ becomes all in all.

Any talk that this is an annihilation, a death to our wills,
is fine rhetoric but true in only a very limited sense. This is a
liberation of our wills from the thrall of sense, it makes it one
with the will of God, more fully alive than in any limited self-
will, guided by our own desires. This is the freedom of the
children of God.

The vow is taken once, but the conformity, the at-onement
goes on through our lives.

A time may come when we feel that a command is not
relevant to us, does not fit the inspirations that the Holy Spirit
has inspired us with. It is difficult to know the difference between true inspiration and our own desires masquerading as
coming from him. The only test is our humility and obedience
and love in contradiction. If we cannot be sure ourselves, the
superior is even less able to be sure. The only trustworthy sign
is the true holiness of the person concerned; his charity, his
humility, and his obedience. This situation is more common
than it was—though even in the early days there are famous
examples: Boniface and Leoba. It is probable that others earlier asked to go on the foreign mission and were refused. But
Boniface received the answer yes; he did not go without the
blessing of the abbot. So with us, we may have an inspiration
for some great work. This may be a need that has to be answered. But it may not be ours to give the answer, only to
bring the idea before the community. We have to possess our
souls in peace: *Obedientia et Pax*. God will himself decide the
time and the person.

The whole of life is a positive abandonment in love to the
providence of God, which is operating every minute of the day

185

and night, working through each individual life and in a whole epoch, through history. We should long with love to conform our whole being, mind and will, our whole personality, to that stream of God's loving guidance. If we build our obedience on the faith—knowledge that all is under God's providence, even the disagreeable things—then those hard commandments of a superior will be done for the right reason, as God given and not out of grim determination only. God's will is most manifest in the desires and wishes of our community, the abbot and our brethren. *Ecce quam bonum et quam jucundum habitare in unum.*

CHAPTER FIVE

POVERTY

1. Poverty and the Aggiornamento

THE first thing to do is to find the meaning of Christian poverty in the Gospel. It is the first of the beatitudes: Blessed are the poor of spirit, for theirs is the kingdom of God. There are three elements in this statement: beatitude or joy, poverty of spirit, the kingdom. The teaching of Christ on poverty is not given as a stern law but as an invitation to joy. And with this teaching is attached a promise of the kingdom of God. Nor is the poverty mentioned simply destitution or material poverty as such, though that will be its natural expression, but a spirit of poverty.

This spirit is exactly the opposite of the spirit of the Pharisees as described in the Gospel, who were self-satisfied, particularly with their knowledge of the Law. This spirit of poverty is also the opposite of the spirit of the rich, who are secure in their own power. Christ's picture of his poor was that of those who trusted not in their own ideas nor in their own riches, but those who confided all their needs to God their Father. There are two prayers in the Gospels that give us the spirit of poverty as we should understand it: the *Our Father* and Mary's wonderful hymn, the *Magnificat,* full of that joy which comes from putting all one's trust in the Lord, having no riches of her own—joy in the fulfillment of the kingdom and the future joys of heaven.

So this New Testament idea of the spirit of poverty is a

spirit of detachment from earthly things, from a Pharisaic trust in one's own knowledge of religious law and the power of wealth alike. It betokens a dependence on God for all that we need, both material and spiritual. From this detachment comes the joy that we are already sharing in the riches of God; it creates in us an openness of soul ready to receive—we are in the position of the *orantes* in the early Church, with arms stretched out. This same joy will make it possible to renounce all things and follow Christ wherever he leads.

The *Decree on the Appropriate Renewal of the Religious Life* of Vatican Council II has important things to say on the spirit of poverty and lays special stress on the imitation of Christ. To be a religious means "to follow Christ more freely and imitate him more nearly by the practice of the evangelical counsels" (Art. 1). "In fidelity to their profession and in renunciation of all things for the sake of Christ, let religious follow him as the one thing necessary" (Art. 5). "Poverty voluntarily embraced in imitation of Christ provides a witness which is highly esteemed, especially today. Let religious painstakingly cultivate such poverty, and give it new expressions if need be. By it a man shares in the poverty of Christ, who became poor for our sakes, when before He had been rich, that we might be enriched by his poverty. (See 2 Cor. 8, 9; Mt. 8, 20.)" (Art. 13).

Before we start discussing what we should give up, we must imitate Christ at a deeper level, that of self-surrender (Phil. 2, 7 f., a text that comes over and over again in the thinking of the Council Fathers). This is the spirit of self-abandonment to the will of God, and is far removed from any specific outline of economic structures. In order to be conformed to Christ we have to be in touch with him by communing with him in prayer and meditation on the Gospel. Then we will see how Christ himself practiced poverty in fact. We should not attempt to follow slavishly how he lived but take note that he was at home with simple people, with the poor. As Fr. Häring points out, religious communities should be open and free to new manifestations of ways of imitating our Lord in this matter.

As love is the center of the Christian life, it is reasonable to examine how the spirit of poverty nourishes this life. Since poverty is the detachment from all things other than God in Christ, it provides the setting for great love, not only of God but also of our brothers. Also it provides a witness that we are not attached to earthly things but to those which are heavenly.

Fr. Häring shows that the spirit of poverty is closely linked with the vow of celibacy; they are both detachments from earthly loves. If we show that, while we have taken a vow of poverty, we still remain very attached to things, then it will appear to people that we are finding a substitute for family love in the love of things.

During the course of the Vatican Council there was much discussion of *the Church of the poor,* a phrase very dear to Pope John. We could be a church for the poor, administering largesse like Dives from our own rich man's table, but not be poor ourselves. Our poverty as a group depends on our attitude to our poverty in the common life. We should turn to the Acts of the Apostles, 4, 32–37. There the emphasis is not on common possession but on *sharing* all with one another, those who had need were given what they needed. So no one had what was superfluous; it was given to the poor. How is the Church, how is a religious house going to put that into practice? Certain works require considerable capital; it would be unrealistic to think all members must be poor. All must be ready to share.

Monasteries and convents have almost a natural propensity to become wealthy. They pay no taxes; friends lavish upon them gifts of money, land, buildings, art works. By their very profession the inmates are industrious and abstemious; as with the early Puritans, riches come unsought but inevitably. Monks and nuns claim no wages, their wants are few. Even if these institutions pass through hard times, they have by their corporate nature a better chance of survival to better times than private individuals, farmers or small businessmen for example. History bears this out: monasteries and convents, particularly the former, accumulated wealth as dams water.

Benedictines do not take a vow of poverty, not because they are exempt from this counsel but because it is subsumed in the all-embracing vow of conversion of manners. But St. Benedict certainly left us his mind on this counsel. So we should examine his Rule. It is rare that he writes with vehemence; he does on the vice of private property for monks. Repeatedly he inveighs against individual monks owning anything. He is like a farmer stopping up all the holes against the fox. And he is not talking about a bank account; it is the minutiae of ordinary life that are his concern. He lists them. No one may presume to give or receive anything without permission of the abbot, nor have anything as his own, nothing whatever—he hammers it home—neither book nor writing pad, nor pen, nothing at all. Elsewhere: for monks should not even have their bodies or wills under their own command. All things necessary are to be received from the abbot. Even suppose friend or parent bring a present, it is not to be accepted for personal use until explicit permission is received from the abbot; and if he thinks fit to hand the present to another brother, the initial recipient should not grieve.

On the other hand, the abbot is not to be rigid about these matters. To everyone according to his need, as Scripture says (Acts 4, 35); but again not simply to those who clamor, but to those who have a genuine need. St. Benedict pins it down to the minutest detail, whether it be cowl, tunic, stockings, shoes, belt, knife, pen needle, handkerchief, or tablet.

How different is this list of material things to the destitution of the Syrian monks!

The Rule is severe about clothing. It is from the abbot that the monks receives it. Old clothing is saved and given to the poor. Shoes and stockings are part of the monks wardrobe; it should even be better when going on a journey, but returned when the monk reaches home again. Two of everything in general is the rule. Cleanliness was for St. Benedict, if not for the Syrian monks, kin to holiness.

When the monk comes to make his vows, his parents must be made aware of what he is doing and vow also to disinherit him (ch. 59). But the chapter proceeds: in order to prevent the son receiving the inheritance, St. Benedict suggests—and little did he know what proportions his suggestion would take on in the Middle Ages—that the parents, if they wished, should give their property to the monastery during their lifetime, and they would have the use of its income so long as they lived—that is, mortmain. On this, particularly in England, monasteries grew rich with land.

It is very striking that St. Benedict is not conscious of the danger that a community as such might become dangerously wealthy; for all his revulsion from personal possessions, communal property does not seem a menace. Where he set his monastery high up on a distant and fairly barren mountain, the danger was slight. We in our age, when nothing is remote and property has so many insidious forms, must examine both personal and communal property in monastic houses with care.

The Personal Problem. Our minds have been so conditioned by a legalist spirit, we are satisfied in our consciences by the phrase *"ad usum."* We might even find it within our swallowing capacity to gulp down a plane, provided it had painted on its fusilage "for our use." So long as by a legal fiction we think of everything we have and use as not our own, by this single magic phrase, we are happy to possess almost anything—movie cameras, automobiles, expensive watches, binoculars, skates, skis, record players and TV sets, transistors, the latest in electric shavers, heaters, table lamps, to say nothing of *objets d'art,* even perhaps a sum of money we are keeping—safe, of course, with the procurator—for this or that book or record, or just a hypothetical book or record. *Ad usum!*

Clothing too is *ad usum,* but beware if anyone suggests borrowing an overcoat, umbrella, sweater, shoes for tennis. The young have athletic tastes, golf clubs, tennis rackets—in the plural, and with all the accoutrements. It is owning we give

191

up; but with a handy permission, we may use anything. It is all right, it is only *ad usum*. We are better off now perhaps than we would have been in the world, besides having no responsibilities. "Go, give up all, give to the poor, and come follow me."

Trips away from the monastery or convent are a problem. Custom varies. In some congregations a time away each year is regularized, ten days, or more, either in a mountain retreat owned by the community or with the family or friends. For those who are allowed to "go into the world" for a period in the summer a real problem exists. In an agricultural society on a farm, in a simple culture out in the country, a monk could relax without being dissipated. But in our sophisticated society eager friends want to give the returned solitary a good time, meaning an entertaining time. Friends are so generous: trips to Florida or Cape Cod or Europe may not cost the monastery a cent. Of course, it would be against poverty to be spending all that money on a first-class fare to the south of Spain, but if the friends pick up the bill . . . The superior may be nonplussed and a little hesitant, especially if the friends have been good to the house—perhaps built the library and set up a fund for the further education of the young religious; it would be ungrateful to refuse. After that a precedent has been set. Next year there are other tempting offers, which can hardly be refused when the first was accepted. People tell us that these trips are very economical. But economy is not the same thing as poverty. These trips were taken for pleasure and relaxation. Financially, the monastery or the convent did not lose a dime, but they did not bear witness to poverty, or share in any way in the poverty of Christ who trudged the tracks of Palestine preaching to the poor as a poor man himself. The poor of today still stand by helpless as they see the rich ride past.

It is essential that we consider it our individual duty to live as frugally as our superior will allow, even austerely, reducing personal wants to the minimum and personal expenses likewise. A monk should accept a cheaper object rather than the best, and cheaper modes of transport. After all, busses do get one places. Sometimes, when time is important, planes are inevitable. Even a plane has tourist class.

The Community. It is possible for the individual religious to be frugal but the house as a whole to lack the spirit of poverty and so fail in its witness. The right tone will depend on the superior and the bursar or cellarer, but much too will depend on the spirit of the community as a whole. It could be demanding or careless about these things. At those crucial decisions in conventual chapter when a major issue is decided, then the spirit of the community is tested; they cannot shuffle off responsibility on anyone else. It is the members of the community who have taken the vows to live like Christ and these same members must practice their own vows, together.

It is possible for a monk to be as poor as a church mouse while his community is sleek as a city cat: individual poverty, community wealth. In older days that situation was a useful social condition. The monasteries all over Europe were centers of cultural, economic, and social development. The monks were able, by communal activity, to draw the countryside out of penury and want into order and a modicum of frugal wealth. They were centers of civilized and organized life. Their wealth was—often—the old-age insurance of the poor, the unemployment insurance, sickness benefit; rough and ready, to be sure, but a fact. In England, the East Anglian monasteries drained the marshes, the northern ones cleared the "forests," plowed the land, things which the simple, unorganized peasants, unlettered, lacking in initiative as they were, could not do. The Cistercians showed the way to sheep farming and breeding, indeed to the wool trade.

The situation is certainly different today. Monks do not on the whole have the lead in economic, agricultural, financial matters—except in some underdeveloped countries. Yet, by abstemiousness, industry, and thrift, monasteries still do accumulate land and wealth.

The question is: What attitude should the community take towards this wealth? The community as such cannot hide be-

193

hind anonymity in this matter any more than can or should the shareholders in a large industrial company. The community is a moral person, making moral decisions; and the members of that community in their joint discussions and voted decisions are all responsible to God for the acts of their conventual chapters. We cannot claim responsible monasticism on the one hand and deny it in practice on the other.

In our day, also, poverty is present everywhere, even in the wealth-laden states. No country has universal opulence. Even in the United States, riches and poverty stand side by side. What is the right attitude for religious? Do what Christ would have done, perhaps? What would he have done? —Go to the poor and help them. Yet here we are in our comfortable, if not quite luxurious, monasteries.

This is no easy problem, there is no easy solution. Consider the sort of typical circumstances that we have to deal with in real situations: A new monastery has to be built, which is a rather exciting undertaking for the whole community. The old one had, perhaps, been designed and built by the old German brothers who came over from Bavaria in the mid-nineteenth century. It has no artistic merits, a barracks of a place. It is solid, of course, but very inconvenient. The plumbing may be pre-historic, heating almost non-existent; but it served the times. There was not much money to spare in those days. Now, one sees, it is a little different: a kind friend is eager to have the new building nicely built; and over a five-year period she will foot the bill. So the community are hard at work with the architects, the best in the Middle West. Showers down at the other end of the passage are so inconvenient, the community have decided to place all the facilities between each pair of cells. It is more expensive, of course, but it does save precious time. Then the architect has persuaded them, a little against their instincts, to engage some famous European furniture designer and maker both to design and make all the furniture for the cells, refectory, and guest rooms. The oak will look lovely. It will also be a little expensive. Then there was the question of the stairway. An extravagance? But it was pointed out that

194

all European monasteries worthy of the name had splendid stairways.

Remember that we are speaking of men of Christ specially dedicated to poverty and this will not seem an overdrawn picture. Christ did not live in such a house, with flamboyant stairways, showers and toilets for each member of the holy family. Nor do the poor of today. Where is the witness to poverty in all this? When a poor man knocks at the door, will he feel at home, or rather that he is in an alien place of the rich?

We are not presenting any simple solution, for there is none; we are raising questions and looking for principles. Let us take another case. It is said of the Cistercian foundation in Kerala in Southern India that for years the monks made no real contact with the local people, even with the Catholic ones. There was a certain deference, but a real barrier between the Hindu and the European. The monks were living an austere life according to the standards of Europe, with very simple furniture, tables and chairs, an iron bedstead. But the local people had no furniture, they sat on the floor, slept on the floor, ate off the floor. The monks decided to follow suit, eliminating their "rich man's" chairs and tables and bed, thus approximating to the local standards of poverty. Immediately the attitude of the people changed. A witness to solidarity with the poor had been established. One can point to this example with the pride of a Christian, and say that there are men who lived up to Christ in their monastic vows. What precisely is so admirable is that the community saw a need and a way to respond to their profession of poverty and acted directly and as a group upon generous motives.

It is part of the whole criterion of poverty that monks are poor men. Poor people in their own homes and lives (insofar as either are in fact their own) cannot afford luxuries. They have to be satisfied with the necessities of life, which, in most European countries, at least, are usually available somehow. By this standard it is wonderful to have an old monastery built by Bavarian lay brothers, with blessedly simple beds and chairs, an austere stone stairway. Simplicity and frugality have their own beauty; such an atmosphere reminds one of the vows, of the community's corporate clear conscience, of the united desire to share with Christ his life of want.

The problem has world-wide dimensions, for the poverty of the world is now well-known by all and is sometimes desperate. What may seem frugality in one country is luxury over the border. Is there any absolute standard, even for the Western world? One thinks of the Poor Clares, who still do without tables and chairs. It is not easy to accuse them of being archaistic or unrealistic when they do present such a shining example of poverty.

An important principle of religious dedication through poverty is that the more one accepts the amenities of life, the less the witness to poverty is real; and when they are taken for granted, it is killed at the root. Any *display* of wealth in life or buildings made by a monastery is out of place. In countries like South America or throughout Asia it would be a scandal, but even in rich countries, poverty is at our doors. And whatever has been spent on ourselves over and above frugality could have been used for the crises of hunger and deprivation which are normal in underprivileged countries. Distance no longer means anything; we cannot be lavish on ourselves when hundreds of millions are starving.

With all these considerations in mind, we suggest as a firm criterion of monastic poverty the frugality of simple people in the monastery's locality, —not that of the destitute, nor of the very poor, but of those many families which have what the area regards as not far above the level of subsistence. There is, in a word, to be no superfluity.

However, there are other considerations, both of circumstance and even more of spiritual poverty in other, less obvious, manifestations. The work of a community may weigh heavily in decisions about material poverty. For instance, an adequate diet for a community that had little active work would be insufficient for a very active one. Poverty is a means to God, not

196

to the hospital, which is where a half-starved and ill-fed monastery would be leading its members.

Many monasteries and convents have schools or hospitals or colleges. These works have been undertaken for God, and therefore should be carried out very well. This may require money for expensive equipment and even more for the salaries of laymen. To pay the janitors and cooks and teachers or nurses a low salary and plead the vow of poverty is making others keep our vow of poverty which they have never been called to. Granted fair salary scales, then superfluity and lavishness in equipment, in building material should be avoided. Beauty is for the monk to reside in simplicity—and such beauty should be considered, particularly in schools and colleges, for it has a great civilizing effect and makes a deeper impression than many lectures on art.

We have talked much of poverty especially its material expression, but we must hold fast to the spiritual meaning of all our actions. Poverty is not an end in itself, but a gesture which contains and facilitates our dedication to God alone. When a man or woman, monk or nun, monastery or convent has all the amenities of life, this is no mere superficial fact. It enters into the very marrow of the soul, creating a sense of self-satisfaction, a repletion that lulls the soul into complacency and a forgetfulness of the high meaning of his life. Certain kinds of security are inimical to spiritual growth. How hard it is for a rich man to enter into heaven; how much harder for a rich religious or a rich community. The heart may become easily entangled in the earthly pleasures available to the rich: music, society, art, good food, travel, even those simple luxuries like good linen, warm clothes, new books, and just civilized living and conversation. They may well be innocent pleasures. But they may also, without one's perceiving it, encroach on the singleness of purpose which a monastic environment is meant to foster, and may even engross the soul, keeping it from moving forward to God.

A life of poverty, in which there is little earthly to cling to

for consolation, no rich food, no good linen, no concerts or
ballgames on friends' tickets, no soft chairs or available ciga-
rettes, frees the soul and mind for engagement with God. When
one is at home in the world and in one's self, then one forgets
the call to a more perfect home and the burden of self which
meeting Christ had taught us to recognize. Silence, in which
the "voices" of pleasant encounters or experiences are absent
and worldly comfort is minimal, leads the heart to listen to
God and cling to him. The soul, as it were, abhors a vacuum;
if it is filled with earthly things, it is content; if it is emptied
of all this, it receives its Lord with joy.

St. Thomas Aquinas expresses it all clearly in his *Summa
Theologica*:

> Now, man stands between the things of this world and spiritual
> goods, in which latter eternal happiness consists. So the more he
> clings to either of these, the further removed he is from the other,
> and vice versa. The man, then, who clings completely to things of
> this world, in such a way as to make them the purpose of his life,
> making them the reason and the guide of his actions, by so doing
> cuts himself totally off from spiritual goods. Now a disorder of this
> kind is avoided by keeping the commandments. Men are not bound
> to put to one side totally the things of this world in order to attain
> heaven. For a man, using earthly things, but not as an end in
> themselves, can do so. But he will attain heaven more expeditiously
> by giving up totally the good things of this world—this is why we
> were given the evangelical counsels.[1]

Poverty for religious is not just a matter of dollars and cents
or material surroundings. There are many aspects of our lives
which we possess; and having them at our disposal we are to a
certain extent rich. These things too must all be used re-
sponsibly and frugally as gestures of our complete self-commit-
ment to Christ. For instance, the dedication of one's time to
other people is a real poverty, not imposed, but as a generous
gift. Poverty is not material want; it can often be far more
really expressed and lived in the donation of our work under
obedience to our students or patients or, as the Good Shepherd

1. I, II, q. 108, art. 4, c.

198

Sisters practice, to disturbed children. In such circumstances the body expends all its energies, along with the person's spiritual vitality. This is more real a poverty to many than is, say, seeing that all the lights are out to save five minutes of electricity, or that we do not waste any paper in a letter to parents. The vow of poverty is this sacrifice of self and of the world, insofar as either is held by us in possession, for Christ's sake. Some would even prefer to speak of the vow of poverty as one of commitment to Christ, and so avoid the view that it is an economic arrangement, like a labor contract.

Poverty has taken many forms in the history of the Church on earth, and there are many ways of following Christ the poor man. They are not to be seen as intrinsically better or worse, but as different responses to different calls of God. God calls us through situations, and as history progresses, so do needs and witnesses change. For the early Church poverty was practically equivalent to the flight from the world. The monks were conscious, however, of their duty to the poor. They farmed their land and of their surplus grain they would send shiploads down the river to the poor of Alexandria. In the time of St. Benedict and in the early Middle Ages this tradition continued. But with the appearance of St. Francis a new insight was made available to the world which has affected us ever since. For him poverty was the essential way of union with Christ, much as for St. Benedict obedience and humility were. Francis was sent as a sign by God for men to see Christ in the poor, to see self in riches. Those who, like Francis, come to us as signs express the reality of a particular religious dedication in vivid form, so that men will stop and look and learn. But each of us, having learned the lesson, must carry it out in the way proper to himself, and the Order as a whole in a manner proper to its own spirit.

One final remark. Today we are rightly and seriously concerned with the physical poverty and economic distress of millions. Whether we have taken the vow of total commitment or not, we as Christians cannot be unconcerned with the condition of starving humanity. We cannot in conscience be wasteful

199

of material goods that they need. Charity urges us to be personally and communally frugal, and then to give generously where help is so desperately needed. Above that, monks or nuns have in their vow of poverty a commitment to the poor of the world, a real kinship with all those in want and distress; they belong in Christ to the poor, to whom he came. Their vow must be a strong stimulus to keep from clinging to the things of this world which have already been renounced for Christ's sake, and for the sake of his poor, where he is to be found. Monks should truly be poor, and in taking on the concerns and wants of the poor will be taking on Christ.

2. The World

"The world" has many overtones. What does it mean in the Bible, in monastic literature, and in today's theology as expressed in the documents of Vatican II? For monks this inquiry is important because it is usually supposed that the monk has left the world, but which world? It is important for every Christian, too, for has he not renounced in his baptismal vows the devil and all his works? [1]

In the Hebrew Bible the world was expressed by "heaven and earth" (as in Gen. 1, 1). The Greek Bible used the word *"kosmos."* The single word *"tebel"* in Hebrew referred to earth only. For the Greeks *"kosmos"* was the ordered universe, including men and gods. When the Jews used this word in the Bible they meant the universe as created by God, distinct from God, including man. Man is in the world to rule it (Gen. 1, 28), and he will include it in his destiny, either dragging it down with him by sin, or lifting it up to glory by good deeds.

Therefore, the world in the Bible is looked at from a twofold point of view. Since it comes from the word of God, it is beautiful and good. "God saw that it was good," is the refrain of the creation story in Genesis 1; and Augustine never tired

1. The biblical discussions rely much on *Vocabulaire de théologie biblique,* Edited by Xavier Léon-Dufour and others, Paris, 1962.

of using that phrase against the Manichees. But for man, once he has sinned, the world is the instrument of God's anger. The waters of the flood were used by God to punish the wickedness of primitive man. The plagues which attacked Egypt at the word of Moses were another embodiment of the hostility of the world, the disordered forces of nature—which are still in God's control.

In the apocalyptic writings of Jeremiah and Isaiah and Joel, at the last judgment the world will share the doom of destruction with sinful man. But for those who are saved, God will create "a new heaven and a new earth" (Is. 65, 17).

When we reach the New Testament, the idea of "world," apart from the obvious cases where it means the universe, at times means self-sufficient men and very often the sinful atmosphere of pagan society.

The Christian must "keep himself untainted by the world" (Jas. 1, 27). "Do not bestow your love on the world, and what the world has to offer; the lover of this world has no love of the Father in him" (1 Jn. 2, 15). In this passage we seem to be more concerned with the pleasures of this world as such, earthly pleasures. The text goes on: "What does the world offer? Only gratification of corrupt nature, gratification of the eye, the empty pomp of living. These things take their being from the world, not from the Father" (1 Jn. 2, 16).

But the world did take its origin from the Father—so what sort of world is John writing about? It must be the world as infected by sin. The key to an understanding of this text is in the phrase at the beginning, "Do not bestow your love," meaning that the world must not take the place of God in one's love. "The world and its gratifications pass away . . ." (1 Jn. 2, 17). Could we say that this is a way of speaking of detachment? There is no talk of retiring from the world, but rather of keeping it at arm's length in one's love. This is starkly stated by James (4, 4): "Wantons, have you never been told that the world's friendship means enmity with God, and the man who would have the world for his friend makes himself God's enemy?" It is the old teaching of James' master: "You cannot serve two masters." It is either God or Mammon. James goes on: "The Spirit which dwells in you loves with a jealous love." That is, he will have no rival.

In the passage of Romans, "You must not fall in with the manners of this world" (12, 2), St. Paul seems to be referring to the proud ways of unregenerate men. "I warn every man who is of your company not to think highly of himself . . ." (12, 3). But he was speaking of all earthly pleasures when he wrote, Through the cross, "the world stands crucified to me, and I to the world" (Gal. 6, 14). This, however, is a personal decision not necessarily applicable to all. In 1 Corinthians 7, 29 ff., Paul goes further, telling the Christians that complete indifference to this world is now the rule of life. "Those who weep must forget their tears, and those who rejoice their rejoicing, . . . and those who take advantage of what the world offers must not take full advantage of it; the fashion of this world is soon to pass away." But notice he does not say we must not take any advantage of the world's perfection and perfectibility—rather "full advantage."

This word "world" is a Johannine one. It occurs many times in the fourth Gospel and in the first epistle. In the Gospel it stands for the opposition to the teaching of Christ. "If the world hates you, be sure that it hated me before it learned to hate you" (15, 18).

The Bible contains many examples of flight from the world, withdrawal into the desert; and the call of the desert was strong in the early Church. The whole People of God was called into the desert in order that he might fashion them, weaning them from the pleasures of the "world." It was in the desert that God made his covenant with his People; it was there that he welded them into a strong force able to win the promised land. All this was for the monks a parable of their own lives.

The great prophet Elias went into the desert, and was he not fed by God himself, who sent him an angel? The last of the prophets, John the Baptist, lived in the desert. And he too became the hero of the anchorites and cenobites who left the cities and lived in caves. John the Baptist did not, in his preaching, curse the life of cities, he simply warned that the time was at hand and penance was needed. He told his hearers to be just. His flight from the world was then a personal choice. Christ himself spent forty days in the desert; St. Paul did too for several years before he began to preach the Gospel.

It is then evident that there was no need to go outside the Hebrew or the Christian traditions to find justification for withdrawal. It is there throughout the history of the Jews and in the New Testament. But in the New Testament in no case is it a permanent condition in which the hermit remains for life, or one in which he does not attempt some active work for his fellow men. The Baptist preached. Christ himself was away a little over a month only. St. Paul withdrew in order to be fortified in the work which was to last till his death.

In the cases of our Lord and of Paul there is no indication that the withdrawal was a refusal of civilized life. It was simply a way of being alone with God. When we come to an analysis of the word "world" in the New Testament, we find many elements. Like most basic words, it had many current meanings and is used in these meanings by the same author, as in the Gospel of John. We have to be very careful as we read to recognize which meaning is foremost in each passage.

It cannot be denied that today there is a wave of optimism about the world. Pope John set the tone when he refused to go along with the "prophets of doom." The lay institutes or Christian movements within the Church seeking perfection in the world are signs of this new appreciation of the "world."

Monastic life is said to be a flight from the world, by which some think it is meant that the world is quite wicked and dangerous. The religious life is taking baptism seriously, and baptism is death to this *world*. "You know well enough that we who were taken up into Christ by baptism have been taken up, all of us, into his death" (Rom. 6, 3). Must then the religious and even every baptized person be dead to and abandon the world? The sentence previous to the one just quoted from

Romans spoke of sin: "We have died, once and for all, to sin." It is sin that we are expected to shun. This is one meaning, since it is one element of the reality, of the "world"—sin.

The more we examine the New Testament, the more it is evident that we must be extremely cautious in interpreting the words it uses. The writers had a very different culture and education from our own. While our language is full if imagery and metaphor, Aramaic is full of different ones which seem rather primitive and violent to us. We can be caught unawares and take a metaphor literally. Thus "world" in ordinary speech means this earth and all the material things and people, even the spiritual forces in it. But we must be on our guard. In biblical language—that is, the combination of Hellenistic Greek and Aramaic—its meaning has at times become restricted to what is evil in the world. But there is only one ultimate evil, and that is sin. Sin is not itself a physical entity, it is a choice men make and all the consequences for them.

Our Lord himself once was very plain about what he meant. He prayed to his Father: "I am not asking that thou shouldst take them out of the world, but that thou shouldst keep them clear of what is evil" (Jn. 17, 15).

The word "death," used so often in this connection, also is a metaphor for detachment. Now detachment from something does not mean hatred of it, nor even the shunning of it. It is a capacity to give the world up when the situation requires it. It means a proper and not excessive liking for something. Detachment from this world means being free of a *bondage* to things or people, a liberty of spirit with regard to them. Monasticism acts as a sign of this detachment by expressly standing aside from them. It does not say the world is bad— but that God is better.

From Scripture we gain an idea of the "world" which is as complicated as the religious reality which it describes—creation, mankind, nature—sometimes as bearing the effects of the sin of men and used by God to correct men; the allurements of "this world's" pleasures which can be sufficient to turn a Christian's heart away from love of God. It meant, especially in St. John, people dedicated to ends which are restricted to any of the temporary ends of human achievement, and who did so in a blind way, so as to refuse to listen to Christ's call.

What did the world mean to the early monks? On the whole it seemed to signify the domination of sin in ordinary society, the allurements which led to spiritual dullness or death. The world was a *place*—the economic and social life of human communities located in towns. One could flee from it to the desert. The world was where everyone lived together without visible concern for salvation. The dedication called for by Christ could be found in ordinary lives and trades but was not manifestly different from the dedication of selfishness. The ambiguity of life in the ordinary world was seen as a temptation to confuse true dedication with its specious double. And we may well imagine that such a situation was possible; there are periods when ideals fall off and need to be seriously and unambiguously reaffirmed by the witnesses whom God calls. The practical judgment as to what action is needed ought to be left as the prerogative of the men living then in the situation, unless there are weighty external reasons for doubting their prudence. And though prudence was not the first battle-cry of the desert monks, it was the chief fruit of their experience. They went out in fervor, and there learned moderation.

It is obviously impossible to do or provide a survey of the attitude of the early monks to the world. We would have to spread our net to Mesopotamia and Persia, east and west Syria, Armenia, Palestine, Asia Minor as well as Egypt, to say nothing of the western countries. Then, too, each monk will have a different explanation of his vocation. Here are the ideals of Antony, presented in the life of him by Athanasius:

So, children, let us not grow weary nor think we are toiling a long time or that we are doing something great. For the sufferings of this present time are not worthy to be compared with the glory to

205

come that shall be revealed to us. Neither let us look back upon the world and think that we have renounced great things. For even the whole world is a trifling thing compared with all of Heaven.[1]

An important qualification upon any early monk's expression of his spiritual attitude to the world is the warning that his life and practice may be genuinely holy and full of openness to all God's truth, while his theological understanding is limited by conventions or circumstances beyond any man's control. Thus, relying on the researches of Arthur Vööbus,[2] we may say that the Syrian and Persian monasticism in its earliest stage was more radical than the Egyptian and at times rejects the world as intrinsically bad. This becomes evident in the very crucial area of sexual love. They spoke of marriage as essentially evil.

To repeat some descriptions of Syrian monks given by St. Ephraem who lived during the first half of the fourth century:

These monks left their villages and civilization and lived a life which reduced them to the state of wild beasts. They lived with animals, ate grass with them, and perched on rocks like birds. . . . they had a thirst for mortification and self-annihilation. Not only did they persist in severe fasting and extremes of self-deprivation, they even went so far as to despise life itself . . . taking no precautions against attacks from wild animals or snakes.

They are described as figures smothered in squalor, wild-faced with long hair . . . dreadfully disfigured by hunger. . . . They have given up working or living in towns; they roam the deserts like animals, wandering from place to place and eating grass and roots. They pass the night in cramped caves, climb rocks and live like birds; dig holes for themselves on mountain peaks. Their whole appearance is wild, repulsive and matted with filth and dirt. . . . Some dress in rags, others are covered with straw, others actually naked. Filthiness is characteristic of their way of life. Ephraem adds that they thirst for mortification and their activity consists only in prayer.[3]

1. *Op. cit.*, vol. 1, p. 34.
2. *The History of Asceticism in the Syrian Orient,* 2 vols., C.S.S.O.—vols. 184, 197, Louvain, 1958, 1960.
3. *Ibid.,* vol. 1, pp. 153–154.

206

Here we have a description which implies complete rejection of civilized life and even of life itself. St. Benedict's acceptance of beds, of cleanliness, of cooked food, of wine, of stability, of the arts and crafts, of decent clothing and many other items of civilization is in direct opposition to the picture we have above of the Syrian form of monasticism. Indeed, it became clear with time that there had infiltrated into the latter some strains of Manichean thought which almost transposed it into something non-Christian. A number of saints, not least St. Basil, reacted against it. But the atmosphere of a heresy lasts far longer than the doctrinal formulae. We must then continually maintain that *the world is evil only in the human use of it.*

We repudiate this extreme outlook of some Syrian monks, but, whatever its origin—Gnostic or Manichean—it did penetrate into the thinking of monastic writers. It is the kind of thinking that would make living in the world a second class kind of life; that would make monastic living the only true Christianity; that would even dare to say that the monk is living *the* perfect Christian life, as though there were no other perfect Christian lives.

All this talk has been completely denied by a great passage in the *Decree on the Apostolate of the Laity.*

Many elements make up the temporal order: namely, the good things of life and the prosperity of the family, culture, economic affairs, the arts and professions, political institutions, international relations, and other matters of this kind, as well as their development and progress. All these not only aid in the attainment of man's ultimate goal but also possess *their own intrinsic value.* This value has been implanted in them by God, whether they are considered in themselves or as part of the whole temporal order. "God saw all that he had made, and it was very good" (Gen. 1, 31). This natural goodness of theirs takes on a special dignity as a result of their relation to the human person, for whose service they were created. Last of all, it has pleased God to unite all things, both natural and supernatural, in Christ Jesus "that in all things he may have the first place" (Col. 1, 18). This destination, however, not only does not deprive the temporal order of its independence, its proper goals, laws, resources, and significance for human welfare but rather perfects the temporal order in its own intrinsic strength and excellence and raises it to the level of man's total vocation upon earth.[1]

There is a footnote to this edition which reads in part:

This section clarifies the Church's teaching on the essential goodness of the things of this world and acknowledges that they have true value . . . It thus lays the foundation for the Christian renewal of the temporal order. The age-old detachment of the Church from the "evil world" is no longer valid. Christian laymen must engage in the world, contribute to the perfection of its own values, and enlighten it with the truths of the Gospel.[2]

We should remain detached from the evil in the world, recognize that the world, far from *being* evil, is of its nature good and only evil by the evil use made of it by evil men. Therefore, those uses should be shunned. On the other hand, to use and transform the good in the world, that is the task of laymen and monks, each in their own ways.

Must we not admit that in our day we have discovered a new attitude to creation, one that is more positive, less fearful, more authentic. This splendid passage from the Council in its decree on the laity is a reassurance that this new insight is approved by the teaching authority within the Church. This insight is *not of course absolutely new;* it became very common at the time of the Renaissance and had among the saints its adepts, St. Thomas More, St. Francis de Sales. It had its devotees among a pagan group too which was turning away from the Gospel and towards a Greek hedonism. This caused reaction; and a Puritan wave inside and outside the Church stemmed the movement towards a more positive attitude to the world. But, now that the hesitations are over, we must accept all the good that is there and sanctify it.

Should this change the attitude of the monk? Yes. His flight from the world is not a flight from the world as such, but a flight to God in obedience, an obedience that conforms his will absolutely to Christ. He chooses God absolutely, without a rival.

1. *The Documents of Vatican II,* p. 497.
2. *Ibid.*

He recognizes that marriage is a wonderful institution and designed by God; he recognizes that the physical universe is full of marvels and beauty, that science is, in all its fresh insights, a discovery of God's own universe. *But like a lover the monk wants to sacrifice all else for this one love that he has for God.* And if a critic remarks, But what of the command to love our neighbor?, the monk will reply that he will do so as an outflow of his love of God, putting his neighbors' needs before the throne, and within the framework of his chosen life positively helping his neighbor. He may have to come out of his retreat if his neighbor's need is great. There are, however, many ways within the area of his retirement that he can help his neighbor, by counselling, teaching, preaching, writing, praying.

The monk must not feel that he is not cooperating if he does not rush around doing good works. There are spiritual as well as corporal works of mercy. The chief are prayer and penance. But the monk must not give the impression that he is escaping, or turning away from something that is through and through evil. He praises God every day in Lauds for his having created this wonderful world we live in. He mourns only his own sins, those of others and the misery that many live in, the world over. These he helps with his alms, his prayers and, if within reach, with personal physical aid.

Some in this world are too attached to it, not heeding God or his commandments; others are so engaged in this world that they forget God and his care of us. For these the monastic life stands as a reminder. Conscious that no man can be in his life the whole witness of Christ in the world, and considering his own gifts, the monk chooses the life of utter dedication to God, which will include seclusion.

There is no denying that, as history unfolded, monastic practice in the West has taken two fairly distinct forms with regard to separation from the world, the Benedictine and the Cistercian. The one allows for more or less separation according to the practice of each congregation and each house. The other keeps all contact to an absolute minimum, indeed refuses on principle to undertake any direct apostolate except that of prayer and penance. The reasoning of the pure contemplative is more or less as follows: the greatest help man can give to man in the spiritual order is by prayer and penance; but he can also help by example, by being a living sign. A Cistercian house, therefore, concentrates on prayer and penance in a signal way, as a sort of apostolate. This requires faith of a high order, because the results are normally not visible. The monk following the life of prayer normally sees no results. It depends for its power on the action of grace, on the fact of faith that we are all united with the glorified Christ and share in his power of saving, once we ourselves have been baptized into his death and glory.

This hidden life is becoming increasingly difficult for the men of our generation. Contemplatives feel the urge to go out to show charity by visible actions as well as by faith in the value of prayer and penance. Monks have not contracted out of the society of God's People, they have commitments to them in love—which begets a real desire to embody their love in direct action. No solution to this problem can yet be seen: but it cannot be resolved by abandoning the contemplative life, which is so clearly a part of God's will for the full expression of his life among men and has such a solid history in the life of the Church.

The Benedictines have in the main accepted some apostolic work. But they must remain segregated, at least in the Basilian sense of having quarters that are away from the world and a spirit of silence which allows the monks to be generally recollected. Benedictines are not active religious, but are often on the verge of becoming so. Awareness of the real value of such a life and vigilance are required, or else the meaning will be lost.

One can end with a note of cautious optimism. We have to admit that the only evil in the world is sin, but sin is *in* the world. It follows that in the world there are great dangers for certain people, not only to virtue but also to being able at all to lead a life dedicated to God. These need the help of religious life, since it would be next to impossible for them personally to have complete dedication to Christ in a life immersed in human affairs. They need the support of religious life, let us frankly admit the fact. They are running away from their own tendencies to misuse the world. So, they put themselves under the salutary yoke of obedience which, in their case, alone can perfect them.

But of course this does not mean that these think the world is bad. In fact, having conquered themselves, or rather having been conquered by Christ, they can re-enter the world and help build it up as God wants it built up. So monks and contemplatives generally have a great part to play in the world today. They have learned to see life as God sees it and as the layman, who has got to redeem it, desperately wants to see it. Benedictines really have to be with the Church today in this sense, in this new recognition of the role of the temporal in God's plan. They must be dedicated to the world, not on its terms, but on God's.

CHAPTER SIX

PRAYER

1. Personal Prayer in the Modern World

IT could be asked: Why is personal prayer put first? The answer is that liturgical prayer is in the ascendant and needs no defending, and also because no prayer is true prayer unless it is first personal. We are living in the most activist age that has ever existed in the story of men. Unless a man is fully occupied doing something he is not considered a real man. Men have been caught up in the fascination of their own inventions which can outstrip them in activity and productivity. Modern man is spurred on by the sight of those very machines that outdistance him in speed, leaping across continents and oceans at the speed of sound and faster. Always faster life goes: the traveller has already arrived at his destination almost before he has set off. There is no pause, no plodding down the solitary ways of the world on some silent pilgrimage, only the hum of the engine, the clatter of iron, the hurly-burly of the air and bus terminals. Speed, ever more speed; efficiency ever more efficient. Where is the tranquility and peace of mind, the silence and the calm in all that commotion?

Is the Church herself not a little affected by this bustle? It would be unfair to say that the contemplative life or the life of prayer is not mentioned in the documents of the Second Vatican Council; the first decree of all was devoted to the prayer of the Church. But, apart from that, the contemplative life is mentioned very little, though naturally with great respect and veneration. Yet this was an area which perhaps needed as much careful discussion and elucidation as any other in the Church of today. The world needs personal prayer, the realization of the God within, more than it has ever done. We are all ready to roll up our sleeves and do something active; but even the contemplative and the mixed-life religious are somewhat disheartened in their prayer life. If that is so, what will be the effect of this on the world around?

One of the greatest witnesses needed today is the one which shows that someone really believes that God is present and that we are made to worship him, to plead with him; that he is a Person and not an inexorable force; someone who loves and not some cruel fate.

After having given a very short outline of the history of private prayer, we shall examine the effect of the liturgical revival on the recent revival in contemplative prayer; then examine some of the problems that arise as a result of greater knowledge of Eastern mysticism; we shall then have to examine the scriptural basis for inward prayer. Further, our age itself sets up certain obstacles to a congenial atmosphere for contemplative prayer. Finally, a few words will be said on an approach to personal prayer.

1. In the very early Church we find such writers as Origen writing about inward prayer; his thought is impregnated with the idea that we are the image of God; a disciple of his, Gregory of Nyssa, in his commentary on the life of Moses is profoundly aware of the great discovery that God can be found within. An unknown, the pseudo-Denis, in his great work *The Divine Names* went far in the direction of interiorization—already in these authors there may be echoes of a long tradition from over the Himalayas. But in the West also, with Augustine and Gregory—a splendid introduction to their teaching can be found in *Western Mysticism* by Abbot Cuthbert Butler —there is the same insistence and joy in the practice of inward prayer. The whole Eastern tradition was brought into the West by Cassian, when he describes the teachings of the Fathers of the Desert. How much that is from the Fathers of the Desert

213

and how much from the enigmatic Evagrius it will probably always remain impossible to decide.

In the Middle Ages the tradition continues, side by side with the continuing liturgical prayer; there are all the eremitical revivals of the tenth and eleventh centuries, there is Anselm with his meditations, Bernard and his warm devotion to Jesus, Ailred in the same tradition; then more down to earth and no less mystical the tradition of inward prayer in which we still have relics from medieval England: the Ankren Rule, *The Scale of Perfection, The Cloud of Unknowing;* the revelations of Julian of Norwich; not far behind, the Rhineland School, the astonishing Eckhart, Suso, and the consoling Tauler—and many others. But it was at the climax of the Reformation period that this tradition reached its *apogé* with the Spanish mystics, chief of whom were Teresa and John of the Cross, but there were many others; and in France there was Francis of Sales; England had Benet of Canfield and Fr. Baker.

What happened, that in the following centuries this stream dried up? The chill fear of illuminism and quietism was the cause. Men and women were left with an unintelligible liturgy and substitutes: private devotions, from the nine Fridays to devotion to the Infant of Prague, this special saint, that special shrine. Inward prayer was suspect.

In the late nineteenth century a revival occurred in England led by Evelyn Underhill, Cuthbert Butler, Hedley; the editing of the ancient texts of Teresa, John of the Cross, the English mystics; theological treatises on the subject by such writers as Sandreau, Garrigou-Lagrange, Abbot Chapman. A great revival seemed to be in train; but hot on the heels of this revival came that of the liturgy, and, in spite of its many positive features it has affected inward prayer.

A liturgical revival among the religious and faithful began with Fr. Lambert Beauduin, O.S.B., at Amay and Chevetogne, passed across the frontier to Germany, France, and the United States, picked up momentum in the Thirties, and achieved an unexpected and total victory at the Second Vatican Council at its very first session.

The liturgy is not just a way but the way of the Christian life for all good Christains. It is the Church's worship of the Father with Christ its Lord. All other forms of prayer are subordinate to it and derive from it all their power and efficacy. It is Christ's own worship of the Father. It is the source and summit of all prayer.

That could be a hard saying for one upon whom many aspects of the liturgy jar: the heavy-handed hymns, the impossible organist, the untrained community-singing of poor words to worse music; the badly performed ceremonies. It is, therefore, important to see where contemplative prayer fits in. What of the hermits of the early Church and the revival of the eremitical life in our own day? Surely, some might be tempted to say the summit of prayer is that union with God that is experienced in the soul, one of veiled understanding and a love which clings to the unknown in faith. The liturgy might be considered as the overflowing sacrament or sign of this deep communion with God that is experienced in the soul. But the liturgy is both the sign and the reality. Its center is the Eucharist, where the sign is precisely that: the sign of communion. But is is not only sign, it effects what it signifies.

Further, this sign and the effect last on after the performance of the rite itself. It should and normally does last the whole day unless sin has broken in. Then once again the following morning it is not recreated but renewed and enriched. The heart of the whole action is this union with Christ and his Church, the reason for which Christ instituted the sacrificial meal of the Last Supper. The liturgy is not just a sign but the reality too, and the reality—the *res*—is union with God. It could be looked at differently. At Mass the whole man, the whole Church expresses its homage to God with Christ with the full cooperation of the whole of man, spirit, mind, body, and all that man can devise to express it in art, words, music, architecture, gesture, and symbols.

The new personalist and existentialist framework for theology have both confirmed the liturgical approach to God, each in its own way. Religion is a personal encounter with God.

Where is God recognized so well as a person and as coming forward to meet the Christian as in the very sacraments that Christ instituted, in order to have them as a bridge over which he moves towards us, and particularly in the Eucharist. Besides, the Christian revelation is an existential fact, something that happened and is happening all the time for each redeemed soul. Whatever may have been the gropings of men before the coming of the Messiah, now that he has come, he is the way to God. He is God. There is no other name under heaven by which men may be saved. We must make our commitment to Him, encounter the divine in him, in his word, in his Church, in his sacraments, which bring to us his death and resurrection.

The emphasis on the Bible and biblical spirituality has also reinforced this manner of prayer. To read the Bible is to be brought back again and again to the ever present *fact* of Christ. Our religion is truly an historical one. It is more. Christ not only lived once in Palestine, he is with us today. We encounter him in the Church. The Bible is a historical record, the record of God's dealings with men throughout history. This is the way that God has presented himself to men, not in some nebulous theory of the *One*.

Now, contemplation, whatever be the starting point—a Christian mystery, sacrament, or the beauties of nature, a consideration of the attributes of the divine, a phrase in the Bible—is essentially a communing with God in the center of our being, in the silence of reasoning, that wraps the soul in a peace.

This spiritual activity seems to dispense with words, with images, with ritual, with sacraments, almost dispenses with the Church herself. It could be called a flight beyond the means to the end for which all those means were instituted. Reading some of the accounts of the Fathers of the Desert this is exactly the impression one receives. They would appear to have been partially though certainly not antagonistically remote from the Church and even from the sacraments except at rare intervals. Today, after the constitution on the liturgy, that becomes an impossible position to take up.

The liturgy is the summit towards which the activity of the Church is directed; at the same time it is the fountain from which all her power flows. For the goal of apostolic works is that all who are made sons of God by faith and baptism should come together to praise God in the midst of his Church.[1]

But it is important to point out that the constitution of the liturgy does not claim that the liturgy is the *only* legitimate form of prayer, far from it. The document goes on:

> The spiritual life, however, is not confined to participation in the liturgy. The Christian is assuredly called to pray with his brethren, but he must also enter into his chamber to pray to the Father in secret (see Mt. 6, 6); indeed, according to the teaching of the Apostle Paul, he should pray without ceasing (see 1 Thess. 5, 17).[2]

In other words the question is a typical example of the principle of "both/and"; we should not assert either that Christians should only pray the liturgy, or that they should only pray to the Father in the privacy and secrecy of their rooms, but both pray the liturgy with their fellow Christians and also pray alone with God.

Another question has arisen in recent times. In the study of comparative religion we find mysticism widespread: not only Christian, but Hindu, Buddhist, Taoist, and Islamic. The list could be much lengthened. Historically, we find mysticism among the Platonists, particularly Plotinus and his followers. What is more, there seems to be general agreement about the technique for achieving this state. This training or ascesis has been accurately described by all these, Hindu, Buddhist, and Moslems. Certain elements are so strikingly the same, for example, the account of the purgative, illuminative, and unitive ways, that one wonders whether the phenomenon is Christian

1. *The Documents of Vatican II,* p. 142.
2. *Ibid.,* p. 143.

at all. Is Christian mysticism an Indian occupation masquerading as Christian? This is an area where much study still needs to be done, at the textual, psychological, metaphysical, and theological levels. There are pioneer works, such as those by Louis Gardet on Islamic mysticism; Père Johann on Hindu mysticism, and Dom Rutledge likewise; Heinrich Dumoulin, Merton, and others on Zen; Zahner's summary.[1] But an overall master-work still remains to be written.

One thing is sure, that within the net of mysticism many distinct experiences are described. At their lowest are the Huxley-style experiences that can be induced by a drug, but which undoubtedly are abnormal. On the whole they seem little more than a super-excitation of the emotions and even of the senses, especially the visual one. Then there are those mystical experiences of a historical order described by Arnold Toynbee in his *Study of History*. But going further back in history we find Rousseau with his nature mysticism and stranger yet Newton experiencing a mathematical mystical experience. We shall leave these aside to confine ourselves to that experience which occurs apparently at the very center of one's being.

It has been maintained that much non-Christian religious mystical experience is really nothing more than the experience of one's own being as such. Normally, we only experience the activities of our own being, thinking and willing, the emotions, and so on. But this experience reaching down beneath the surface of the phenomena touches the spring of life, of existence. This, so it is claimed, is an extremely profound experience. We are encouraged to think this is the real explanation of some of the experiences described, because the very theory of being given by the adepts claims that this is the whole of reality. We are identical with the all. This might mean that there is no real me and only the all exists, or it could be a misunderstanding, that is, someone who having experienced this marvellous "me" takes it for the *All*. The fact is there is

1. See "Contemplation" in *Dictionnaire de Spiritualité,* Edited by M. Viller, Paris, 1932–.

no way of proving either explanation right by reason alone, because reason is by-passed in these experiences, and because words have no clearly established meaning in this connection. In the Christian tradition it is likely that some mystics have reached a natural mysticism, possibly akin to the above—an experience of the self mistaken for an experience of God. This may account for the apparently pantheistic manner of speaking about the experience. It was for this reason that Master Eckhart got a bad name. On the other hand, he and those like him may merely have been inadequate expositors of a real Christian experience which anyway is not describable.

We might ask at this point: Is God able to be experienced at all? The answer must be in the negative if we are speaking of his essence. He is infinite and all our experience is finite. But he might be experienced through his effects, in his action and in ways which do not pass through our reasoning mechanism. This is mysticism and contemplation.

In true Christian mysticism there has to be a relationship, two poles—an I and a Thou, a personal meeting between two, a going out of the self to the Other, who is God. On the other hand, this movement may not be recognized as such. The Other may be so overwhelming that the presence of self becomes obliterated from consciousness. But when the mystic came back to normal consciousness it would be hotly denied that the self did not exist, and the self's existence strongly asserted. This assertion would, however, come from normal consciousness and from theological propositions.

We cannot force God to "show" himself even in his effects. We are always the suppliants, the beggars. All we can do is to place ourselves into a suitable "posture" of our nothingness and wait upon God.

Both St. Teresa and St. John of the Cross are positive on this point: all experience of God is a grace that cannot be snatched, only received. For both, the human side consists in freeing the soul from stain, from sin, and the roots of sin, all of which act as a veil to our supernatural sight. The difference between them is that St. John of the Cross sets little or no store by the ecstasies and illuminations that come in prayer except the intellectual ones; while Teresa, who suffered much from ecstasies, is grateful for them and the experience of God's action they gave her.

There is here a large question that naturally presents itself. Is this Christian at all? It is so remote from ordinary life, from normal Christian behavior and prayer patterns. We might comment that one great difference exists between much Eastern non-Christian mysticism and the Catholic variety. The former is very often concerned with knowledge, a gnosis, an awareness. Christian mysticism is an awareness that goes out into love. This is bound to be, because prayer for the Christian is a union between the creature and the Creator, between the redeemed and the Redeemer. It is personal. Often this Eastern mysticism even claims to be achievable by the person concerned, unaided from outside. It is considered as a natural process, won by practice. This is particularly true of much Buddhist theory.[1]

Zen Buddhism, in the form that it has sifted through to the West, would be in the same category. All Christian contemplation is a *gift* from God. This would make Christian mysticism distinct from much outside the fold. Is it, however, possible that there are mystics, in the Christian sense, in other religions? Once it is admitted that persons in good faith, not Christians, may have sanctifying grace, then it would follow that the effects and results of this grace would manifest themselves in their souls, particularly if they lived a truly holy life. If that is so, then we have another confusion in our world pattern of mysticism. Some Catholic mystics may be so on the natural level, some non-Christians—particularly Islamic ones—may be mystics on the supernatural level. Consequently, we need not be surprised at the existence of so-called non-Christian mystics, but we should rather rejoice.

An answer to the question of whether there is a specifically Christian mysticism or contemplation is first to be found in Scripture itself. We know that in the earthly paradise Adam

1. See Humphrey Christmas, *Buddhism,* London, n.d.

and Eve spoke with God. In whatever way we are expected
to interpret those early chapters of Genesis, one thing is clear:
that a very close relationship existed between our first parents
and the invisible God. The same is true, to a limited degree,
with Abraham, but the texts are obscure. Information is clearer
with Moses. He climbed the mountain of Sinai and there he
even dared to ask to see God face to face. The answer was that
he would not be allowed, except—and here is an astonishing
piece of anthropomorphism—that he could from behind, so that
he would not see God's face. Perhaps it is not so simple as we
think it. The point, and it had to be put crudely, was that God
in himself was invisible to man. Yet Moses receives his vision
and the result was that his own face was so transformed by
the sight of God's glory that the People of Israel were blinded
by the splendor of it; and Moses had to cover his face with
a cloth.

Elias in his turn is granted an experience of God. The old
images, the old signs of God's glory are discarded consciously;
he will not experience him in the wind, nor in the thunder, nor
in the earthquake, either, but in the sound of a gentle breeze,
signifying something inward.

In the New Testament the accounts of Christ's own prayer
are mysterious and hidden from us. To the practical Western
mind it is astonishing that he spent perhaps 31 of his 33 years
of life on earth in complete obscurity—and in view of who he
was, in close union with the Father. Two years, at most three,
he gave to the active life of preaching. Even that short span
was begun by forty days in the desert in prayerful solitude.
Before he chose his apostles he spent the night in prayer. He
used to disengage himself from the crowds and escape into the
Galilean mountains alone. We know, from the manner Judas
set the trap to seize him, that Jesus used to spend his nights
regularly, when preaching in the daytime in Jerusalem, out in
the Garden of Olives east of the city walls. He was praying
there the night of his capture.

The Precursor, John the Baptist, was himself a solitary,
living the life of an ascetic in the desert near Jordan. He al-

221

most more than Christ himself was the model for the contemplative ascetics of the early Church.

St. Paul followed Christ's, his master's, example, withdrawing into the desert before undertaking his apostolic labors. On one occasion he describes—if ambiguously—a mystical experience that he himself had (2 Cor. 12). He was carried up into the third heaven. So extraordinary was it that he did not know whether he was still in the body or out of it. Mysteries were revealed to him, but they were beyond speech. Now, this sounds exactly the sort of mystical experience we are looking for, an encounter with the Absolute. But there is one very important point stressed by St. Paul himself. This experience was not apart from Christ. He wrote, "There is a man I know who was carried out of himself *in Christ,* fourteen years since . . ." This ecstasy was in Christ. Here, then, is the classical example of the mystical state in the Christian context: in Christ, and beyond reason . . . "and heard mysteries which man is not allowed to utter."

In the first epistle to the Corinthians (13, 12–13) he sums up the difference between our knowledge of God now and in heaven. Now we only have a "confused reflection in a mirror" (Knox), but in heaven "I shall know as fully as I am known" (Jerusalem Bible). It is only through charity that, in this life, the barrier between men and God is broken through. He writes to the Colossians, "I would see them well ordered in love, enriched in every way with fuller understanding, so as to penetrate the secret revealed to us by God the Father, and by Jesus Christ, *in whom* the whole treasury of wisdom and knowledge is stored up" (2, 2).

Martha and Mary have long been taken as examples of the active and the contemplative lives. This may be putting too much into the story that concerned simply these two friends of Jesus. But it remains true that the Fathers of the Church almost to a man did so interpret the passage and in so doing gave their own attitude to the "two lives"; so Cassian, Augustine, Jerome, Bede, and later Bernard and innumerable others. Jesus here seems to be looking at a wider horizon than just a meal. He said, "Mary has chosen the better part," meaning surely the better approach to life. What was that approach? It was described in the verses that came earlier. Mary *sat* at Jesus' feet—the word "to sit" is used in the New Testament in a contemplative sense, it is a sign of attentiveness, receptivity. She *"listened* to his word." This reminds us of the first word of the Holy Rule: *"Ausculta."*

The time has come to examine this whole teaching of the Bible on our immediate relationship with God. Man, according to the book of Genesis, was made in the image and likeness of God, an astonishing remark when we consider our littleness and when associated with the statement in the same chapter that this same God made the whole universe, earth, moon, sun, and stars. Yet was man made to God's image. St. Paul takes up this fundamental idea in 2 Corinthians: "Our gospel is a mystery . . . [to] those whose unbelieving minds have been blinded by the god this world worships, so that the glorious gospel of Christ, God's image, cannot reach them . . ." (4, 3–4). There it is clearly expressed that Christ is the image of God. In Hebrews we find Christ described thus: "a Son, who is the radiance of his Father's splendour, and the full expression of his being" (1, 3). Here is something more than an image, a being on the very same plane of existence with the Father. St. John expresses it even more profoundly in the Prologue of the Gospel: Christ is the "word," the *"logos."*

Then in other passages of St. Paul we find the doctrine of man as being re-formed, re-created in the image of Christ, incorporated into Christ. "You must be quit of the old self, and the habits that went with it; you must be clothed in the new self, that is being refitted all the time for closer knowledge, so that *the image of the God* who created it is its pattern" (Col. 3, 10). And in Romans, "All those who from the first were known to him, he has destined from the first to be moulded *into the image of his Son"* (Rom. 8, 29).

These texts and others establish the doctrine of the restoration of men in the likeness (image) of God, through Christ, who is the very image of God. In this way God lives in us;

Scripture sometimes says Christ, sometimes the Spirit of God. This impress of God on the soul creates in it a likeness of God even in this life.

In his first epistle St. John put it this way: "We are sons of God even now, and what we shall be hereafter, has not been made known as yet. But we know that when he comes we shall see him, then, as he is" (3, 2). Already, then, in this life, this new-life is in us making us able to know and love God in a dark way, through a glass darkly. God is present to the soul. "We will both come to him, and make our continual abode with him." St. Paul repeats, we are the temple of God, of Christ, of the Spirit.

Once sinful man has been purged of his sinfulness, received the grace of baptism, the nourishment of the Eucharist, then the new life of union with God begins to be active. This is the beginning of the contemplative way. In this life this union is in faith; and all we feel and experience is not God himself, but only an effect of God. Yet this experience, we do know, was one repeatedly described in the early Christian Church; we find it expressed in the writings of Origen, Gregory of Nyssa, Augustine, Gregory the Great, and many others. So we may conclude that there is an authentic Christian contemplative or mystical tradition that reaches back to the New Testament itself and the great Fathers of the Church.

The end of man, the purpose of his existence, is union with God in Christ; that was the reason for his creation, the reason why Christ was born, died, and rose again. All men have this possibility within their grasp through the mercy of God and the merits of Christ. This union is possible in this life: it takes place ontologically by grace, which is itself a likeness to God in the soul, it makes man co-natural with God. God is in fact present to the soul as object of knowledge and love. The knowledge in this life is by faith, in a darkness which in heaven will be light. So even now men may seek God in the darkness of faith and do receive from God "inklings," premonitions, beginnings of an understanding of him. But all this is only obtainable through the humanity of Christ, through the ministry of his Church, his Scriptures, his sacraments. By being united to Christ and his Church—if only by an unknowing desire to do God's will, whatever it might be—the soul reaches in its innermost being to God. The normal way for the Christian to reach God then is through the established signs which nourish both his faith and his love.

When a Christian prays in public with the People of God—of which he forms part—and when this public act is one established by Christ himself as the supreme act of worship of the Father by the New Man, then when both the inward and the outward man are fully engaged and committed to the act, we surely have the summit of human worship. This was precisely what St. Benedict was doing when he set up his school of divine service.

But it also remains true that both leading up to this corporate visible and audible act and flowing from it are the communings of the individual soul with God. The liturgy nourishes private prayer, and private prayer provides the necessary personal commitment for the community act which the liturgy is. There is time for both.

Who is this God we worship in our Churches and in the secret recesses of our hearts? They tell us he is dead, he is no more. Science has killed him, war blown him sky high; astrophysics has left no place for him to live in; men get along pretty well without him. Research has shown how human is the picture in the Bible that its writers describe. There is no going back, the God-is-dead writers say. Progress is inevitable, inexorable. Words, images, ideas that satisfied our fathers no longer satisfy us. God is irrelevant, they say; he is dead.

Modern life is no longer God-centered. The very structure of our cities resembles not at all the medieval town or village, nestling round its church or monastery. Now it is man's own habitation that rears its proud head to the sky: the bank, the

225

office building, the factory, and no thunderbolts fall. Silence from above. Men seem to do without God, merrymaking, money-making. No prayers are said. God is in his grave.

The reason the above gloomy picture has been drawn is that religious as well as laity in the Church have been infected with the ideas it portrays. In their prayers they cannot escape it. Let us face this problem of faith.

Two approaches are possible, and both useful at different times. The first is simple but often difficult: to make an act of faith. Believing is not seeing or understanding; it is an acceptance in the dark. This darkness is not a new idea but an old one, even if it has been overlaid for a century or so with a false, deceptive apologetic, textbook kind of clarity. The God of the Bible is the hidden God, whose very name remains a secret; the unknown God St. Paul referred to. Nothing we can say of him can reveal him to us as he is. As he said to Moses, "I am who I am," meaning, as recently some have interpreted it, "I am what I am," which is almost saying, "No name can grasp the nature of my being." For all his pleading Moses was never permitted to see him face to face. In any case, how could words express the essence of God, least of all scientific language, which is one of numbers and measurement. Possibly poetry leads to the threshold, the poetry of the Bible above all, and that of the mystics; but even they end in the darkness, the night of understanding, acknowledging that all speech is straw compared to the ineffable reality.

The second approach is to reason it out. We must acknowledge that much of the old way of speaking of God is dead with us. We no longer savor the sugary emotionalism of the nineteenth century. Fiercely we strip away unworthy images in art or thought. God is a stupendous mystery and cannot but remain so. We cannot fathom the depth of his wisdom. As the Portuguese proverb has it, God writes straight with crooked lines. More than that, God's ways are not our ways. Any attempt—like that of Job's—to draw aside the curtain is doomed to fail. Even the philosophical approaches of the medieval Scholastics appear unreal to many today. We shuffle off medieval thinking, perhaps, a little too readily. Take, for example, St. Thomas's attributes of God, which he admitted were negative, stating what God was *not*—infinite, not finite; immense, not measurable; spirit, not matter; immutable, not mutable. We know nothing, some say, nothing whatever about God. But this is the *via negativa* taken to an extreme, and the wrong extreme. Of every positive attribute we can conjure up, we have to say, with the Hindus, God is not that nor this, but not because he is less, rather because he is infinitely more. A coin may not be a sixpence. But that is not sufficient reason for saying it is worth less, it may be worth much more. God is not less than finite but more.

Then, this earth we are engulfed by, galaxy upon galaxy, quasar upon quasar, we are less than nothing compared with all that expanse. That is only, as it were, the horizontal plane. When we add to our imagination the vertical plane of time, time before we were and after we cease to exist, that is, on this speck of dust, *we* are smaller still. How can God be interested in us? But once again we are allowing ourselves to fall the victims of a fallacy. Size is not the measure of greatness or importance; if it were, the large man or the large woman would be more important than a small one. But this was put in a splendid manner by Pascal in one of his *pensées,* which should be read whole.[1] The gist of it is this: not all physical size in all its mighty extent is worth one thought; and not all the knowledge of all men is equal in value to one act of charity. They are three different planes of being. So a human soul that is capable both of thinking and of loving is infinitely more valuable than any amount of sheer space and matter.

Besides, the scientists, wonderful as their achievement has been, are still where men have always been in this very area of human relationships. War is no less dangerously near today than it was thousands of years ago and is infinitely more damaging; the human family remains the point of tension in spite of all the freedom and the psychiatry. Man can do without God in the discovery of his laws, except that the mind that finds

1. No. 792, Modern Library edition.

227

these laws is itself a gift of God, and the laws themselves were designed by him. But man cannot do without God's guidance by revelation and by grace in the work of love. Leave out God and hell is created on earth, freedom vanishes, fear and not love rules. It will be the manifestation of love by Christians in life which will be the conversion of the new pagan world.

To return to contemplative prayer. We have examined the varied fortunes of this traditional Christian attitude, its present unsure status; we have seen the pressures that are being brought against it directly and indirectly; the attack on faith which is always an attack, conscious or unconscious, on prayer. We have tried to establish its rightful place beside liturgical prayer. And now let us examine the practical problems, in our day and in our life, of a life of prayer.

St. Benedict told the novice master to find out whether the novice truly sought God. He did not mean as we often do, primarily in other people, but primarily God in himself. Of course, St. Benedict was not denying the other, but first a monk seeks God in himself. This he does when he goes to church or to the silence and solitude of his cell. Elsewhere we have emphasized St. Benedict's teaching on prayer.

Some Practical Thoughts

Prayer must be fitted into life as it actually is in our twentieth-century setting, in our particular life.

Of course, it is possible that in some indefinite time in the future there will be plenty of time to pray. But when will that occur? One has to deal with *now*. Those spacious days, curiously enough, are often frittered away. It is the busy person who finds time to pray. One reason may be that for a monk the work afoot is under obedience and, therefore, does not in fact interfere so much with the life of prayer as might have been supposed. Our sights must not be raised to the indeterminate future but always be kept on what can be accomplished in the present set of circumstances, no matter how unpromising they appear to be.

There are two problems: how to pray during the time of prayer; how to preserve a spirit of prayer in those long stetches when we have much else to do.

The presence of God is the basis of prayer. He is present by his love which is infinite and unswerving. We know that he loves us because he made us and then after redeemed us. He, therefore, knows all about us, knows us through and through. We are, as it were, enveloped in his wisdom. By his creative power he made us and further keeps us in being by the greatness of his power and the strength of his love. So we can be confident that we are related in all these close ways to God.

But God is Three in One; there is the divine life continually in act. This life, present to us, *we share*. We know it by faith; we have Christ-in-us by grace. It is the meaning of the New Testament phrases: "living water"; "We will take up our abode with you"; "You are the Temple of God."

The first basic fact of the supernatural life, that we are present to God, leads to the second which is our unworthiness, because of our natural littleness, and because of our sins. But humility must always be linked with hope. So in spite of our nothingness we cling to God.

The approach to God must of its nature lead to a cry, "Your will be done." — "Speak, Lord, your servant hears," a willingness to obey, to love. This is true charity.

From these fundamental attitudes will flow insights into what Our Lord does want us to do. It will almost surely be related to people we live with, the work we are engaged in. That is right.

At this point we should take up the New Testament to read, to receive the *special message* that God wills for us today. This first part, namely, reading, may be long or short, according as the words strike home or not, and the meditation that follows will vary accordingly.

The prayerful attitude during the day is not an easy one to maintain. Here are a few helpful ideas. The presence of God is not only to be found in the depth of our souls. God's footsteps, as it were, are visible in all nature, animate and inanimate.

He left his impress when He made them all. It is very evident in such spectacles as the ocean, the stars, in such splendors of nature as the Grand Canyon. But it is present also in the little things of flowers, insects, an ordinary stream. In a way each gives a glimpse of some attribute of God, power, wisdom, beauty. But even the chaos we sometimes find reveals the paradox of the God's hidden mysteriousness, his unknowableness in this life, not in the sense that we cannot know that he is, but the unknowableness of all that he is. To stand before the mystery of the universe is to stand before the mystery of God. He is *Deus absconditus*. He is present in the working out of his providence, the gradual evolving of the universe of which we form a small but conscious part.

More marvellous still, Christ our Saviour and God is present among us when we are together. This was one of the most significant teachings of Christ. "Wherever two or three are gathered together in my name, there am I in the midst of them." Christ, God-Man, is present in every sacrament given; the sign is the sign of his presence. Of all the sacraments the most intimately linked with his presence is the Eucharist, not only the presence in the species, but particularly the presence in union between Christ and the Christian. God the Word is present too in the reading of the Bible; he reveals himself at such times. The Bible is the revelation of God, but not a static, historical revelation merely, it is a revelation, a presence of God here and now to the one who is reading his message. This is God speaking to us now, opening our mind to the marvels of his actions in the past and today and for his Church. God is present in any event, particularly important events, sudden changes of fortune, new obediences. God is particularly present in the words of a superior, a priest, a bishop, the holy father himself, in the words of the teaching Church, guided as it is by Christ and his Spirit. God is present in our work, the obedience of our life, the *sacrificium laudis* that we perform every day. Those children, that sick person, these studies, these chores, Christ is present in them. Perhaps specially there, in a hidden, pervasive way, a presence of the cross.

230

2. *Lectio Divina*

This phrase as a name for spiritual reading has become again
the normal one as a result of the writings of Dom Jean
Leclercq.[1] He has pointed out that there is a difference between what people have for some time called spiritual reading
and *lectio divina,* for the latter emphasizes the prayerfulness
of the reading. It is *lectio divina* that St. Benedict wrote about,
not spiritual reading as an intellectual occupation, a toned-down
theology. What surprises modern monks is the amount of time
that he gives to it in the Holy Rule. It has been worked out by
several authorities that *lectio divina* receives about four hours
a day in the Rule's horarium, and that all together in the
morning. These four hours could not possibly be four solid
hours of prayer, which would hardly be a prudent way of
guiding "beginners," as St. Benedict calls his monks. Like so
much else in the Rule, this subject is treated without very in-
formative details, and we are left largely to our own conjec-
tures. We do know, however, from the *Rule of the Master*—
who is very close to St. Benedict in time, place, and ideas—
that the young monks, for instance, used part of this time for
learning the psalms, that for some of the time a monk would
read aloud to others, especially of course to those who could
not read.

There was no moral theology, as we know it, in those days;
there was, for that matter, no dogmatic theology either. Nor
would there be a Scripture course, though there would be much
reading of Scripture and some reading of the great commentaries already available, such as those of Augustine, John
Chrysostom, and Origen. The Scholastic dedication to order
and precision, the philosophical analysis in handbooks for students, had not yet occurred in the Western Church. The approach to learning was rather an eclectic one, whose object was

1. For an excellent book on this subject, see his *The Love of Learning
and the Desire for God,* New York and London, 1960.

231

to learn of the love of God, and which relied heavily on the language and patterns of Scripture.

Lectio divina, then, is prayerful reading. We are very fortunate in having today books in many areas which can be used for *lectio divina*—that is, which can be read prayerfully. It has not always been true that one could read books of moral theology, dogmatic theology, and Scripture prayerfully. In moral theology, especially, there were textbooks whose distinctions and legalism and "professionalism" could never have provided one with food for prayer. The same was often true of Scripture and dogma. And so we are very fortunate to be able to read books today like those of Bernard Häring on moral theology which speak to us with both deep thought and deep spirituality. Books which are academic or apologetic are not without use, but their use is not prayer.

One of the greatest inspirations to all fields of theology (in which books are now written which can be read prayerfully) has been biblical studies. We are frequently sidetracked, in spite of the best intentions, from reading the Bible, which should be our greatest source of prayer and enlightenment. But even if we were to bring our vague resolves into effect and actually read the Bible more frequently, we would still not profit unless we have acquired the art of prayerful reading. There are two dangers to avoid; the first is too rapid reading, the second is one which is too academic. One may read the Bible too rapidly because great stretches of it, especially the New Testament, are very familiar. When we find ourselves doing this, it means that we have been reading not prayerfully but for information—the way one reads the newspaper. And if this has been our frame of mind, then the words have sped past without sinking in or coming to life, because the "life" we were looking for was a matter of facts and information. This reading skims the surface, and is not *lectio divina.* The second danger is reading too academically. The Bible is also easily misread in this way because there is a large amount of background which can be supplied to explain the full context of each sentence. The linguistic, historical, and cultural information which can be provided for a complete explanation of Scripture is of great importance; but to attend to it is not to attend to the voice of God. Lengthy commentaries are necessary for some purposes, but not for *lectio divina*. Further, a certain amount of commentary is very helpful to *lectio divina;* but it should be like an interpreter helping two persons of different languages to speak to one another.

Lectio divina is not simply prayer, it is not simply study; it is a mixture of the two. It is a study which leads to prayer, it is thought becoming thoughtful through attention to God himself as the author of thought. The content of the thought itself inspires us to wonder and appreciation, which lead us to God. This is most likely to happen with Scripture itself, for it has always been God's own word in a special way. The Bible is not written for "edification," but is the passing on of God's own message by men commissioned for that job. The real facts of the message are the ideal source of our prayer, for they are indeed the source of our being related as we are to God. Our prayer should be principally inspired by the Incarnation and Redemption, for it is these which lead us to God himself.

It would certainly be a false kind of *lectio divina* that refused to admit a careful study of the texts and of their implications. But the scholarship that precedes *lectio divina* is either simply a different activity—and so when we study the Bible we leave ourselves less open to God's word (for good reasons) and only later or at intervals actually read "spiritually"—or it is, and most men must find it so, not immediately to the point, because the sense of the faith and even general historical and cultural knowledge which we have are already sufficient for God to speak to us in his Book. Whichever way we regard scholarship, it is a good thing: either it is a necessary preliminary, or it is to be broadly assumed. In no case are we in danger of becoming fundamentalists, or depreciating the real value of linguistic and historical understanding of God's word. The communication between God and man which takes place in Scripture and in the holy reading of Scripture depends on a knowledge of its original language and culture; but this knowledge is

233

not itself *lectio divina,* nor is its acquisition in detail a pre-requisite for such reading, because the Church possesses and shares in all her members a true sense of the voice of God. Though it would be foolish to rely exclusively on this sense of faith when reading the Bible, still it is important that we understand and qualify the importance of scholarship towards *lectio divina.*

It might be well to take some examples of Bible reading which dwell on Scripture in such a way as to start from study—or rather an openness to listen hard and a readiness to find real differences from what we are used to—and lead to prayer. We shall take the prologue to St. John's Gospel and the description of the Last Supper in 1 Corinthians.

As soon as we begin, we are made aware that the Bible is a single work, that it has a unity of purpose and meaning which make it necessary to refer to many parts of it when trying to understand one text. Christ's fulfillment of the promises made to Abraham and David and the prophets is reflected in the fact that the New Testament is constantly referring to the Old. The new message of salvation is not spoken without a present memory of the former words of God. Sometimes it is only a word, sometimes an image, sometimes an event or action, sometimes a person or personal characteristic. Many Bibles provide cross references, which are in themselves very valuable, but need to be carefully used; used, that is, as side-comments in a conversation, not as facts to remember for an examination. To look up *all* references is probably the surest way to dampen the conversation which *lectio divina* is meant to be.

Further, such references may at first sight not mean much, but gradually, as one realizes how conscious these authors were of the Old Testament, taking from it so many categories to explain the meaning of the new message of Christ, the obscure echoes prove to be of great value for the understanding of a passage. An example of the depth to which this can go is the Infancy narrative of Luke, so brilliantly analyzed by Abbé Laurentin.[1]

1. René Laurentin, *Structure et Théologie de Luc i-ii,* Paris, 1957.

Let us take the opening words of the Fourth Gospel: "In the beginning was the Word . . ." The word for beginning, *arché* in Greek, has also the sense of origin and source, what is first and foremost. The Hebrew background to it is Genesis 1, 1: "In the beginning," where God speaks the word of creation. The logos, the word, is also in Greek more than just our usual English equivalent; it means a spoken word, a saying or speech, an argument or case or cause, an idea or concept, reason. For some philosophers it meant the order of the universe. For the Hebrews in the Old Testament, the word of God was his spoken word of authority, transmitted to his people in the Torah and the prophets. Or it was his creative word, as we find it described in Proverbs 8, 22. But the sense in John is not the word the prophet utters, because the word is with God and is what God is. This is perhaps as far beyond the vision of the original authors of Proverbs and Ecclesiasticus as the New Testament is beyond the Old, but the Old Testament was meant to be open-ended and was so until the last Word was spoken which closed it by fulfilling its promise. We do not mean to read things into the Old Testament; rather we are recapturing its genuine openness when we allow that the deep mysteries which were therein contemplated have in fact come to fuller light.

O Lord, make me open to the fuller mystery of your word; you do not want my mind to be a closed book, but a continuing conversation with your Word in you and in the world which you called into being.

From the beginning, God has spoken. St. Paul wrote to the Church at Colossae that Christ, the Word made flesh, "is also the head of the Body, that is, the Church; *he is the beginning, the first-born from the dead.*" Similarly in the Apocalypse 3, 14: "To the angel of the church at Laodicea write thus: A message to thee from the Truth, the faithful and unerring witness, *the source from which God's creation began.*" Christ is God's last word, his Amen, to the world to which he spoke *in the beginning.*

In verse 14 of the Prologue, he who is the Princeps, simply God's idea or thought, because the *logos* is also distinct from God, is "in God's presence" or "is related to God." So we must say that the Word is not just another name for God, but still God. A great mystery. Is this a glimpse, O God, of your own being—Power, Intelligence, Love? This is your showing us by an inspired word something of your mystery. We are called to share your life in this word. By grace and truth I am lifted into your mysterious life, O God the Father. I am really informed by your word, not because I receive information, but because in listening to you I hear the truth and am told of your love, and while the word is with me I am with you for your Word is with you—and is what you are. May I never lose that word, that insight, that charity.

The life of the Word with God is imparted to the created world, the world which God created and recreated. It is the whole world to which God speaks, as he first did in Genesis by a word of command which established the world first of all as good. This is prominent in the Prologue of John: Everything was made by Him. Creation is an act of God, and God's word creates, because it contains God's own authority and power. In Proverbs 8, 22 ff., God's word is again associated with the dependence of the world on its creator. "God has given me being at the beginning of his purposes," says Wisdom. This "has given me being" does not mean "has created"; the word is a different one, as though the writer were avoiding the idea that Wisdom was created. "From eternity was I established," from the beginning, the Source, the Creator of all, who is with God and is God, who is Wisdom and before all things, became flesh.

What does flesh mean? Not just what we normally mean by it, neither the palpable covering of our skeletal frames, nor concupiscence, but physical man. Man, of course, is always physical, but the word "flesh" naturally is a vivid image of man as a living body. We scarcely realize how important that word was then and for long after. The Zoroastrians, the Gnostics, later the Manichees and the Albigensians, all refused to accept that God became flesh. For them the material world was corrupt and corrupting, and wisdom's aim was to be rid of gross and heavy matter. But "the Word became flesh," became a physical

236

man. Thus does God sanctify the material world, to which he spoke his word in the beginning, but uniting it to himself in his Word.

The mystery of the really audible Word, heard on this very planet, is simply beyond our words, and nothing we can say in reply or response is an adequate embodiment of what we have heard: that God has come to his world, loved it and united Himself with it, remade it in his image, and sanctified it. By being one with a part of it, he becomes related to the whole immensity of it, but especially with men, for the Word became flesh. We cannot for long discourse to ourselves on such a mystery; rather, we give up ordinary words and respond in hymns of praise and wonder and thanksgiving, or by silence. As the truth of this tremendous mystery penetrates the heart I become more aware that it is you, Jesus, Lord, Word of God, Wisdom of God, before me, waiting for your presence to dawn on me. And all I really want is just your presence, as if, after a long separation, two people in love have come together again. Your love amazes me, for myself and for all men and for the whole world. It is a very mysterious love, deeper than I can think: for you are yourself majestic, the world's Lord, and here you have come so close to men, for you became flesh, and close to the world, for you lived with us, and still live in us. What love is this, O God? It is Godly love. I love you in return, and praise you; you must never leave us, for you have the words of eternal life.

How natural it is to pray in these circumstances.

Chapter 11 of St. Paul's first epistle to the Corinthian church is the earliest account we have of the Church's Mass (23-27), and it is fuller in detail on the "institution" than any of the others. And it is nearest to the accounts preserved in the liturgies.

After only twenty years of being Christian (at the most), the Corinthians were losing their sense of awe at the meaning of the sign—that is, charity. "There is no room for praise here."

Recalling to them his original preaching, he recounts the institution by Christ. "Do this . . . for a commemoration of me." St. Paul's account is the only place in the New Testament where these words occur. Suppose 1 Corinthians had not survived, what play might have been made of the omission—except in the text of the Mass. How haphazard is our historical evidence for all things Christian, and how important is the living stream of tradition.

No doubt, St. Paul saw the Last Supper and the ritual repetition as a commemoration of Christ's death: "So it is the Lord's death you are heralding." But for him it is more: the death is a sacrifice: "My body, given up for you," and "this cup . . . is the New Testament in my blood." This is a tremendous saying.

So we search for an understanding of the idea of testament and covenant. We are taken back to the moment of the Passover, to the divine command transmitted to the People of God to commemorate the great event of their liberation from slavery in Egypt. The Last Supper was a grafting on to that rite, with all its implications: new People of God, new covenant, not written on stone; new liberation, this time from sin, a new kingdom, the heavenly one.

Besides this imagery there comes in Our Lord's own words the echo of another theme, that of the messianic meal—much more discreet, but perhaps even more essential to the Mass. Once again it is rewarding to search the Scriptures for a deepened realization of what that concept applied to the Last Supper and to the Mass would imply. Who is not moved to gratefulness and wonder? A covenant: God has committed himself to us forever: an alliance of love, a marriage. There are so many ways of expressing the closeness of God to us: we are your church, we are Christ's body, his bride, and you, Lord, are the husband. We belong to your household, as friends, as faithful servants, as sons in Christ. We are grafted onto the stem, which is Christ. We are made new in him by a new creation. He lives in us, for we are temples of the divine Trinity. In all these ways we are close to you, O God, one with you in will and life. To deserve this we have done . . .

nothing. We are beggars and sinners, so all we can do is to beg
. . . for forgiveness of our sins. You lovingly grant us this in the
Eucharist, so we offer this *sacrificium laudis* with complete
gladness and thanksgiving.

Another approach to sacred Scripture as *lectio divina,* besides
dwelling on a single passage and its echoes, is to choose some
virtue or truth or doctrine and collect the teaching of both the
Old and New Testaments on it, for instance the teaching of
Christ and his apostles on humility, or joy, or charity. Or one
could take the titles of Christ and deeper one's understanding
of some of them by comparing passages, for instance, "Son of
man"—there are two meanings in the New Testament and it is
prominent in the Old Testament in Ezechiel 2, Daniel 7. One
could take the idea of the kingdom in both the Old and New
Testaments, or the idea of obedience, of love, of virginity, of
poverty and the poor, Our Lord's teaching on prayer and the
example he set, collect the actual prayers of the New Testament,
especially those in the Apocalypse, the heavenly liturgy. One
could take some of the symbols which run through the whole
Bible: water, light, the cloud, the image of God, the rock, the
shepherd, the Temple, the City of God (Jerusalem); or various kinds of sacrifice, what sacrifice was and is acceptable to
God. But once one begins, there is no end to the possible and
fruitful ideas for spiritual reading in Scripture.

As to *lectio divina* with particular reference to young religious, it is important to note that certain subjects are particularly important and relevant for them, certain others not. Thus
the Canticle of Canticles is a superbly beautiful piece of literature and may be fruitfully considered as a spiritual allegory,
but is not ideally suited to the young. What are the subjects
they should study in depth at that period of their monastic life?
  1. Charity: the love within the Godhead. We find this expressed in the first epistle of St. John. The love of God for men

is, in a way, the "theme song" of the whole Bible. God's love is shown in the act of creation—the createdness of the world is a golden thread which turns up in many places: not only Genesis 1 but in a number of psalms and in Job. God's love is shown in his promise of redemption to come, in his preparing a chosen People, to whom he sent his prophets, for the Redeemer's coming, and in sending his divine Son. We must see the New Testament as the sublime manifestation of God's love—in Christ's redemptive life and death and resurrection and ascension, in his words and teaching, in the founding of the Church. Our love for God is shown in obedience, as we are taught in each verse of Psalm 118. Nor should we fight shy of love as a sacrifice. The liturgical renewal is bringing a more profound appreciation of the meaning of sacrifice: a giving of oneself in love, made manifest. The Mass is, of course, a meal, but a sacrificial meal, one where the participants unite to praise God and give themselves back thankfully to him, with and in Christ. In the New Testament this love for God is repeatedly associated with obedience, obviously not the purely external forms of it, but a willing and generous spirit of acceptance. All the Old and New Testament strictures on wrong kinds of sacrifice, especially in Hebrews, give us a sound outlook on sacrifice, and therefore on love. Fraternal love, which for Benedictines takes the prominent form of fraternal obedience, is important in the New Testament in the example of Christ and in his teaching and in the teaching of the apostolic Church.

2. Humility. We tend to be theoretical about humility. We should seek it rather in the concrete theme of the Poor of Yahweh in the Old Testament, and the Servant of God in Isaiah, who reach forward to perfect expression in Christ, the poor man and Servant of the Lord. The close connection between poverty and humility is evident in Hebrew, where one word can be used for both "poor" and "humble."

3. The essential concept of grace, or Christ's life in the soul, is also one to be studied in depth—and in depth and height—

because its ramifications are immense and the ways it has been expressed in sacred Scripture almost beyond counting. There is grace as a personal gift, as life, light, water, a living spring, a priceless pearl. There is grace as uniting us to the body of Christ: making us a part of the People of God, citizens of the kingdom, branches of the vine. And thus, in poring over the Bible to explore the meaning of grace, we find the Church, that mysterious entity which continues the life and witness of Christ through the centuries.

4. Faith is another important theme. We could begin with Abraham, and take in all the men of faith who encountered the saving word of their personal God, especially the apostles, and its extension to all who hear the preached and authoritative word of Christ's disciples.

These are what the young need in a special way, for the Bible and its themes are not abstract. Rather, God is encountered with a complete human response—in poetry, in moral injunctions, in theology; thus man responds with his imagination, with his will, and with his mind. All these modes of response are summed up in the heart, the inmost sanctuary of the soul. Sometimes it is very simple: God is our rock, our fortress, our shield. Sometimes it is sublime, as in the splendid poetry of Job and Wisdom. It is at times most feeling, as when it is said that even if a mother were to abandon her new-born child, God would never abandon us.

Must *lectio divina* always be holy Scripture? It certainly has a uniqueness that no other text has: it is the word of God in a special, quasi-sacramental way. Encountering Christ in the words which his Church has recognized as the primal, authentic account of him carries with it a grace which does not accrue to any other such written record of an account of Christ. And yet there are times when we need specific help, and the tradition of the Church has provided us with many wise men whose understanding of Christ is couched in language closer to

241

our own than is that of Scripture. The saints and theologians who have had deep insights into the meaning of God's life among men can often be of great assistance.

Broadly speaking, there are five periods of different spiritual writing: the patristic, the medieval, the *pietas moderna,* the Tridentine, and the contemporary.

The patristic literature is often difficult to us for several reasons. It is verbose, it is immediately concerned with problems that are not ours, its equipment for dealing with Scripture is inadequate, and the translations are often poor. Still some of our ancient Christian literature has immense appeal: the letters of St. Ignatius of Antioch, the accounts of the early martyrs (especially St. Polycarp, the martyrs of Lyons, Sts. Perpetua and Felicity), some of Augustine's works (*The Confessions,* the sermons on St. John's Gospel, the concluding ten books of the *City of God*). Lives of the saints were not as frequent then as now, but Athanasius on Antony, Gregory on Benedict, Cassian on various Desert Fathers still have their attraction and value. Works like Hilary's *On the Trinity* or John Chrysostom's great Scripture commentaries take quite a bit of reading for hurried men of this century. Yet there are already important works on prayer: Denys on the divine names, Gregory of Nyssa, Origen on the Canticle of Canticles, and parts of Augustine and Gregory the Great.

The Middle Ages is also weak in biography. The fascination for the miraculous kept interest in the real virtues submerged. Here and there we find gems: the biographies of Benet Biscop, Cuthbert, and Wilfrid by Bede, that of Catherine of Siena by Raymond, the contemporary life of Ailred of Rievaulx. Nor is it strong in readable biblical commentaries, excepting those of Bernard and Thomas Aquinas. There are passages of the *Summa,* for instance those on the passion of Christ, which can hardly be excelled for solid thinking with a biblical foundation. Other medieval writings with real power are those of Bernard, of William of St. Thierry, the sermons of Ailred, the writings of Catherine of Siena, and that unique group of works usually referred to as the medieval English mystics. These concentrate on the personal side of religious devotion, not the liturgical (although they were sometimes thought of as the very way to make the liturgy a real prayer).

The period of the *pietas moderna* is summed up in the *Imitation of Christ*. With it should be reckoned the German mystics: Eckhart, Suso, and Tauler. They are not quite what we mean by medieval, and yet not Reformation either.

The Tridentine period is restless in many of its writings. It has the writing of the greatest mystics: Teresa, John of the Cross, Francis de Sales, Olier and Bérulle, and even Augustine Baker, who is not to be despised but who is difficult to read. It also has the beginnings of lives of saints in the modern sense. We know enough about the people concerned to form a picture of their personalities: Ignatius, Bellarmine, Francis Xavier, Campion, Francis de Sales. Perhaps the finest example of biography is Trochu on St. Francis de Sales—its one defect is its enormous length.

The life of a saint could be undertaken for many reasons, not least to prove that he was a saint. Then the miracles and extraordinary virtues are stressed—the former making him unreal, the latter inimitable. Or sometimes a life is written to fit the figure of the man into the times in which he lived; then the book can be weighted down with historical and religious irrelevant details.

What do we now look for in the life of a saint? First we want to see and be sure that he was human, just as we are. He must therefore be limited, faulty, beset with problems, and very imperfect. Then we want to see how he managed to overcome his failings, or rather how he suffered himself to be a failure in union with Christ the Victor. People's own passions are often their greatest passion. Saints are not born, they become holy as all men must, through stress and strain, through suffering and salvation, through patience and faith. It follows from this that for us the most interesting part of the story is the moment of conversion, the bottom rungs of the ladder, and not the success story when thousands flocked to his confessional or crowded around his cave or convent. Unfortunately, men notice holiness in other men only after tremendous struggles have already been nearly won; the glorious end is more frequently recorded than the inglorious beginning. Those saints with well-documented early lives are few: Augustine is alone in antiquity, Francis de Sales, Teresa, possibly the Curé of Ars (though the material has not been printed), Soeur Thérèse. Lives of holy people in modern times must have details on modern living and its problems and how these men and women, filled with the life of Christ, met and lived with these problems. The lives of men and women of all walks of life can be filled with Christ's spirit—teachers, business men, politicians, waiters, miners, postmen, philosophers, and football players.

The poor quality of writing which has for long characterized saints' biographies may well explain why they are out of fashion. Yet not to read about the saints is an impoverishment, for it is they who embody Christ's teaching in every age and in every type of character. Just as we are happy to read about the "heroes" of the Old Testament—Abraham, Moses, David— and about the "heroes" of the New—Peter and Paul, John and James—so should we be happy to read about the "heroes" of the entire new dispensation. We are far more moved by the particular than by generalizations: generalizations may impress us, but particular things alone have a personal effect which challenges us. Theorizing on the virtue of patience cannot do nearly so much to affect our own attitude to present opposition as the description of a holy man being patient when faced with definite antagonism. The saints are the ones who have the Spirit living in them most fully, not just in them but flowing from them and inspiring all their actions. It is in them that the charismatic action of God is now visible; they are the ones who have had the insights which will be of most importance to their generation and often for generations to come. We would be denying ourselves a gift of God if we turned our back on the example of the saints.

To understand the meaning of a holy man's life, the milieu and theological background are important. We are now particularly interested in the saints as psychological cases, and this too is very important. Most of all one should know the saint through his writings, especially, as Newman used to say, through his letters, for these are the most spontaneous writings of all. Nowadays it is possible to read the processes of canonization: this is how Trochu did such splendid work on the Curé of Ars and on St. Francis of Sales, and Ida Görres on Soeur Thérèse.

One must look around carefully for the particular example of sanctity that is most relevant to one's own problems. Not all are important to each one of us. If one were to object that the Christian life is the same in every walk of life, then one would reply that it very seldom seems so. Only two saints have been readily available for men of all kinds—St. Francis de Sales and Soeur Thérèse; they did work out a spirituality of ordinary life which most people can profit from very much (though neither has quite the liturgical and social spirit of involvement that we now expect). Each saint is different and each Christian will learn from some of them but not from others. The members of an orchestra play in unity, but on different instruments and with different notes. In one the big drum of justice will have a leading part; in another the gentle mellow tone of patience on the cello; while in another the warm and swift sound of the strings of charity will take the lead. A doctor is faced with spiritual and moral problems that never or rarely occur in other lives. A housewife requires a set of virtues which a spinster or recluse does not exemplify. Just as different jobs require different tools, so a person faced with a temptation against faith needs a different virtue from a person whose problem is chastity.

Benedictines have a difficulty peculiar to themselves. The tens of thousands of Benedictine saints lived in an age when hagiography was not historical or psychological as we demand that it be. There is no distinctively Benedictine saint, to whom they can look as, say, Jesuits and Carmelites can. But the Benedictine way is such an open and adaptable one that one in fact is quite right to look to other types and Orders for examples of holiness that appeal to each one of us. Benedictines do not have a set type. For the teacher there is John Bosco; for the contemplative there are the many English, German, and Spanish mystics.

The contemporary period of spiritual writing is one of great variety, one in which piety is to be found in many places besides books with "soul" in the title. Among contemporary writers, we would especially recommend Guardini for his humanism; Merton for his very attractive and compelling writing on prayer, Jungmann and Nocent on liturgy; Richard on the Redemption; Laurentin for Mary; Dillenschneider for the Holy Spirit; Lagrange for the *Gospel of Jesus Christ;* Congar and Mersch; Masure, Héris, and de la Taille on the Eucharist; and Butler and Marmion on the Benedictine spirit. The list is fragmentary, but it is not meant to be a bibliography; it is just an indication of the large amount of genuine spiritual reading that is now available to us. They are all in some way or another a response to the word of Christ, and they all derive their special efficacy from the one book which should be our most frequent meditation—the Bible.

3. The Liturgy

Since this book is not a compendium of monastic spirituality but an examination of certain monastic questions and issues and themes which are of concern to Benedictines today, no attempt is going to be made to cover the whole subject of monastic liturgy, but certain problems should be briefly mentioned.

It is scarcely necessary to discuss the question of the vernacular in the liturgy. It is a matter over which there is almost no dissent. Prayer, to be effective, should be in a language which is readily intelligible to the one praying. Very few people are really bilingual, fewer yet are fluent in Latin. Therefore, prayer in Latin is often just love's labors lost. In any case, a great reform of the liturgy is under way, and this problem should soon resolve itself.

The liturgy—Mass and Divine Office—is the central core of the Benedictine monastic life. St. Benedict provides a regular schedule of times and psalms for prayer, but he is silent on the theory of liturgy. He accepts it as so natural a Christian occupation as not to need explanation. We in our day, emerging from a relatively individualistic era when prayer was really a private occupation, feel the need of an understanding of corporate prayer which follows a schedule and which is so different from private prayer. Without an understanding, the whole process can become an unintelligible burden. The liturgy, since it is prayer, is not explained as other jobs in the Church are by its tangible usefulness or its natural satisfaction; it is not just another activity.

And yet prayer is part of the Church's life, because the Church is not just an organization, a world-wide religious group, which happens to be rather highly organized and very rich. The Church is a deep mystery of men: it is a union formed in response to the word of God and it has an inner life, which is its secret and its joy. That secret is the life and Spirit of Christ. Now it is he who lives in us. The Church is a mystery of persons who substantially share the gift of God's love, in which no one is absorbed or destroyed but rather individually enhanced and enriched. The Church is the whole Christ, everyone who shares his life. It was to achieve this that Jesus Our Lord accepted death and was raised from the dead. By this he draws all men to himself, in order that the Father may be glorified in all.

The Church is the summing up of the unity of love which man has always wanted. The creation of man and woman was not complete until the two were made one flesh; so too the redemption of man is fully complete when we are at one with God as a united human family. Now this unity which we are striving for is only found through Christ and only in him do men really unite to glorify the Father fully.

The liturgy—Mass and Divine Office—is the manifestation of just that: the union of men in the name of Christ to praise the glorious love of God. It is there that we do what Christians

247

are in fact always somehow doing by joining with other men for the direct or indirect sake of God's glory. But, since it is not just another activity like other activities, it must obviously proclaim itself as such.

To realize better the real point of the liturgy and of our liturgical life as monks, there will have to be some reforms and rejuvenation. The present forms are not perfect. They must be made more natural and free. This is largely a matter of the language and the way that the psalms and readings are used.

Meanwhile monks and nuns have a tremendous witness to enact for the modern world: the embodiment of Christ's communal prayer—for the world. It need not be very grand and ceremonious; rather it should be simple and sincere, of a sort that rouses recollection and devotion. Mere outward show is like sounding brass—all noise and no melody. Benedictines have, therefore, a considerable responsibility in their daily Office not only to themselves and to the Church, but to God and to the world.

At the community Mass, the most important act of the day for all its members, the whole community should be gathered. The community Mass expresses in the most perfect way the worship of each and every one of the members of the group: the offering to the Father of the perfect Victim, in whom we are united with the Father. It is in the Mass that the unity in love of all the community is not only expressed but created, nurtured, enriched, restored. Nothing should be allowed to steal a member from that supreme act of the day. Of its very nature it is a communal meal, of its nature the *sacrificium laudis* of all mankind, but especially of those in each place where it is offered. Where if not in a Benedictine house can this be done more fittingly? The family of mankind is represented by each Benedictine family celebrating and sharing together this chief sign and token of our belonging together in Christ. Further, a monastery is a Christian community which is particularly dedicated to love and service of God. The Mass is their sign and sacrament of this generous love for all men in honor of God. And around the Mass the Divine Office is sung day and night to prepare for it and to thank God for it. But we never rest content in the Mass itself, it takes us all beyond ourselves and our community to a transcendent union with the one Lord; therefore, there is another sense in which the Divine Office directs our attention not to the Mass, but beyond the created signs of our worship to the union which they signify and promote.

The liturgy should, for Benedictines, be more closely associated with the contemplative life than with the active. The contemplative life, that is, the contemplative side of the life, is the great heritage of the Benedictines, but it could be lost by excessive zeal to be of assistance to the active Church in the various apostolates. The greatest service the Benedictines can give to the Church is to preserve, deepen, and extend their contemplative lives. A contemplative is not one who has a heightened intellectual appreciation of the Godhead, nor is he one who has special ecstasies or visions or locutions. He is one who lives continually in the presence of God, who lives with Christ and is conscious of the inspirations of God's life in him, the Holy Spirit. He is not simply one who concentrates on his ability to think about God, but one who sees God in all things and in all people, recognizes God's hand in all happenings, friendly and hostile, calamitous and gay.

Thus the contemplative life is simply a life or pattern of life that is designed to bring about this *attitude of being* with the greatest ease. Precisely the liturgy is designed for this by drawing the brethren together, and so to recognize Christ in their midst, especially Christ in his supreme act of self-giving love. Precisely too the hours of the Divine Office are for this—drawing the monk back to the Church and to the presence of God, in love and thanksgiving, in sorrow and supplication. So too the silences, providing as they do opportunity for encounters with Christ in recollection, are an important part of the contemplative pattern. Benedictines at Mass are to be seen in the light of Benedictines at common Office; their Office is to be seen in the light of their silence. In this way is the Benedictine liturgy, the work of God in a stable family, different from other forms which the Church's worship may take.

What good to the Church is all this? The perfect subjection of one follower of Christ in his whole being to the divine will is of greatest value to the whole body of the faithful. We are all one; the good of one affects the well-being of all the others. Our devotion to union with God, *because it is in Christ,* cannot but be a devotion to the unity of men in love, whether our chief daily acitivity is one of direct apostolic service or not. For in Christ the union of man with God *and* the union of men with men are both perfectly achieved.

We may add that the Church and the world need contemplatives. Our age especially needs contemplative men and women, in or out of monasteries and convents, who see God in all, —who see him especially in this very age, so full as it is of novelties and wonders, of problems and dangers, of heroic opportunities and national catastrophes. For this age lacks just that: the insight to see God in itself and to understand this wonderful expansion of knowledge and activities from God's point of view. Our age is like a giant child, moving with great strength but a faltering step, in an uncertainty resulting from failure of contact with God and the assurance of his love and fatherly protection. Only by the contemplative spirit can this interior confidence be acquired, only by that spirit can peace be spread in the world.

Nor must we forget that prayer has an intrinsic power which makes it in itself one of the chief forms of the apostolate. If we try to pray, we are praying; and if we pray then God hears our prayer. The contemplative need not fear that his life of prayer is unrewarded. It is rewarded in proportion to his faith; he somewhere in the Middle West, the effect somewhere perhaps in China, a faltering Christian made strong.

INDEX

CARMELITE MONASTERY
LIBRARY
SARANAC LAKE, N Y